GLOBAL UNDERGROUNDS

GLOBAL UNDERGROUNDS

Exploring Cities Within

*Edited by Paul Dobraszczyk, Carlos López Galviz
and Bradley L. Garrett*

REAKTION BOOKS

Published by Reaktion Books Ltd
Unit 32, Waterside
44–48 Wharf Road
London N1 7UX, UK

www.reaktionbooks.co.uk

First published 2016, reprinted 2017

Printed and bound in China

A catalogue record for this book is available from the
British Library

ISBN 978 1 78023 576 9

CONTENTS

PREFACE:
Global Undergrounds
Geoff Manaugh

The signs are everywhere around us, evidence of another world. A line of drains extends across the sloping lawn of a local park; blacked-out windows on a Brooklyn town house suggest the building is not quite what it seems; the sound of wind blowing out of a hole in the ground of an empty meadow implies the presence of a massive space beneath. We live amid interpenetrating systems of space, knotted topologies that do not immediately reveal themselves but, instead, lurk in the shadows, under streets, below grade. These are the worlds – always plural – of the underground, and they are as tucked away as they are exhilarating to find.

In the autumn of 2013 I talked my way into a press conference held some 60 metres (200 ft) underneath Central Park, heralding the turning on of the first valve of New York City's famed Water Tunnel No. 3. The whole thing had the air of an old-school rave: we were never given an actual address, but were instead told to meet at a specific corner in Manhattan and to look out for a white van. Once inside the van, we were told not to relay any information of our itinerary for others to follow; yet, only minutes later, we rolled up to what was literally just a door in the hillside. You've probably driven past it yourself, if you've gone through Central Park by car. We hopped out, a guard popped open the door – and there, hidden inside like the stage equipment of a James Cameron film, were the elevators. And stairs. And pipework. This was the entrance to a subterranean valve chamber, a control room for the flow of New York City's freshwater drinking supply. Considering how easily this space behind such a simple door could be commandeered, it was no wonder the city wanted to keep it secret.

There we gathered, sixteen flights of stairs down from the surface world, listening to Mayor Michael Bloomberg opine about the long-term value of urban infrastructure. The cavernous, vaulted backdrop of the valve room loomed behind him, cathedral-like, a hydrological super-stadium buried with little fanfare at the literal centre of the city. It felt as though I had conned my way into a water cult, a new Age of Aquarius, an elemental ceremony performed among behemoth machines beneath the streets of Manhattan.

The underground lends itself well to mythology. There is great narrative resonance in going beneath the earth's surface, as if suddenly one's life has come to rhyme with the heroic spelunkers of the ancient world – with Orpheus descending into the darkness for his wife, Eurydice, or, of course, the Renaissance hells of Dante, whose subterranean journey still haunts subsurface explorations to the point of cliché. Hercules went to hell to capture a monster, the three-headed dog Cerberus; Theseus, vanquisher of labyrinths, went to hell to capture women. Even Jesus Christ, if you believe the Athanasian Creed, had his own colossal cave adventure, descending to hell in an act known as 'the harrowing', releasing a crew of saints wrongfully imprisoned there. It was the ultimate jailbreak.

Indeed, if our cities didn't have undergrounds, we would need to invent them. Even in a subterranea-rich city like New York, urban legends arise of more rooms and corridors beneath our feet. There are the caverns of Grand Central Station, but there are also the mythic cow tunnels of Manhattan's West Side. A fabled bit of NYC food lore, these half-real, half-imagined hallways may or may not have been how cattle were formerly led into Manhattan to be slaughtered. Vague blueprints have even shown up online, purporting to show their location, and the city itself has announced that, if the tunnels are real, they will be subject to historic preservation. The deeper implication here is that, even where cities don't have an underground, somebody will be compelled to come up with one simply to help make sense of what happens above. Tunnels can be matters of faith as much as pieces of everyday infrastructure.

On the other hand, the poetry of descent can often be too seductive for its own good. It is all too easy to be swayed by the romance of it all, and consequently much harder to notice the politics: the fact that the underground is so inextricably associated with the under-represented, the oppressed, the forced-out, the resistant. This is where labour is performed, where the city is constructed, its goods processed, where minions toil and pollution accumulates.

An extraordinary example of this is found in Mexico City, a place of great underground archaeological interest, but also a city falling out of balance with itself: owing to the depletion of groundwater, the foundations of the city are subsiding, throwing off the angles of its

sewer system. These pipes and cisterns thus get backed up, unable
to flow using gravity as their designers intended. The city has devised
an extraordinary solution: sewer divers. Human workers descend
blindly into the muck, wearing full-body protective SCUBA gear
seemingly more appropriate for deep-sea diving; they are then led from
above by attentive technicians, who whisper geographic instructions
to them via headphones. Walking through swirls of human waste and
subsurface tides of discarded street rubbish, the divers have found
corpses, trees and even half a Volkswagen. This is work that literally
keeps the city running – or flowing, as the case may be – yet it is work
that, almost by definition, remains invisible. The underside of the city
is where the detritus goes, where waste, excreta and materials thought
to have lost all value collect. Sorting through all that combines the
political significance of overlooked urban labour with the strangely
Freudian interpretive overlay – or is it undertone? – of the return
of the repressed.

At other times and in other places, the signs that something
lies below are almost impossible to discern – but the underworld
nevertheless persists. Consider the extraordinary example of the
English city of Nottingham. Nottingham sits atop a burrower's fantasy:
labyrinths within labyrinths of private artificial caves carved from the
region's sandstone. Stairways in the backs of pubs, old cellars below
houses, the lower reaches of shopping centres and car parks – all butt
up against this hidden world. The vast majority of these nearly 500
caves leave no indication on the surface; there is no particular way or
even reason to deduce that they exist. Yet strange signs here and there
point the way to small components of the subterranean assemblage –
sometimes very literally. For example, in the basement of a shopping
centre, amid way-finding signage for shops and lavatories, there is an
arrow pointing the way, almost comically, to 'Caves'. Along a handful
of Nottingham's residential streets, there are locked steel security doors
with no clear connection to the buildings either side; anyone attempting
to guess at the purpose of those doors would be hard-pressed to
imagine that they actually lead to an old sand mine whorled beneath
the city through an elaborate network of old shafts and chambers
carved into the darkness below.

I had the pleasure of taking a marathon tour of many of these
caves with a Nottingham-based archaeologist. His name, of all things,
was David Strange-Walker. Strange-Walker and his organization, the
Nottingham Caves Survey, are determined to preserve these neglected
underground spaces in whatever form they can – which, for now, means
three-dimensional laser scans of their complex interiors. This raises
a key point: the artificial sandstone caves of Nottingham are largely

unknown outside the city, overlooked even within Nottingham itself, and widely abused by the people who now own them. Strange-Walker pointed out that many businesses and homeowners, learning that they have a cave beneath their foundations, will use that space as nothing more than a private landfill, a place to dump their rubbish. But these are historical artefacts – historical spaces – as much deserving of preservation as any statue in the British Museum.

Put another way, our historical museums are filled with narratively rich, materially compelling human artefacts – but the spaces from which those objects come are equally worthy of preservation and study. Sometimes the space itself is the heritage; in the case of Nottingham – or Cappadocia, or the Paris catacombs – it is history from below.

Other entrances to the underground are carefully hidden – deliberately disguised or camouflaged. Near my own apartment in Brooklyn, for example, is a classic New York brownstone that nevertheless seems a bit odd: the windows are blacked out, almost vampiric, with no light coming or going from either side, and no residents ever seem to step outside. Look closer, by peering through a crack between the front doors, and you'll see emergency transit authority signage inside the front hall. This isn't a house at all, in other words, but an emergency exit stairwell and maintenance shaft for the New York City subway system. The house's roots stretch all the way down to the 4- and 5-line tunnel that runs beneath the East River near by. The implication here is not only that your neighbour's house isn't quite what it seems, but that a New York City town house has the ultimate basement: a deep shaft of stairways that is, in essence, a private entrance to the subway.

Portals to the underworld abound, of course, and their moments of discovery can be both inspiring and strange. Consider Derinkuyu in Cappadocia, Turkey: a man was simply cleaning out a room in his basement when he accidentally knocked a hole in the wall, revealing one of the largest underground cities in the world hidden on the other side. Or think of the Dupont Circle tunnels in Washington, DC, carved in the early twentieth century by an excavation-obsessed lepidopterist named Harrison G. Dyar; they were revealed only when a truck fell through the street. Those tunnels – located mere blocks from the White House – were initially thought to be connected to a Communist conspiracy. Or flip through the annals of burglary and bank crime, where groups like the 'Hole in the Ground Gang' from 1980s Los Angeles or Albert Spaggiari's crew in Nice pop up like moles beneath safe-deposit vaults, revealing both an uncanny knowledge of those cities' sewer systems and the fact that, even today, there is a vibrant subterranean fervour at the criminal heart of the modern metropolis.

The underground is also a kind of back-up for things that simply can't happen on the surface. Deep physics experiments, such as the neutrino detector assembled piece by piece in an old Minnesota iron mine near the US–Canada border, or the Hadean Hadron circles of CERN, reveal that what we can't find above ground, we simply engineer below. This is also darkly true for survivalist fantasies, which hold that some fiery apocalypse will require us to entomb ourselves if we hope to see the future. According to groups such as 'preppers' – who seemingly look forward to hunkering down after societal collapse – where the surface is blown away, all we'll have is what is left below.

From the mythic to the poetic to the political, what occurs beneath our feet is the secret knotting of the world, and it can be studied as such. This is where surface forms are woven together by camouflaged roots, and where buildings lead to caves lead to mines lead to bunkers in a dreamlike sequence that can be unusually difficult to catalogue. The vertiginous undoing of solid ground is this book's goal and speciality, revealing a worm-eaten world of catacombs and hiding places. Overlooked, romanticized, misused and vital: the underground is filigreed with significance and buzzing with unexpectedly intense activity. It's time to descend.

INTRODUCTION:
Exploring Cities Within

Paul Dobraszczyk, Carlos López Galviz
and Bradley L. Garrett

Cities are sinking. We refer here not to rising sea levels but to the insatiable human desire to dig. Sprawling tendons of tunnels now stretch through the underbelly of every major city on the planet – conduits for transport, utility, communication, shelter and storage.[1] The excavation of these spaces, at ever-increasing depths and speed, has changed our lives in ways that we tend to take for granted. This book is a broad collection of eighty stories of underground spaces that moves across every continent and through millennia. It is the most sprawling collection of subterranean stories assembled to date.

Such a book can never be comprehensive, but we nevertheless harbour three clear objectives in compiling these accounts. First, we wish to continue the process of unpacking the history of global undergrounds in the spirit of the cultural historian Rosalind Williams, author of the seminal book *Notes on the Underground* (1990), making it clear that human relationships to underground spaces have been intimate and diverse through time. We wish to defy any notion of the underground as simply a space of inaccessible functional infrastructure built by other people in other times.[2] Second, we want to challenge notions of densely urban areas as the exclusive preserve of subterranea by including entries about underground spaces that might at first seem suburban, rural or indeed rather wild, but where connective imagination facilitates a richer understanding of the urban in an age of unprecedented mobility and network. Third, we seek to invoke subterranean imaginaries in spaces and times that are conceptual or semi-subterranean, or that are yet to materialize, making clear that the emergence of global undergrounds is an ongoing process. Through these three aims, we hope to expand our thinking about what it means to inhabit a world where the material stuff beneath our feet is constantly in flux, where layer upon layer of things, people and substances circulate, dream and dwell. In other words, we want to make it clear that we are all entangled in the subsurface.

Global undergrounds are places of hope, fear, work, memory and resistance – spaces not just tangentially connected to our daily existence on the earth's surface, but intertwined with it, inexorably and fundamentally. While to some, underground spaces are novel, bizarre, foreboding or off limits, the assembly of this collection of work shows that they are nonetheless central to our ways of being in the world and will become more so as cities sink and stretch to accommodate compounding population and materiality. The underground spaces in this book represent breadth and diversity across space and over time, encapsulating both long histories and futures in the making.

We are not alone in our preoccupation with the underground. In what might be termed a 'vertical turn', the politics of subterranea is a topic that a range of thinkers have turned increasing attention to. In the words of the urban scholars Stephen Graham and Lucy Hewitt, the 'flattening of discourses and imaginaries [that] tends still to dominate critical urban research in the Anglophone world' must be challenged.[3] Graham and Hewitt suggest shifting the geographical imagination to underground infrastructure and super-tall structures as a means of combating 'horizontalism', a view of the world that recognizes problems associated with urban sprawl, for instance, while often ignoring the many layers of sprawl beneath and above us.[4] The driving force behind this concern follows on from the architect Eyal Weizman's writings in *Hollow Land* (2007), in which he used the example of the West Bank to describe the increasingly asymmetric warfare taking place around the world. To Weizman, airspace and undergrounds have become some of the world's most contested spaces.[5] Since the publication of *Hollow Land*, a clutch of new literature has sprung up that thinks through the geopolitics of the vertical.[6] Yet much of this work has continued to see subterranean space as space out, over and under what we know – continuing to render it conceptual, forbidden and even exotic, the foreign territory of the 'other'. The geographer Gavin Bridge has opened out a more politically (under)grounded potential for our engagement with subterranea:

> Shafts, tunnels, mines and other holes into the ground serve as conduits connecting the plane of existence (the surface) to a radically different space below. As conduits, their function is to connect – to enable movement by bringing two spaces into relation.[7]

Bridge's notions of conduit and connectivity are useful to us in at least three respects. First, we see the undergrounds collected in this book as intertwined spaces: in opening our imagination to the vertical, we do not wish to pitch it against the horizontal, for the cultural entanglements that move along and within both axes are enmeshed and inseparable. Second, conduits also connect places and meaning; undergrounds are vehicles of powerful narratives, from personal stories of labour and descent into shelter to more structural topics that perpetuate asymmetry across class, gender or wealth as we move up and down. Third, undergrounds crystallize one of the functions that is most essential to cities enmeshed in global networks today: circulation. Rather than imagining a separate infrastructure that is solely the domain of urban planners, tunnel and hydrological engineers or labourers (suggesting a sectional understanding of the city where people, goods, capital, information and waste circulate, cut off from the turbulent rhythm of streets and daily life), we want to foreground the connections between space and politics that converge underground.[8]

Wherever possible, we have tried to collate narratives that are based on experience, and we suggest that in reading this book you remain mobile in your own imagination to envision the underground as a

Aldwych cables in the GLC pipe subways under the Strand, London.

collection of spaces and events in need of chronicling (in a historical sense), but also as places of connection between surface, subsurface, practice and matter. Matter, as you will read, ranges from effluvia and debris through to human remains, archaeological finds, train carriages, seeds and nuclear waste. Practice covers shelters from war or religious and political persecution; everyday travel; exploration of off-limits places whether through tours or more alternative and alluring routes; both recovering and uncovering hidden natures. This approach moves us away from a sense of sites, surfaces and linearity, and closer to – following the philosopher Peter Sloterdijk's suggestion – spherical constellations of meaning that envisage urban space as an enclosed sphere stretched by shared habitation.[9] No other definition better captures the multiplicity of the vast connections and movements contained within these covers. Central to these are the human dimensions of the underground that each entry explores: whether built to escape war and destruction or planned as a conscious critique of time running ever faster, these are spaces that speak of intimacy, enclosure, sharing and dwelling. These are spaces of function and meaning and also spaces of becoming. Product and process merge under the surface through a subtle meld.

One very important component of a richer awareness of the underground is a reflection on where we look for the discourses and practices of subterranean space and how they have been transformed in the past. This view tends to privilege those who have the power to plan, transform and manipulate urban space: the architects, engineers, emperors, kings, popes, aristocrats, wealthy merchants, artists and politicians who often have the resources to dig. While we should never lose sight of the important historical contexts of those excavations, there are other stories that can be recovered: testimonies to labour, beliefs, mythology and subversive tunnelling and underground dwelling. The long histories of cities like Rome, Xi'an, London, Mexico, Naples and Paris are as much about processes of sinking as they are about reaching for the skies, not just through the successive stacking of material remains but through the laying of foundations. Recalling the cover of Harry Granick's book *Underneath New York* (1991), where an enormous hand reaches down from the sky to grab three skyscrapers and pull them up from the ground, we are reminded, at seeing the tangle of wires, pipes, conduits and foundations underneath, that these vertical cities now often perceived from the air do not stop at street level. Indeed, they never have.

The book is divided into thirteen sections: Origins, Labour, Dwelling, Refuse, Memory, Ghosts, Fear, Security, Resistance, Renderings, Exposure, Edges and Futures. Most, if not all, of the entries push us to think about themes not included and work to underscore intersections we had not anticipated. Central to that engagement is a questioning of what we call 'urban' at the porous intersections between nature and culture in cities, suburbs and wilds of various kinds.

How can, for example, a mountain deep in the Arctic Circle in Norway, built to house supplies for a doomed future, be a space that urban inhabitants hundreds or thousands of kilometres away might identify with? Imagining the morose future pilgrimage to the area to collect the seeds of annihilated plants to take back to labs and farms seemed one way. Equally, we wondered whether the storage facility for nuclear waste in the middle of Yucca Mountain in Nevada, a place where Western Shoshone and Western Paiute people came together in the prehistoric past, would ever be as truly 'lost' as its builders hope. We were challenged to think through the ways in which our urban existence inspires the creation of 'wild' places that must remain wild owing to our toxic legacy. How are we to conceptualize an artist's project to stage a unique experience of the cosmos inside a mountain in the Arizona desert? Who does he think will come? What is it he wants them to experience? Is the Swiss–French border near Geneva, where the Hadron Collider is buried, now as urban as a university campus? And is it significant that the Collider was built on the site of a fourth-century Gallo-Roman urban ruin? Questions like these enticed us.

Initially we sought more recognizable connections between cities and the sub-urban. As more implicit entries came in, however, we found that our imaginations were kindled – and there is nothing more you can hope for as an editor. Together, the entries thus comprise a broad approach to the social, cultural, political and environmental dimensions of urban and sub-urban worlds stretching from physical characteristics to meanings, representations and imaginings. Taken as a whole, the entries constitute a survey that fleshes out 'the awareness that we are in a very real sense not on the earth but inside it'.[10] It is that insider's awareness that speaks to a more phenomenological sense of 'being in the world' that no doubt bolsters spheres of meanings even as it descends. Undergrounds are uniquely placed as sites of enquiry to provide powerful insights into what 'being in the world' actually means, since that world is, by stretching vertically, becoming more urban for more people on earth.

Our allocation of entries to the thirteen themes in the book might seem arbitrary, given the overlaps inside those spheres of meaning. However, while it might make sense to bring Rome, Cappadocia, Xi'an, Mexico City, Maastricht and Istanbul together under Origins, for instance, we also saw connections to other themes that we could not ignore. The terracotta warriors of Xi'an, for example, made relatively early in history, also speak of labour, dwelling and ghosts. Likewise, architecture – real and imagined – under the East Antarctic ice sheet is as much about bringing to light the construction of nuclear facilities that could never withstand the materiality of ice as it is about the 'environmental front line' that Greenland and Antarctica represent for our own urban futures as that ice becomes ever more vulnerable.[11] The themes are also a means to treat less exotic undergrounds, such as metros and sewers, differently. Telling the story of Philadelphia's Broad Street subway, for example, reveals the African American labour used there and the erasure (whether intentional or not) of their history from that space. The metro in Prague, in turn, spoke to us of memory and resistance, while sewers and drains in cities such as Melbourne and Las Vegas were both shelters and dwellings, places to hide and regroup for better or worse. Significantly more upsetting are the lives of drain-dwellers in Bogotá, where people shelter in sewers from the brutality of the police and roaming death squads on the pavements above – a reminder of the failure of increased security to create a 'cosmopolitan hub of commerce and creativity' in Colombia.[12] The underground there revealed a disjunction between rhetoric and reality, as it often does. Spheres of meaning incorporate multiple forces: positive and negative, and anything in between.

And so the list of connections that the entries stress is long and rich, calling forth a vertical imagination that is deeply entrenched in time. Underground spaces are populated with the bodies of workers often invisible in historical accounts or with people who live underground by choice or force. The entries detail the waste that we inhume, from household to nuclear, and that never disappears; the multiple layers of memory, their distinct non-linearity and their manifestation as unforeseen spectres, particularly in the process of spatial rediscovery, the fear of war, death and terrorist attacks. They speak to us of security in an age characterized by surveillance from above – remote but also mundane and part of everyday life – where underground spaces become reservoirs, conduits for traffic, arenas of resistance against aerial attack and drone wars. Resistance, in turn, involves places of social insurgency, but also stories of nature: for example, rivers that resist and survive, subverting the use for which at some point in their history they were intended. We encountered renderings that, perhaps, are more conceptual but no less poignant, especially when constructed by film, newspaper photographs and other media. Media exposure allows us to revisit physical processes of excavation and think through the role of new technology in reworking relationships between bodies and spaces. We found edges that mark out the boundaries of the subterranean from Russia and Cairo to New York,

Bratislava and Cape Town; futures that point to past directions but also to novel conjectures about time, environmental preservation and the scientific quest to understand the origins of the universe.

We could have neither seen nor anticipated the wealth of connections that this global survey of undergrounds has laced; yet there is much that cannot be done within these pages. For instance, the non-human underground – spaces carved by elements rather than by people – is outside our remit.[13] Similarly, there were cities that we were not able to include or sites about which we found little information or no writer who had experience with them.[14] This book may be the most expansive and comprehensive collection of stories of global undergrounds assembled to date, yet, we certainly do not want to claim that these themes represent an exhaustive account of the urban underground; on the contrary, we assert that the many meanings of the subterranean suggest more – much more – than we could hope to accommodate within the confines of this book. What we wish this book to do as it circulates through the world is less documentary and more aspirational, looking towards a further expansion of the notions of verticality that are beginning to be unpacked in earnest now across the social sciences and humanities.

There is one last aspect of the collection that is worth explaining. A number of entries suggest actual descents underground through holes into tunnels, vaults and bunkers – worlds less fantastical than Lewis Carroll's trippy rabbit hole. However, the entries here share with Alice's Wonderland the qualities of crossing a threshold: through your reading you will, like Alice, meet new characters, discover and explore and in so doing become wonderfully disorientated. Ludvig Holberg's *Nicolai Klimii iter subterraneum* (Niels Klim's Underground Travels), first published in 1741, went underground long before Carroll did. In the story, Niels returns home to Bergen, having travelled extensively in Europe, and discovers the mouth of a cave at the top of a mountain, known to locals as Flöien. Through it he descends into an unknown underground world, where, having fallen and reached a planet called Nazar, he writes:

> This night light comes from the Firmament, which is nothing else than the reverse of the earth's surface, where the hemisphere gives a similar light than the moon casts upon us; so that only consider this, we can say that in the globe under question nights differ little from days, except that during the night the sun is absent, and that this absence makes the evenings a bit cooler.[15]

Niels's voyage takes him to cities in Nazar where he learns about the character of its inhabitants, their religion, governance and laws, universities, and other more remote places and imaginary beings. But this is a world presented as the reverse – and, we might add, the complement – of the world from which he comes. The light is similar; the journey preserves the familiar moon and sun; nights and days come closer. If metaphorically only, this is the spirit that we hope you find embodied in this book: the familiar made strange, the unfathomable rendered not only present but disturbingly near. We would hope that you, like Niels or Alice, are prepared for the underground to open out to you.

Keeping in mind our ambitions laid down at the outset of this introduction, our aim is to point to, and demonstrate, a fruitful way of exploring multiplicities, one that engages as many different perspectives as can be reasonably gathered; one that is predicated on *exploration* rather than on *explanation*. For some, this may seem like an abdication of the responsibility to commit, a revelling in ambiguity for its own sake; yet we believe in an orientation that listens, gathers and assembles rather than orders and makes coherent. We wanted it to be flexible enough to create new and unexpected constellations of meaning for readers. The book is a spherical constellation of urban undergrounds, if you wish. The angle from which you read it is entirely your choice.

Overleaf
Roseberry GLC pipe
subways, Islington,
London.

ORIGINS

The vertical axis has always been principal to the experience of our species: very young children learn the meaning of 'up' and 'down' long before they have mastered the concepts of 'left' and 'right'.[1] But when did our vertical orientation first result in human-built underground spaces? Wherever we look for the origins of cities – in the Indus valley, Central Anatolia or Southwest Asia (cities that are 4,000, 5,000 or even 12,000 years old) – they often feature burial sites where rituals of death transformed underground spaces into sites of symbolic and material meaning.[2] Early examples are the royal tombs containing offerings for the dead in Mesopotamia, a region often called the 'cradle of civilization'.[3] Perhaps most spectacular are those contained in the funerary complex near Xi'an in China, where excavations have revealed an army of underground warriors and a moat of mercury.

Although new technology has allowed digging to take place in ways it never has before, it is clear that people were creating underground spaces long before the nineteenth century – the period that is largely viewed as the starting point for the cultural significance of tunnelling.[4] Although the first underwater tunnel was built in about 2160 BCE in what is now Iraq by the engineers of Queen Semiramis of Babylon (connecting the royal palace to the Temple of Jupiter on the opposite bank of the Euphrates), credit for the deed is often given to Marc and Isambard Kingdom Brunel, who built the Thames Tunnel in London some 4,000 years later, between 1825 and 1843.[5]

The urban underground that we take for granted today – the subterranean world of infrastructure – only emerged with any force in the Roman period.[6] The Romans invested urban underground space with a new kind of meaning: namely, as a site of order and rationality. Their elaborate sewer networks, underground quarries and heating systems brought technology beneath the city, technology that would complicate the existing associations of the underground with death and burial. Yet, as historians have demonstrated, the Roman underground was not merely utilitarian, for even their sewers were sacrosanct sites – spaces of ritual, myth and magic.[7] This is not surprising, since across the world, not least in the Mediterranean, sewers often stem from springs, life-giving sites where water bubbles from the earth.

The Romans' adept engineering of the urban underground, including vast cisterns and reservoirs, was handed down to Christian successors who imbued those spaces with their own distinct religious meanings. Some of the earliest Christian burial sites – the catacombs in Rome – testify to the renewed power of the underground as a site of transition from death to the afterlife. Engineered as both burial chambers and spaces for the enactment of rituals by the living, the catacombs provided a subterranean focus for the abiding Christian as a safe haven for future resurrection. And just as these early Christian burial sites were places of security protected from a persecuting world above, so later followers would make their homes in wholly underground cities on the plains of Anatolia.

The early Christian period thus handed down to us two of the principal – but contradictory – meanings of the underground: on the one hand, of safety and security; on the other, of danger and death. We may now live in a largely secular world, but that has not resulted in any lessening of these ancient meanings; for the two primary reference points – birth and death – remain unknowable parts of human experience, bolstering the conceptualization of subterranea as a place that can only ever be imagined.

On yet another continent, the ruins of the Templo Mayor in Mexico City have incited a different kind of enactment and meaning. To birth and death, we might add the reappropriation of time, not to mention the layering of sacrifice, conquest, destruction and rebuilding following the Spanish conquest. The Aztec calendar stone, or Sun Stone (Piedra del Sol), once a central connecting thread to the heavens, was found buried in the main square of Mexico City, excavated and mounted on the facade of the Cátedral Metropolitana de la Asunción de María (Mexico's Metropolitan Cathedral), the largest Roman Catholic cathedral of the Americas.

The physical spaces that honeycomb human habitation across the world today are no less imbued with multiple meanings than these ancient examples. This section of the book works to reinforce the long legacy of the human underworld, a space of ancient, intractable and often unexpected convergences.

Taming the Quagmire: Cloaca Maxima, Rome
Nick de Pace and Julia Solis

Entering the Cloaca Maxima ('greatest sewer') in Rome may bring tears to your eyes. Not because of its immense age, architectural beauty or historical significance, but because the fumes from the raw sewage are so noxious that they easily irritate any exposed skin. That is why members of the underground association Roma Sotteranea make sure that any visitors they bring into this sewer are protected from head to toe.

One especially scenic access point is in the Roman Forum, the ancient marketplace whose picturesque ruins have become a popular tourist destination. From a hatch amid broken pillars and monuments, a ladder leads into an arched stone tunnel large enough for a train. This, one of the main arteries of Rome's original sewer system, opens into a network of tunnels, all built to contain the city's effluent. The Cloaca Maxima – one of the world's oldest wastewater systems – is not used much today, but it played a significant role in the development of Rome.[8] Infamous as the collector of all that is foul and rank, its greatest contribution to history was not strictly for sanitation, as we might imagine. Rather, it radically altered the formation of the city through diverting and urbanizing a swampy morass that would eventually become the Roman Forum, the symbolic centre of the Roman world.

Outfall of the Cloaca Maxima, Rome.

grooved faces of rock, while the tunnel's cross-section changes from
semicircle to rectangle.

Unlike many underground spaces that have been opened up
for tourism, these tunnels are cold and completely unlit. Visits are
conducted with electric lanterns held by the participants, and guides
make a habit of interrupting proceedings by asking everyone to turn
off their lights so that they can appreciate the darkness that usually
infuses the tunnels. Without the residual light that we experience in
all spaces above ground, the darkness experienced in these tunnels has
its own unique atmosphere: oppressively heavy and utterly still. At the
beginning of the tour, participants are shown a map of the tunnels
drawn on to one of their walls, the torchlight revealing a veritable maze
of spaces that resembles the street-plan of an enormous medieval city,
an organic space that defies comprehension, even as the map suggests
otherwise. In the moments of darkness, the memory of this labyrinth
heightens the power of the tunnel spaces, as the overview of the map
is collapsed into the tiny space of a blind body.

Yet, despite the darkness of the tunnels, they have been inhabited
in one form or another for centuries. The evidence of this is scattered
throughout, including Roman stick figures incised into the walls;
elaborate eighteenth-century chalk frescoes; wartime depictions of film
stars such as Bette Davis; and bas-reliefs of mythological subjects from
the 1970s. Several of the larger spaces have been converted into chapels,
the rock carved out by pagan forebears subsequently fashioned into
Christian spaces, complete with sculptural altarpieces. Yet the shapes
of these spaces resemble not so much churches as something more
primitive and ancient than even the Roman culture that produced
them – an Egyptian tomb perhaps, or even a Neolithic burial chamber.

The signs of human presence one sees in many parts of the tunnel
complex are unusual not only in persisting for so long untouched but
also because of their contradictory but coexistent iconographies – the
pagan and the Christian, the elevated and banal occupying the same
space. In the city above ground, these marks would have been either
erased over time or 'cleaned up' into a more consistent (and probably
Christianized) visual record. In the dark space below, they have survived
as reminders of the essentially heterogeneous nature of urban life. As
the geographer Steve Pile has reminded us – building on Freud's notion
of the palimpsest – in the city 'many histories occupy the same space',
even if the traces of those histories often disappear without leaving any
material record.[14] In the city below, however, those traces often remain
untouched, leading to a heightened awareness of the overlapping
historical trajectories of urban space and an appreciation of all the
stories that might yet be told.

A Skiff, Fish and Wells: Basilica Cistern, Istanbul
Carlos López Galviz

The Basilica Cistern in Istanbul is one of the best preserved and most impressive structures of the late Roman Empire. Built during the reign of Justinian (527–65 CE), it served the water needs of the nearby Topkapi Palace as well as of local residents. The cistern covers an area of 9,800 square metres (105,500 sq. ft), and can store 100,000 tons of water brought to the site from the Belgrade Forest, about 15 kilometres (just over 9 mi.) northwest of the area that is now known as Sultanahmet, once the very heart of the Byzantine city of Constantinople. The vaulted roof is supported by over 300 marble columns, the majority of which were taken from existing and often remote buildings in the city and elsewhere, a practice characteristic of both Roman and Ottoman builders. Among the features that attract most tourists are two stone plinths carved with Medusa's head: one rests upside down, the other sideways. According to Greek mythology, whoever looked at Medusa's face was turned into stone. Gorgoneia – amulets invested with protective power – featured Medusa's face throughout classical Greece, and they appeared on several buildings across the Mediterranean. The position of the plinths is believed to have reversed the myth while keeping the guardianship of one of the

Roman cistern in the former Constantinople, today's Istanbul.

most important reservoirs of potable water in the city, but experts
still disagree about their origin and purpose in the cistern.

At least three open-air cisterns were built across Constantinople
during the late Roman period. Two are now used as public markets;
the other has been turned into a sports arena (Vefa Stadium). The
second largest underground reservoir is the cistern of Philoxenus,
also in Sultanahmet and, like the Basilica, open to visitors. Both cisterns
had fallen into disuse when a European visitor, Petrus Gyllius, made
his way down, aided by a local resident, in the mid-sixteenth century.
Gyllius recounted:

> I went by chance into a house, where there was a descent into
> it, and went aboard a little skiff. The master of the house, after
> having lighted some torches, rowing me here and there across,
> through the pillars, which lay very deep in water, I made a
> discovery of it [the cistern]. He was very intent upon catching
> his fish, with which the cistern abounds, and speared some of
> them by the light of the torches. There is also a small light
> which descends from the mouth of the well and reflects upon
> the water, where the fish usually come for air.[15]

Gyllius was seeking the remains of the Stoa Basilica, from which the
cistern takes its name. The Basilica, which housed a famous library
of about 600,000 volumes, burned down in about 475 CE, leaving the
Imperial Portico and Imperial Cistern standing alone on its site for
centuries. For later visitors, the cistern – together with Hagia Sophia,
the Hippodrome, the Colonnade of Arcadius at the Avret Bazaar and the
Valens Aqueduct – was among the city's most impressive structures.[16]

There is no mention of the Medusa plinths in Gyllius' account;
they would have been covered by water at the time of his descent. The
journey took him among columns that would normally have stood above
ground, whether supporting the entrances of temples and churches,
marking the limits of parks and gardens, or simply projecting upwards
to the open sky. The everyday quality of the cistern was made apparent
by the several wells that Gyllius saw: watering holes that served the
needs of local residents. The sounds of cameras, phones and the often-
perplexed murmur of tourists have now replaced the 'mighty noise' of
the water filling up the cistern, which Gyllius reported. Fish are back
after the most recent restoration by the Istanbul municipality, completed
in 1987, and the plinths are now lit in different colours. Medusa, hidden
for centuries, is no longer a guardian; she is now a different kind of
amulet, perhaps one that everyone attempts to take home, having
recorded the splendour of the craftsmanship that is evident through

the carvings. Cameras have replaced mirrors, and the cistern has featured in *From Russia with Love* (1963) and, more recently, *The International* (2009). The myth is now commodity.

Old, Deep and Discreet:
Cappadocia's Underground Cities
Bradley L. Garrett

With the majority of the world's population now living in cities, conversations are flaring up once again about how we can make better use of what is below us, not just as conduits for underground transport and storage, but as spaces for living. However, much as we might like the idea of increasing urban density by moving underground – constraining horizontal sprawl and facilitating sustainability by building down rather than out – making the decision to move underground is complicated by the particular geologic characteristics of cities, conflict with the human-made remains that already exist there, and even more difficult-to-pin-down problems such as how living without natural light affects our mental health.

Our lack of understanding of how to make the move below the surface is not for want of precedent, however. For more than 1,500 years human beings have lived underground in parts of Cappadocia, in what is now Turkey. There are an extraordinary 22 known large-scale subterranean cities in the region, the most sprawling of which is Kaymaklı, which is said to have at one time supported a population of 60,000 and even included extensive areas for deep-level animal husbandry. The deepest city is Derinkuyu, which reaches 90 metres (295 ft) below the surface in some places. As a matter of necessity, the Derinkuyu network is equipped with 52 ventilation chimneys 80 metres (250 ft) in height, a feat of engineering that would even today be challenging to orchestrate.[17]

Although these cities were originally built out of convenience, facilitated by an accommodating geology (for protection from heat and the cool storage of perishables), eventually political necessity took precedence. During the Roman occupation of the area, secret churches were constructed underground where Christians could worship without fear of persecution: the underground facilitating the underground.

As such pressure eased and the cities were abandoned, new visitors found interest in them as historic and cultural sites. Tours are now offered of small parts of the system, although many parts remain unsafe to visit. It is currently not known how far these cities extend, and certainly future archaeological discoveries will change our estimates of their total size and open new areas to visitors. However, there is only one collection of 1,500-year-old subterranean cities in the world that is still teaching us new things about how and why human beings might want to live, work and trade underground today, and that is in Cappadocia.

Engineers and architects, in analysing these spaces, have suggested that they

> have attributes that provide lessons to contemporary practitioners . . . the spaces provide sound insulation against excessive weather conditions, the inner climatic conditions of the caves and their low levels of humidity provide perfect storage potentials for agricultural products and wine, and the caves also possess higher potentials to withstand earthquakes.[18]

In short, the properties of thermal, elemental and environmental isolation of these underground cities are now attracting the attention of a new generation of civil engineers, looking to the past for answers to the possible problems of the future.

One of the many maze-like junctions of Derinkuyu.

In a report by *The Guardian* newspaper in 2014 on the underground cities of Cappadocia, it was suggested that 'we can use underground space for all the urban services that do not require daylight – transport, waste management, retail – [releasing] pressure [on] above-ground space for living, recreation, greenery – creating compact and more sustainable cities.'[19] While these insights may not be surprising to those of us used to living in cities where much of our time is already spent underground, we may find ourselves stretching to imagine that at some point we may spend the majority of our time under the surface of the earth. But given the pressure cities are now facing, we should consider this as one possible development within the next few decades. Perhaps if more people took a trip to Cappadocia, this possibility would seem less remote and perhaps even appealing, especially while standing in a naturally defensible, climate-controlled, ornate subterranean church steeped in history.

Under Kingdom: The Layers of Mexico City
Dhan Zunino Singh

With his idea of roughness (*rugosidad*), the Brazilian geographer Milton Santos has claimed that all cities can be read as layers of modes of production that historically accumulate and overlap like sediments. In his estimation, roughness is 'what remains from the past', such as forms of the built environment, landscapes or debris.[20] In Mexico City, this notion of urban layering is particularly important because in one single site, the Zócalo (main square), the entire history of the nation is condensed. The site embodies the complex layers of power in the city's long history: from the Aztec Empire through the Spanish Empire to the Mexican nation-state. Located in a river basin (now dry) on a plateau 2,250 metres (7,400 ft) above sea level, Mexico City was founded in 1325, and remained on its elevated island until the Spanish destroyed it in 1521. The Spaniards soon rebuilt the city following a typical colonial layout: a chequerboard network of roads with a central square. After independence in 1821, Mexico City remained the country's main urban centre, and it became the capital of the new nation in 1824. Surrounding the city's main square, then, one can see the Spanish-built Metropolitan Cathedral (1570–1813), the independence-era National Palace (1813) and, between and under them, the archaeological remains of the most important building of Great Tenochtitlán, the Templo Mayor (*c.* 1390), discovered during the laying of subterranean electrical wiring in 1978.

Templo Mayor model
at El Zócalo metro
station, Line 2.

The construction of modern infrastructure often becomes an archaeological tool, disclosing the buried past when the ground is newly excavated. Indeed, thousands of archaeological objects have been found in Mexico City since the construction of the metro began in the 1970s. Like many metro systems, in Mexico City the metro tunnels have become sites both of public education and of historical reflection. Thus, one can pass through a tunnel that simulates outer space or see the walls of stations decorated with large murals. Even the maps and posters in the stations fuse the functional with the symbolic. The names of the stations take the form of Aztec hieroglyphs; past and present merge as in a museum. In the passenger tunnels, artefacts of ancient cultures are displayed. For example, inside El Zócalo station are models that capture the long history of the site: a large glass cabinet contains a model of the Templo Mayor as it was in the Aztec era, its white pyramids covered with colourful stripes.

In Mexico City, therefore, a journey underground becomes a journey into the past. Yet often that experience resembles that of a theme park, the 'roughness' of the ruins of the Templo Mayor suppressed into an easily digestible image. On the other hand, the archaeological remains of the temple are below ground level but not enclosed. Buried for centuries, they now reside in a large open hole. A fragment of old urban infrastructure (a brick sewer built in 1900) crosses the ruins. Here, the body of the city is opened up to view as an anatomical specimen and a history lesson ready for cultural dissection.

Visiting this archaeological site, I found myself walking among the stone foundations of the city itself, seeing the city from below, the cathedral and other surrounding buildings now seemingly higher than normal. Although one is never far from the powerful Mexican sunlight, in this journey through ruins one experiences the atavistic feeling of descending deep into a threshold between past and present. I was transported to the city's pre-colonial past, emphasized by an awareness that on these subterranean stones funeral rites and human sacrifices had once taken place. At the same time, the cathedral towers rising over the ruins serve as reminders of the winners and losers in the city's history, however subsumed they all are by the noise of the street above; the life of a modern megalopolis. Here, unlike the flattened history of the city that is displayed in the metro, the complex layers of urban history appear overlapped and embedded rather than as discrete chapters in a book, giving a sense of the never-ending process of construction and destruction of the city.

LABOUR

Lewis Mumford (1895–1990) was among the first to argue that the origins of industrial modernity lay in the speeding-up of the exploitation of subterranean resources – fossil fuels, metals, minerals and building materials – through mining. Of course, underground labour was not a new feature of industrial modernity, since excavation for building materials dates back to the origins of cities themselves; what was new in the first industrial revolution was the development of the mine as 'the first completely inorganic environment to be created and lived in by man'.[1] Industrialization depended on the creation of deep-level subterranean environments for the extraction of resources, environments that were cut off completely from the world above and sustained by artificial technology, whether lighting (originally the Davy lamp, devised in 1815), water extraction (through steam-powered pumping engines) or sophisticated means of tunnelling (such as Marc Brunel's tunnelling shield, first used in the Thames Tunnel in 1825). This paraphernalia of technological tools was, for a long time, in sharp contrast with the nature of human labour in mines: even with the invention of tunnelling tools such as shields and later boring machines, or with the introduction of compressed-air technology, labour with pickaxes and shovels continued to be just as important.

Representations of labourers in subterranean environments have tended to stress the infernal aspects of the work, often with overtones that highlight class and ethnicity. For example, witnesses of the construction of Brunel's Thames Tunnel and, later, London's sewerage system, described (and sometimes pictured) the labourers they saw as somehow monstrous, bound up as they were with the brutal conditions of underground mining.[2] It was as if the guiding principles of these subterranean excavations – science, measurement and calculation – were displaced by the irrational sight of human bodies working in those spaces. Here, embodied identification (of observer to worker) leads to an atavistic reading, perhaps as a means of distancing oneself from the horror of realizing the human cost of industrial progress. Yet there are exceptions, places where underground labour becomes a utopian form of work, one that resists this dominant mode of exploitation. In utopian undergrounds, such as the spaces dug out by the 'mole man' in east London in the early twenty-first century, labour takes the form of a working-out of inner desires, creating a utopian space that defies the conventional logic of capitalism.[3]

Today, despite the almost universal use of tunnel-boring machines for deep-level excavations beneath cities, there are still workers who remind us that underground spaces are ones that are resolutely produced and that their maintenance is an unavoidable and delicate operation.[4] Usually clad in identical high-visibility fluorescent boiler suits, these workers may seem far removed from the pick-wielding, half-naked shadowy figures that excavated the resources that powered the first industrial revolution, but they nevertheless bring the corporeal back into conventional notions of the urban underground as a purely technological space. Today, these workers are no longer ascribed a demonic status, but they retain a sense of the heroic – and embodied – nature of underground work: the acute sense of a new modernism, one that connects the modernization of cities to conditions of employment, whether it be those of miners in now touristic sites or those of metro workers whose rights and wages are subject to the violent fluctuations of global capital.

Absurd Space: Williamson Tunnels, Liverpool
Paul Dobraszczyk

In about 1805 the tobacco merchant Joseph Williamson (1769–1840) moved with his wife to Edge Hill, a relatively undeveloped suburb of Liverpool, and began to build houses in the area. Because this part of Edge Hill lay on top of an old sandstone quarry, the ground was uneven, a fact that Williamson decided to redress by building brick arches over the quarry. The resulting tunnels were the first element of an extraordinary development that spread into the surrounding area. During the following thirty years, until Williamson's death in 1840, many kilometres of tunnels were built, providing work for hundreds of local men left unemployed by the recession that hit Britain in the years after the end of the Napoleonic Wars in 1815.[5]

Visiting the tunnels today – only a fraction of the network created by Williamson is accessible to tourists – one is struck by the absurd quality of the project.[6] Looking at a map of the tunnels so far discovered, one sees that some tunnels join together, while others end after only a few metres. Further inspection of the tunnels heightens this sense of absurdity: one tunnel, barely wide enough to squeeze through, cuts through a wall and then abruptly stops; another passes vertically through the ground, its opening visible through the sides of an adjacent tunnel; and one of the large brick tunnels was built directly over another for no apparent reason.

Many have speculated on the causes of Williamson's tunnelling obsession. Did he belong to a religious sect, and perhaps design

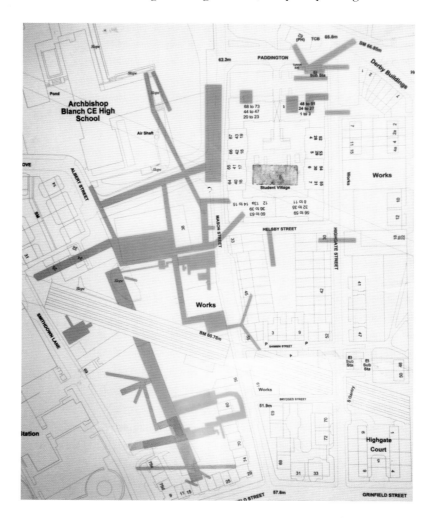

Map of the Williamson Tunnels, Liverpool.

the tunnels as a safe haven from an imminent apocalypse? Did he merely seek solace in his underground spaces after his wife died in 1822? Or was he a showman courting publicity by being deliberately evasive about his reasons for building the tunnels? Despite the lack of evidence for his motives, one thing is clear: Williamson provided much-needed employment for men in his local community, even if that work seemingly had no end product in mind. Indeed, he continued to take on more and more men, despite the fact that some of them performed pointless duties, such as moving piles of rocks from one place to another and then moving them back again, or building tunnels and then immediately sealing them up. Viewed in this way, the project seems like an elaborate joke at the expense of capitalist notions of work – far odder than a simple act of philanthropy or an expression of Williamson's eccentricity. Each one of the thousands of bricks that line the tunnels was made by hand rather than by machine, suggesting a work ethic more akin to the thinking of the anti-industrialist William Morris (1834–1896) than to other contemporaneous subterranean projects such as the Thames Tunnel in London, begun in 1825. In Williamson's tunnels, labour becomes an end in itself, disconnected from cycles of production and consumption, just like the utopian vision of work seen in Morris's late novel *News from Nowhere* (1890).

Today, the presence of the tunnels creates an atmosphere of mystery in the surrounding area of Edge Hill, which is now a run-down inner-city suburb of Liverpool. Walking the streets near the tunnels' visitor centre, one cannot help but notice things in the landscape that would not normally solicit attention: high fences, dead ends, abandoned buildings and bricked-up windows and doors. For, with the knowledge of Williamson's eccentric tunnels, everyday sights take on a mysterious and alluring quality. Now, everything might be a portal to another world, one that could transform the mundane into the marvellous.

Hidden Labour: Broad Street Subway, Philadelphia
James Wolfinger

Sing, hammer, sing![7]

Reporters in 1920s Philadelphia struggled to capture what they saw. The tunnel beneath Broad Street, one of the city's two busiest avenues, grew by 15–30 metres (50–100 ft) a day. Planks covered the road as crews of 3,000 or more men went underground, using shallow cut-and-cover techniques when possible, and deep tunnelling when they had to. The abutments of the Reading Railroad, for example, forced construction crews to burrow 14 metres (45 ft) under the city's surface and build supports for the heavy rail line. City Hall, at the time a fairly new building and one of the heaviest in the nation, sat squarely in the middle of the intersection of Broad and Market streets, and required inventive engineers and steely workmen to negotiate. Above, on the planks, drivers motored along with little idea of the work taking place and no idea who was doing it just beneath them.

'C'mon get hot, get hot!'

But the tunnel below was otherworldly: a workplace that was fantastical, dangerous, sometimes deadly. Reporters succumbing to flights of fancy compared subterranean Philadelphia to Alice in Wonderland, the tunnel a 'picturesque vista of a steel-girdered canyon'. It was a place where Hercules might work, driving steel rails through earth and bedrock. Others recoiled at what seemed unhealthy, perhaps unnatural. 'Ten feet, twenty, twenty-five, thirty – still going down', wrote one reporter. 'The dank, moist smell of earth grows – it is like going into the mouldering cellar of a long-deserted castle . . . It is chilly and cold below. Instinctively one thinks of pneumonia, tuberculosis.'

'Send her home!'

Many reporters noted the workers in the crews, men who, as much as the tunnel itself, fitted the fantastical motif: 'In the light from a few electric bulbs in the ceiling, the cement-covered workmen moved about like gray spirits from another world. Some looked like very strange spirits, carrying dishpans into which more lights were screwed.' Everywhere in the 'Underworld of the excavation' there were pools of water, pneumatic hammers, deafening roars, odd shadows and workmen, thousands of workmen. Not so many of the reporters noted the race of the workers – perhaps it was the heavy clothes, poor lighting and filth of the environment; perhaps it was the racism of the time; perhaps both – but those who paid attention found that many of them, perhaps half, were African American. More than any other group of people, those men did the heavy lifting, the blasting, the shovelling. Laura Lee of the *Evening Bulletin* captured the scene:

> Suddenly we came upon another song, a negro spiritual sung
> while a gang of men, each with a pair of great iron tongs,
> swings a track into place. At the long, high note of the song
> they push the track along and let it drop.

Broad Street
Subway Line
under construction,
Philadelphia, c. 1928.

Elsewhere Lee found a workman, 'powerful muscles swelling', swinging a hammer: 'His mighty blows against the steel shafts supporting the Broad St subway between Locust and Walnut sts, seem great enough to bring the entire subway toppling down.'

'Atta girl!'

The work songs and spirituals these black men sang (their lyrics interspersed throughout this article) kept the work moving but could not stave off an avalanche of injuries and even deaths. The city set up a moving hospital – some called it a 'first-aid shack' – with four nurses and a doctor at all times, and they were never idle. A reporter listed the common ailments as 'crushed thumbs, bruised arms, rusty nails to be extracted from feet, lacerations and abrasions', a painful but mundane list compared to what the headlines reported: 'Subway Gas Blast Hurts 10'; Tube Blast Rocks Broad St Homes'; '6 Hurt by Blast'; 'Tractor's Plunge Kills Tube Worker'; '2 Men Buried'; 'Spectacular Blaze'; 'Fire'. The human toll was appalling, and, as was customary for the time, each article recounted the names of the injured or deceased along with a racial marker: 'Colored'.

Joseph Dumas, colored.
James Alvarez, colored.
Gary Mcgrae, colored.
Arthur Mitchell . . .

The hospital, the articles, the racial notations all provided, as the *Evening Bulletin* put it, 'a grim reminder of the price that must be paid for the great engineering feats that are being accomplished'.

'Ring, hammer ring.'

When the track was finally laid and the lights came on in 1928, all this was forgotten. Dignitaries such as Mayor Harry Mackey and E. T. Stotesbury of the great Morgan bank were on hand to run the first train and talk to the press about how the project showed 'just what the city can do in a transportation way for its people'. The subway was burnished and safe, its stations painted in buff, green and blue. Philadelphia, they thought, would use the subway to pave the way to five million residents, millions in additional tax dollars and a pre-eminent place in the nation. A subway line, of course, should never shoulder such high expectations. But whether the dignitaries were right or wrong about the future, none of them noted the work and sacrifice that had gone into building the subway. None of the photos from the grand opening showed the workers who had dug the tunnel, let alone African Americans. They were wiped from memory and from history.

'When will the book be out?' one of the workers asked the *Bulletin*'s Laura Lee. She replied that she was just working on an article, but then mused to herself: 'One could write a book about it, at that.'

Yes, one could. But who would be the subject?

Salt of a Mining Cathedral: Zipaquirá, Colombia
Carlos López Galviz

It is not really a cathedral: there is no bishop, neither is there a tower, nor an imposing facade. It is buried 200 metres (660 ft) underground in what used to be a halite (rock salt) mine, expanded from a shrine built in about 1932 by the miners to honour their patron saint, the Virgen de Guasá (meaning salt and water).

Zipaquirá sits near El Abra, a cave system in the most northern of the Andean plateaus where three cordilleras embrace a number of plains, Bogotá's among them. El Abra is the site of one of the oldest human settlements in the Americas, dating back 12,500 years. The mine itself has been a site of extraction for centuries, at least since the Muiscas, one of the most prominent indigenous groups of pre-Hispanic Colombia, whose renowned artistry and craftsmanship with gold inspired several legends, the best-known of which is El Dorado.

One of the prevalent ideas in Europe in the colonial period was that the salt extracted from high-altitude mines was of inferior quality to that excavated from lower sites. The high quality of the halite extracted from Zipaquirá – over 2,800 metres (9,000 ft) above sea level – proved the opposite.

The geographer Alexander von Humboldt (1769–1859) visited the mine in 1801. In his account, he stated that the rock salt (*sal gema*) should be extracted through underground galleries rather than the open quarries he had witnessed. Humboldt's advice was to introduce new methods of extraction modelled on European practices, advice that required up-to-date knowledge of the theories of mining extraction adopted in Prussia. As it happened, Jacob Benjamin Wiesner, Humboldt's compatriot and a resident of Zipaquirá for years, had just that knowledge. If change in the mode of extraction was important, it was partly because rather than directing industry, the Spanish Europeans had fallen victim to what Humboldt regarded as the bad manners and habits of the indigenous peoples and had become, in his words, 'lazier and stupider than before'.[8]

Half a century after Humboldt's visit, the wealth the mine had promised remained elusive, or, at any rate, was kept in the close circles of those taking advantage of the resources Zipaquirá had to offer. Hordes of women in rags searching for salt debris near factories and piles of rubbish were a common sight by the mid-nineteenth century.[9]

Modern art installation in Zipaquirá's 'cathedral' near Bogotá, Colombia.

Despite its significant population (around 100,000 inhabitants in 2012), Zipaquirá never became an important urban centre; that was to be the story of Bogotá, 45 kilometres (28 mi.) to the south. As for mining and the underground church, miners continued their work well into the twentieth century and, indeed, to this day. The church was inaugurated on 15 August 1954, closed in 1990 and reopened five years later, following the completion of a new church beneath the existing one. The church, or cathedral as it is known, is now part of a theme park centred on the mine, including the 'miner's route', a guided tour that features a 35-minute ride on a replica train, a climbing wall, an 80-square-metre (860-sq.-ft) subterranean 'water mirror' and a light show with sounds. The new church has become the centrepiece of one of Colombia's top tourist destinations.

> 'Do you recall any miracles?'
>   'Miracles? Not many, no . . . The miracle is the cathedral itself: Colombia's top wonder.'

So said Alfonso Gutiérrez, a miner for more than 33 years, having learned the trade from his father, in a brief interview by the local television station during the Holy Week celebrations in 2012.[10] 'The Virgin covers us with her mantle' and protects us, said another miner. The mantle might very well cover miners and visitors alike, whether they are devotees or not. What the underground church means to Zipaquireños fuses a long history of extraction, the labour of generations of miners, with shows that now entice the most reticent of tourists: a miracle, of sorts.

Human Life Underground: Vale un Potosí, Bolivia
Mariëlle van der Meer

The girl comes running up to me. I've just come stumbling out of a mineshaft and I'm blinking in the fading sunlight. The landscape around me is desolate – a handful of shacks among piles of slate and rubble, so many shades of grey against the grey of the sky. The girl has bright and inquisitive eyes but her posture shows defeat, a heaviness beyond her years. She's showing me a couple of tiny pieces of silver in the palm of her hand and she looks at me with an expression at once hopeful and resigned – as much of a sales pitch as she can muster. She's momentarily distracted as movement in the rubble behind her catches her eye: two little boys come scrambling out – I imagine that they are her brothers – and they are laughing. The girl relaxes, and starts to giggle, too. For a moment all I can hear is the sound of children's laughter and I briefly forget where I am. I smile and think to myself that as long as there are children laughing, there is some hope and beauty in the sharp grey hardness that defines this place.

I am in Potosí, Bolivia, and it's 2002.

Potosí, one of the highest cities in the world, is at the foot of Cerro Rico (Rich Mountain), a mountain that, according to local myth, consists entirely of silver ore. It is also more ominously known as 'the mountain that eats men'. From its foundation in 1545 and throughout the colonial era, Potosí was one of the wealthiest and largest cities of the Americas and the principal supplier of silver to the Spanish Empire. The expression *vale un Potosí*, still used, means 'being valued as a Potosí' – in other words, being of great value. After 1800, the mines were depleted and work shifted to tin production, ushering in a slow economic decline. Some of the mines remain in use, though, and silver is still being extracted.

For some reason that I still don't quite understand, I have let myself be talked into taking a tour of the Candelaria silver mine, one of the few of its kind left in the world still operating without the use of any modern mining technology. That is not because such technology is unavailable here, but because it comes at a cost – clearly a higher cost than a human life. I am told that the life expectancy of the men who work in the mines is about ten to fifteen years from the moment they start, and that most will die of silicosis, a disease caused by continued exposure in the mineshafts to toxic silica dust, which clogs the lungs. This disease is easy enough to prevent, if the mining cooperatives would provide air-filtering masks. Some of the boys are only thirteen when they start working in the mines, so the odds are that they will be dead at 23. I am 25 at this point, so as I visit the mines, I'm acutely aware that I am observing boys who will never reach my age. They go underground every day for twelve hours, and they only ever see daylight an hour or two before sunset; otherwise, their daily life is entirely underground.

I am given an oilskin raincoat and a helmet with a light, and am instructed to go down the shaft in a tiny lift that holds only two people at

Figure of El Tío, adorned with votive offerings, inside the Cerro Rico, Potosí, Bolivia.

a time. I'm paired up with a silent Bolivian miner who looks at me with vacant eyes. I am embarrassed even to be there.

The tour group assembles in a dimly lit cave at the bottom of the shaft. We're being shown some areas of rock where the silver shines through. Our guide prompts us to clamber down a few wooden ladders and crawl through one of the tunnels into the next chamber. Even though I am quite small, the tunnel is barely large enough for me to crawl through on my hands and knees, and at times I have to go flat on my belly. I feel intense claustrophobia, realizing that 6,000 metres (nearly 20,000 ft) of mountain are on top of me. All I see in front of me, in the unconvincing beam of light coming from my helmet, is more tunnel. I swallow; my mouth is parched. The thick air is suffocating. I feel panic rising in my throat. I am dizzy, hot and nauseous. After a 100-metre (330-ft) crawl I finally get into the next chamber. The guide is staring at me silently, and the other tourists are looking as sheepish and uncomfortable as I feel. Around us, miners work. Unseeing eyes, sharp chisels, shared cigarettes. We get to the next little cave, where a statue is propped up. Candles are lit at either side, cigarette stubs and coca leaves are stuck into his mouth, and little ceremonial flags adorn his body. This is El Tío (The Uncle), the spirit of the underworld that inhabits the mines, ostensibly guarding the lives of the miners. He does not seem benevolent, as you might expect of a patron saint; rather, he has the appearance of a grotesque devil with horns, harsh staring eyes and a monstrous penis – the latter being splashed daily by a beastly strong local grain alcohol in a ritual to improve the 'fertility of the mountain', thus keeping alive the cycle that slowly kills the men who make these offerings every day.

Infrastructural Fetishism: York Metro Extension, Toronto
Bradley L. Garrett

A soft glow in the distance acts as a lure, pulling you deeper into the tunnels. You know that at some point you should probably pull back. You can feel small vibrations, tiny shockwaves, ripping down the tunnel now. You don't feel them just through your feet but all around you, like an oversized airport body scanner spinning horizontally around the cement tube. You are constantly reminded by the smell that even though you're moving horizontally, as you would on your way to work for instance, here you are buried. The 'surface' is a distant prospect, no one knows you're here, and should a train actually speed down this tunnel, you would die. You stop walking and listen again. There's nothing. And then the vibrations kick in once more, even stronger now. You put your head to the tracks and it rattles your tooth fillings. You can sense the machine at work and you want to be in it. Somewhere ahead, in the dead of night, like an earthworm, a tunnel-boring machine is casually chewing the Iroquois sand substrata at a rate of 15 metres (50 ft) per day. But is it Yorkie, Torkie, Holly or Molly saddled up for the labour? There's only one way to find out: you must keep walking.

There are many places one could start writing about the Toronto metro. Lower Bay might be the obvious choice – an abandoned metro station that was open for only six months in 1996. Some accuse the Toronto Transit Commission of playing political games in the construction of Lower Bay, pulling in the funds to create jobs to build a station they knew would never be necessary. Now it is used mostly as a film set, a fitting tribute to a station that was perhaps always a fiction.

Despite its reputation as a cultural point of interest, the Toronto metro has always been modest in scale. The two and a half existing lines are not anywhere near sufficient for a rapidly growing city. For several years the York Extension has been excavated to expand the reach of the system – 8.6 kilometres (5 1/2 mi.) of fresh tunnel connecting six new stations at a cost of C$2.6 billion. Yorkie, Torkie, Holly and Molly have made the tunnels that, soon after, are fitted with tracks. Those tracks run from the new terminus at Vaughn Metropolitan Centre and connect to what used to be Downsview station (now known as Sheppard West).

The tunnels, thus emptied of tunnel-boring machine bodies, the bodies of Toronto Transit Commission workers and those of urban explorers trying to reach the former while dodging the latter, will be temporarily vacated. They will then be filled with the bodies of thousands, hundreds of thousands and then millions of commuters who will never walk these tunnels but will scream through them in carriages at high speed.

The privilege of putting ear to track is thus rendered in the present moment, amid the softly settling dust spat out by masticating machines, bathed in the glow and the rumble, where one finds a sense of solace and a sense of place – a feeling that no one belongs here more than you, the quiet lurker, the infrastructural fetishist. Patiently, you contort yourself into an architectural crevice and wait for the hum to die down. The workers have gone home to their families for another night. You begin to creep again. Finally, at the bleeding edge of the excavation, inside the machine cab (it was Torkie) and awash with satisfaction, you sit down, press the green button and begin drilling.

Overleaf
The moment when platforms split into adjacent tube tunnels, long before the tracks are laid.

Wares, Rights and Stars: Delhi's Metro and Bazar
Carlos López Galviz

Nobles, merchants, dancers and prostitutes are part of the history of Chawri Bazar, one of the most iconic wholesale markets in Delhi, founded some 175 years ago. Rapid exchange of urban travellers now supersedes centuries-old trade and enjoyment, as the market is also the deepest metro station in India (30 m/nearly 100 ft below ground). The station is part of the Yellow Line, the second to open and in 2014 one of the busiest of a 190-kilometre (120-mi.) system. The Metro company bored the first tunnels ever built in Delhi for a stretch of 11 kilometres (7 mi.) and despite legislation protecting trees.[11]

The authorities perceive the moving of masses 'as a vehicle for inculcating a culture of discipline, order, routine and cleanliness in Delhi'.[12] Reordering the space of the city as much as its practices has been a strong symbol of the inroads into modernization and progress made by the city and by India as a whole. The system is a powerful symbol of that process, although strong reservations remain about the employment conditions of metro workers. The Delhi Metro Rail Corporation Ltd has outsourced a number of jobs, such as the issuing of tokens and passes, the assisting of passengers and the cleaning of premises, a fact that has unsurprisingly introduced a model of private contractors and subcontractors that limit the rights and wages of the workers themselves. At the other end of the spectrum is Bollywood. An important part of the DMRC's income comes from leases to film companies. In 2008–9 alone, six Bollywood movies used the metro as a location, paying around Rs1,000,000 (well over £10,000) an hour.[13] The question is whether and how underpaid workers and Bollywood stars can meet – figuratively, that is.

Chawri means meeting place; so does *bazar*. Just as the metro has succeeded in presenting an image of change for the better in a metropolitan area of over 23 million inhabitants, other initiatives are needed so that the metro also becomes a place where the ideas, rights and minds of workers and corporate bodies meet. Important steps have been taken in that direction. Chawri Bazar is one of ten designated stations for the 'promotion of social causes', including health awareness campaigns and shelter and other basic services for children and the elderly. At the same time, Delhi's metro is part of the Nova Group of Metros, which together with Community of Metros (COMET) forms a benchmarking conglomerate with members in cities across the world, including Buenos Aires, São Paulo, New York, Montreal, London, Paris, Berlin, Moscow, Singapore, Hong Kong, Beijing, Shanghai and Sydney. Key aims of the group are sharing good practice and measuring

Chawri Bazar station sign
on the Delhi Metro, in
the style of the London
Underground.

performance in areas such as growth, innovation, customer base, safety and the environment.[14] Presumably contractual obligations and employment conditions are part of 'Internal Processes', one of the six different areas in which companies are assessed following a KPI (Key Performance Indicator) model. The global and the local meet in Delhi's metro, therefore. Now it is time to ask what language will be used, whose interests will be reflected and what the consequences will be for whom. After all, this is part of what bazars and metros share: the coming together of people, their wares and ideas, their futures and promises.

DWELLING

I t is but a short step from working underground to living there. The reasons for dwelling underground are numerous: to escape religious persecution; to flee from social or political terror; to find shelter despite being homeless; to look for work in times of hardship; to find security in times of war; or to revel in seemingly unrestrained freedom. The attraction of living underground – whether by necessity or choice – might very well stem from alternative uses of spaces whose function is challenged and redefined by creativity as much as by need. As the phenomenologist Gaston Bachelard (1884–1962) wrote, the house (particularly in childhood) is usually imagined as a vertical object: 'It rises upward . . . it differentiates itself in terms of its verticality [and] appeals to our consciousness of verticality.' As Bachelard intimates, when we dwell in a cellar (imaginatively or physically) we are engaging with 'the dark entity of the house', namely that space which reminds us of the 'irrationality of the depths'.[1] Here, buried space is equated with the unconscious.

In Bachelard's terms, underground 'dwelling' might be a fundamentally positive – if inherently fearful – experience; once we inhabit the depths, we both 'tame' those fears and achieve a new richness of existence. But what of the underground homes born of desperation, or of terror; the Lviv sewers that sheltered Jewish refugees for fourteen months during the Nazi occupation (dramatized in Agnieszka Holland's film *In Darkness* of 2011); the homeless who live in an abandoned section of the New York City Subway, brought to light in Marc Singer's documentary *Dark Days* (2000); or the sewers of Bogotá, where hiding children are routinely hunted down and killed by death squads? In all these examples, the underground is a site of both danger and safety; the storm shelter and the tomb. In a sense, the very fact of an enforced form of underground dwelling should prompt us to engage critically with what it means to dwell in cities, especially when we think about marginalized segments of society.[2] If the underground becomes a shelter that also protects us from the reality of inequality and social injustice, are we not obliged to shed light on such spaces?

We may react in horror at the thought and evidence of enforced confinement underground. Such horror, however, is perhaps rooted in our identification with the fact that we are all, to some extent, already living underground, whether in the depths of our own minds or, as Rosalind Williams has reminded us, beneath an atmosphere rapidly faltering above our heads.[3]

Underground Outback: Coober Pedy, Australia
Mariëlle van der Meer

On 1 February 1915 a young Willie Hutchinson stumbled on a couple of pieces of opal while camping in the South Australian desert with his father during a search for gold. Very soon afterwards the first opal claim was pegged, and a town was born. Coober Pedy derives its name from *kupa-piti*, an Aboriginal expression meaning 'white man in a hole' – which refers to the fact that most of the town's population live in underground dwellings. Coober Pedy is also known as the opal capital of the world, and since it was founded in 1915 a steady stream of opportunists, eccentrics and adventurers have arrived there, all in search of a fortune, of their souls or of a place to call home. With temperatures exceeding 40°C (104°F) for eight months of the year, and a growing collection of caves and tunnels sitting empty from mining and excavation, it seemed a logical step to turn those underground spaces into homes, thereby avoiding the harsh heat and the cost of building new dwellings. Yet what started as a pragmatic answer to the constraints of nature and available space became a trend in real estate, and today underground residences, or 'dug-outs' as they are known locally, are purpose-built. The cost of building a three-bedroom house underground is as high as the equivalent above ground, yet without the need for air conditioning the cost of living underground is far lower.

It was around six in the morning when I stumbled groggily off the Greyhound bus into the eerily bright desert light of Coober Pedy after a mostly sleepless twelve-hour journey from Adelaide. I had decided that I wanted to spend a few days in this intriguing town, to try and get a feel of what it's like to live underground and to get to know more

Underground chapel:
Coober Pedy, Australia.

about the motley crew of characters who had settled down here. At first glance, there wasn't much to see: a few streets; a handful of buildings; a petrol station; everything coloured in the same dusty, faded reddish tones characteristic of the Outback. Then I realized two things that were different: first, I couldn't see a single tree, bush or any other naturally growing shrub (I found out later that the only tree in Coober Pedy is a man-made iron structure); second, on the horizon, instead of buildings I could see a scattering of conical hills, which gave the entire scene an apocalyptic, even alien ambience. No wonder that films such as *Mad Max Beyond Thunderdome* (1985), *The Adventures of Priscilla, Queen of the Desert* (1994) and *Until the End of the World* (1991) were filmed here.

I had booked accommodation in the Opal Cave, or Bedrock Hostel, which, as the name suggests, is an underground abode. It was the first time I had stayed below ground, and I felt a mixture of excitement and disorientation. It was as if there was no here and now: context became irrelevant. Like Alice after her fall through the rabbit hole, I was in a different world, where my habitual way of making sense of my surroundings did not apply. That first night, I slept for about twelve hours; without any sounds, any daylight filtering in, there was no sense of day and night.

Interestingly, Coober Pedy is one of the most multicultural communities in Australia, its population of 3,500 comprising more

than 45 nationalities. It experienced, as did most of Australia, a big surge in population after the Second World War, when a steady stream of mostly eastern and southern European men came to the town to try their luck mining opal. One such character was Crocodile Harry, a Latvian immigrant, whose bizarre underground home I visited during my stay. After accidentally killing a crocodile in Australia's Northern Territory in self-defence and realizing that he could make a decent amount of money by selling its skin, Harry built up his first small fortune in the crocodile industry before moving to Coober Pedy to try his luck with opal. An adventurer, recluse and womanizer, Harry dug out a cave that he (rather dubiously) called his 'nest', with the inside walls shaped like a woman's labia and breasts. These walls are covered with photographs and other mementos of ladies who have lived with him over the years. When I met Harry (in 1996) he was frail, old and ill – and there was something distinctly sad about seeing him surrounded by his perverted shrine to womanhood. I have been told that these days, with Harry long gone (and, one imagines, buried for good in a true underground place), Crocodile Harry's Nest is a popular tourist destination – and has become something of a shrine to the man himself.

While Harry's story may sound rather eccentric, within the context of Coober Pedy it fits right in. There is a distinct feeling of lawlessness in the town – a combination of the uniqueness of the setting, the shared life of the opal prospector and the sense of a parallel (un)reality brought on by the unconventional life underground – that seems to encourage its inhabitants' full and proud embracing and acceptance of 'being different'. Its centennial was in 2015, and it was exactly that which was celebrated: the uniqueness of a town and its characters.

Beneath the Neon: Flood Channels, Las Vegas
Matthew O'Brien

To understand the topography of the Las Vegas valley, look at the palm of your hand. The mounds on the outside of your palm are the mountain ranges surrounding the valley: the Spring Mountains to the west; the Desert, Sheep and Las Vegas mountains to the north; the Sunrise and Frenchman mountains to the east; and the River and McCullough mountains to the south. The concave interior is the basin floor. The lines are flood channels – the more prominent ones representing primary washes – that are widening and deepening over time.

Like your palm, the 1,500-square-kilometre (600-sq.-mi.) valley is enclosed, except for a shallow groove at its southeastern edge. The Las Vegas Wash, which winds across the basin and marks its lowest elevation, escapes through this groove and empties into Lake Mead, the reservoir created when the Hoover Dam plugged the Colorado River in the mid-1930s.

In the heart of the Mojave Desert, Las Vegas – which attracts 40 million visitors a year, making it more popular than Mecca – is devastatingly hot and dry. The city's average maximum temperature in the summer months is 39°C (102°F). Its average yearly rainfall is 115 mm (4.5 in.; Los Angeles averages 330 mm/13 in. of rain a year and Seattle 940 mm/37 in.), and there are often months without any measurable precipitation.

During the spring and summer, however, air from the Gulf of Mexico produces thunderstorms that release significant amounts of rain in short periods of time. The hardpan desert floor (and all the asphalt and concrete) allows little infiltration, and so the slopes of the basin carry the water to the lower and more urbanized elevations en route to the Las Vegas Wash, at speeds exceeding 40 kilometres (25 mi.) per hour. Pavements become streams, streets rivers and intersections lakes. Rubbish bins, news-stands, cars, mobile homes and people are swept away, which isn't good for tourism.

In 1985, following a series of summer floods that crippled Sin City, the Nevada Legislature authorized the creation of the Clark County Regional Flood Control District. The goals of the District included developing a masterplan to reduce flooding, regulating land use in flood zones and helping to fund the maintenance of channels. This was the valley's first serious and coordinated approach to flood control, which had previously been done piecemeal by various Southern Nevada entities. In 1986 Clark County voters, traditionally reluctant to support flood control while casting ballots under clear skies, approved a quarter-cent sales tax to fund the flood Control District. The following year,

One of the people who has taken up residence in the flood channels of Las Vegas.

revenues arrived. Finally, in 1988, construction began on the first project: the channelling of the Las Vegas Wash between Craig Road and Civic Center Drive. The District has been playing a spirited – and unwinnable – game of catch-up ever since.

Along with the Las Vegas Valley, which had a population of 750,000 in 1990 and was in 2014 home to over two million people, the flood-control system is in constant growth. An intricate web that reaches from mountain range to mountain range, like the lines of your palm, it consists of 75 detention basins and 885 kilometres (550 mi.) of channels, more than 320 kilometres (200 mi.) of which are underground. What secrets do the Las Vegas storm drains keep? What lies beneath the neon? The answer is debris (X-rated flyers, beer cans, Bibles), art (graffiti, murals, poetry, philosophy) and people – hundreds of people.

Ernie, a former thoroughbred jockey and current video-poker addict, has lived in a lateral pipe under Interstate 15 for ten years. He painted its midsection beige so that he can detect black widow spiders. He has survived multiple floods while stranded in the pipe, which is a dead end and doesn't drain water. 'I've been lucky', he says with a Tennessee twang. 'Real lucky. I've been through three of the big ones in here. I've been trapped for days when the rain got too rowdy. I'll tell you what. I've seen God. Me and God have had some long talks, buddy.'

Harold, 1.8 metres (6 ft) tall with an Afro, has lived in a downtown drain for five years, on and off. A former chef, he's saving money working odd jobs and hopes to move out of the tunnel soon. His spot includes a Coleman camp stove, an assortment of pots and pans, and makeshift shelves lined with oils, spices and other condiments. 'Anything you want to eat right now, I can fix it for you', says Harold proudly. 'I got it all down here, man. Ham, spaghetti, meatballs. I cook three meals a day every day.'

Gary moved from Seattle to Las Vegas twenty years ago to kick a cocaine habit, making him perhaps the only person to come to Vegas to get away from cocaine. Leaving the coke behind, he found plenty of methamphetamine. Laziness and a meth addiction have kept him on the streets, he said, and he has lived in a drain just west of the Strip for about three years. His camp, illuminated during the day by a ceiling grate (his skylight), consists of a single mattress, an office chair and a wooden spool that serves as a coffee table. Gary says he has colon cancer and doesn't have long to live.

Downstream from Gary's camp, past an impressive graffiti gallery and under the Las Vegas Strip, the ceiling drops and the tunnel turns eastwards. Pipes punch holes in the walls. The smell of mildew is overwhelming. Concrete, cockroaches and a stream of run-off 5 centimetres (2 in.) deep are the only things to keep you company.

'The underworld is a mirror of the world above ground', wrote Klaus Klemp in *Underworld: Sites of Concealment.*[4] But down here in the dark, there are few clues to the gambling carnival more than 9 metres (30 ft) overhead. There are, however, similarities between the drains and the casinos: both neutralize all sense of time, their exits can be hard to find and – despite the presence of people – they're among the loneliest places on earth.

Parts of this text are adapted from Matthew O'Brien, 'Beneath the Neon: Life and Death in the Tunnels of Las Vegas' (Las Vegas, 2007)

Death Squads and Firebombs: Sewers of Bogotá
Bradley L. Garrett

In considering potential living spaces in cities, sewers would probably be at the bottom of everyone's list. They're cramped, they're dirty, they're smelly and they're not easy to get into and out of. However, they are also, for all these reasons, the last place someone might look for you, making them an ideal hideout.

Since the 1990s the sewers of Bogotá, Colombia, have been filled with social and political refugees, many of whom are almost constantly high on *basuco* (a mixture of crack, pulverized glass and chemicals) and glue. Before you pass judgement, however, be aware that many of these people have seen their friends and family burned alive by paramilitary groups who firebombed the sewers trying to eradicate them.

A number of those living in the sewers of Bogotá are simply the poor (considered by many to be 'disposables'). Others have fled underground because they were targets of right-wing paramilitary groups during Colombia's 'Dirty War', which began in the early 1980s. In the 1990s, when the US government directed $300 million in foreign funds ($60 million of which was in arms sales) in an 'emergency aid' package to the Colombian government. What was the emergency, you might ask? It was the rising power of the political left, including trade unions, which threatened the right-wing political order preferred by the US government.[5] In 2004 the *New York Times* reported that 'Colombia is by far the world's most dangerous country for union members, with 94 killed last year and 47 slain by August 25 this year.'[6] These dreadful statistics are part of the story of the Bogotá underground, where hundreds still live today.

Most of the refugees in the sewers, however, are simply the underclasses, forced underground by rampant social violence. For

Two members of a sewer gang emerge from a manhole in Bogotá.

a brief moment, in the early 1990s, a *Los Angeles Times* article gave voice to this humanitarian crisis.[7] There was a minor increase of awareness and an influx of aid. Then, after the cameras had gone and the story had ceased to be a headline, the death squads swept in again, conducting 'social cleansing' retribution raids, fuelled by embarrassment, with a disturbing amount of support from the government and the public.

Many of those who fled into the sewers to avoid the death squads years ago took their children with them. In one sewer, a couple had been living for seventeen years and had given birth to three children. In another, according to Kara McIver, a human rights campaigner, 'a rotating group of teenagers was living beneath one manhole. Once it was determined they could not get into the sewer with their guns, the police poured gasoline into the tunnel and lit a match, burning 22 kids alive.'[8]

These stories are horrible to read. Yet they are a necessary counterbalance to many of the celebratory entries in this book. The underground, in many cultures of the past, was a place of fear, death and horror. Modern technology is allowing us to spend more time underground than we ever have before, easing some of that historic stigma. However, it's important to keep in mind the fact that, for many, the underground remains a place of death and horror. As should be evident from many of the entries in this book, it is far too easy to forget what we don't see, right underneath our feet. There is no more important place to keep in mind than the sewers of Bogotá.

Mateship Below: Melbourne Drains
Darmon Richter

It wasn't until I visited Melbourne that I heard the term 'mateship'. In *The Australian Legend* (1958), Russel Ward describes this cultural idiom as a concept integral to the Australian character, encapsulating not only friendship, but loyalty and equality besides.[9] Ward's own affiliations with the Australian Communist Party might tempt one to liken its usage to that of 'comrade'; nevertheless, the term is applied broadly in defining the spirit of post-colonial Australia.

In an examination of the notorious Ned Kelly gang, for instance, Philip Butterss has highlighted the characteristics of 'anti-authoritarianism, egalitarianism and mateship' as key factors in the invocation of Australia's national identity. The term 'mateship' could, however, be used just as easily to define the culture of those contemporary outlaws who dedicate themselves to exploring the extensive networks of storm drains beneath Australia.[10]

These drains have their roots in nineteenth-century city planning. The Victoria Gold Rush hit its peak during the 1880s, by which point Melbourne was among the wealthiest cities in the world and second largest in the British Empire, after London.[11] London itself was undergoing a vast overhaul at the time, as the Metropolitan Board of Works – under its chief engineer, Sir Joseph Bazalgette – constructed more than 1,900 kilometres (1,200 mi.) of tunnels that revolutionized the city's sewers. Australian architects took their cue from British urban engineering and set about creating expansive networks of storm-water drains beneath their fledgling cities.

In the case of Melbourne – a city built on the flood plains of the Yarra River, and whose early expansion was blocked by broad swathes of marshland – these drainage systems were instrumental in the future growth of the metropolis. Between 1870 and 1910 almost all the region's natural streams were redirected into canals, which in time were built over as new development sprawled.[12] Today, there exist almost 1,600 kilometres (1,000 mi.) of drainage tunnels beneath Melbourne alone, urban caves that spill at regular intervals along the banks of the Yarra, posing what must be an irresistible lure to youngsters with a taste for adventure. On 26 January 1986, Australia Day, three such youngsters, Woody, Dougo and Sloth, teamed up to form an exploration club known as the 'Cave Clan'.

One of the Cave Clan's early discoveries was the brick-lined tomb of the Hawk's Burn, a former tributary to the Yarra River. Among Australian 'drainers', the culture is one of appropriation; they had stumbled across the underground stream on ANZAC Day in 1987 –

the anniversary of the landing of the Australian and New Zealand Army Corps at Gallipoli – and so it was rechristened the ANZAC Drain.

In the 1980s and 1990s the Cave Clan documented more than a hundred drain systems across the city, with the rule that whoever first 'discovered' a drain would earn the right to name it. Thus one finds titles such as 'Bob's Evil Manhole', '3 Days Drain', 'Snake Pit' and 'Dougo's Dunny'. The group's maps became a phenomenological record not only of geography, but incorporating personalities and experiences into a rapidly developing contemporary folklore of the undercity.

The concept of mateship echoes throughout the Melbourne drains, many of which have been put to new use as social hangouts. Old sofas laboriously dragged beneath the surface of the city; empty beer bottles; guestbooks painted on to walls; even the lines of graffiti that advise of easy exit points or potential dangers ahead: these are the ephemera of mateship. In the ANZAC Drain, one large space has been reimagined as a clubhouse. Referred to as the Chamber, it is where today's Cave Clan gathers for annual festivities and awards ceremonies, a celebration of the achievements of the city's drain explorers. More than that, though,

Exploring stormwater drains in Melbourne.

it has become a shrine. On one wall are recorded the names of the fallen: Michael 'Predator' Carlton, for example, founder of the Sydney offshoot of the Cave Clan. Another mention goes to Jeff Chapman, aka Ninjalicious, a renowned Canadian explorer and founder of the pioneering urban exploration zine *Infiltration*.[13]

For deceased explorers, though, there can be no more fitting memorial than their own hand-drawn marks on the tunnel walls. Predator's graffitied tags, which appear far and wide beneath the streets of Melbourne, now form a part of the local legend; they sit alongside those of the engineer Alf Sadlier of the Melbourne Metropolitan Board of Works, who, during reconstruction work in the 1940s and 1950s, would sign his name in tar paint on the drain walls.

In this way Melbourne's drains have evolved into something of a cultural scrapbook, the collected thoughts and experiences of countless strangers united by curiosity. In Tenth Drain, graffiti scrawled on one section of pipe neatly summarizes this culture of anti-authoritarianism, egalitarianism and mateship: 'Hello to adventurers who come to places like this.'

Class Dividers: Lower Wacker Drive, Chicago
James Wolfinger

A single road on Chicago's Lower Wacker Drive has become famous as the setting for numerous cinematic underground sequences, including chase scenes in *The Dark Knight* (2008), *The Blues Brothers* (1980) and the Bollywood film *Dhoom 3* (2013). Even after recent renovations, the 3.2-kilometre (2-mi.) underground road (it is really at ground level, but, like the rest of Chicago's Loop, it was elevated out of the Lake Michigan basin in the mid-nineteenth century), which follows the Chicago River, still has 800 support pillars, blind turns and 30,000 vehicles a day that race down it. A *Chicago Tribune* reporter likened driving on Lower Wacker to being in a video game, where 'a stream of passing cars, trucks and even CTA [Chicago Transit Authority] buses . . . echoing horns and flashing yellow warning lights . . . elevate the heart rate and moisten the palms [especially] when traffic suddenly materializes from entrance ramps and behind concrete pillars'. The visual sensation of the road has made it irresistible to Hollywood location scouts. That most public of images, however, is only part of the story.[14]

Upper and Lower Wacker Drive have their roots in Daniel Burnham's famed Plan of Chicago (1909), which aimed to transform

The multi-layered Lower
Wacker Drive, Chicago.

the city from 'Hog Butcher to the World'
into 'Paris on the Prairie'. The Burnham
Plan proposed improvements to the city's
lakefront, railway terminals and parks, and
envisioned the two Wacker Drives as a means
to improve the ambience of the riverside while
removing the old fish and vegetable markets
that lined the Chicago River. In their place,
the city would have an above-ground road for
businessmen and tourists and an underground
road for delivery trucks and service vehicles.

Since the first section of Lower Wacker
was completed, in 1926, the roads have thus
deliberately served as both creator and marker of urban class difference.
The streets above, such as Upper Wacker Drive and its intersection with
Michigan Avenue (the high-rent 'Magnificent Mile'), to this day appeal
to tourists and well-heeled Chicagoans alike. A stone's throw from
Lower Wacker, such people can stay at the new Trump International
Hotel, shop at Burberry and Ann Taylor, and dine on steak at Smith &
Wollensky. Many visitors take the riverboat tours that run parallel to
Lower Wacker and show off the city's architectural treasures: the Civic
Opera House, the Tribune Building, the Wrigley Building. Seldom, if
ever, do the tour guides mention Lower Wacker Drive, although the
Beaux-Arts boulevard is just 20 metres (20 yd) away, at eye level, and
obvious to anyone on the river.

The class-based nature of Lower Wacker became even more
apparent just a few years after its construction with the onset of the
Great Depression. Reporters believed that the nooks and crannies
along the road housed as many as 1,000 unemployed Chicagoans, who
found shelter there from the region's brutal winters. They popularized
it as the 'Hoover Hotel', although some took to calling Lower Wacker
Chicago's version of the Paris catacombs. Ever since, the city's homeless
have found refuge beside this underground thoroughfare. As late as the
1990s, reporters estimated that over a hundred people lived on Lower
Wacker, and such reporting was strongly reminiscent of the social
reformer Jacob Riis, who a century earlier had described the landscape
as 'downtown's dark and dangerous underbelly', a place of 'mystique
[that] lies below the surface'.[15]

In the late 1990s Mayor Richard Daley, as part of his beautification
programme for the city, sought $350 million to rebuild Lower Wacker
Drive. The city would no longer tolerate a homeless population
underground, living in the shadows, sometimes literally in those cast
by their open fires. City employees locked gates along the road and sent

rubbish trucks to remove the meagre belongings of the homeless. The police forcibly evicted those who would not go on their own. These actions pleased those who thought the government was taking Chicago back; but they appalled others, who wondered how far Americans would stoop to torment the poorest in society. Studs Terkel, the city's great humanitarian and oral historian, denounced the move to 'evict people from a public space where they have been for years, where they have disturbed nobody'. 'What is happening to us as humans?' he asked.[16]

Terkel's question was a good one, although he might have broadened it to ask how we had created a society that had so many homeless living on Lower Wacker in the first place. An astute observer of society – Chicago's in particular – Terkel could not have missed the juxtaposition of comfort and wealth above ground and terrible poverty below. As George Gardner, an evicted homeless man, put it: 'We're one of the richest countries in the entire world, and we got poverty that's unreal. It don't make sense.' It may not, but Lower Wacker Drive certainly highlights it.

Diggers and Deserters: Odessa Catacombs
Darmon Richter

Beneath Odessa, a port city on the coast of Ukraine, lies a labyrinth: a complex network of tunnels that, at an estimated total length of 2,500 kilometres (1,550 mi.), may be the largest underground system in the world.[17] The Odessa catacombs grew out of natural cavities, fissures and caves that were expanded in the seventeenth century to form smuggling tunnels; in the nineteenth century there was a rapid boom in construction and the tunnels beneath the city were developed into working limestone mines. By the end of the century the catacombs were spread across three distinct levels that descended to a depth of 60 metres (nearly 200 ft) below sea level.[18]

The mining operations were interrupted, however, by the Russian Civil War of 1917, and the catacombs reverted to a realm of smugglers and ne'er-do-wells.[19] They would remain like this – a lawless, subterranean kingdom – until the Second World War, when they had an opportunity for redemption.

When Nazi forces drove the Red Army out of Odessa in 1941, an estimated 6,000 Soviet partisans remained behind, hidden in the tunnels beneath the city and living on food and other supplies that were lowered down shafts by the rebels above. From there they would launch surprise strikes on the invaders, before disappearing back into the catacombs.

Tunnel in the vast complex of catacombs and tunnels beneath Odessa.

These partisans survived hunger, cave-ins and Nazi poison-gas strikes; many remained at their posts until as late as April 1944, when the Soviet Army returned to liberate the city.[20]

For the children of Odessa, the myths of the catacombs are an heirloom, their secrets a repository of national pride. 'Diggers don't make maps', one local told me as he led me down into the labyrinth; 'It's against the rules.' Such discretion indicates a partisan mentality, the philosophy of the rebel class, and perhaps explains why the Odessa catacombs remain such a well-kept secret today.

Many people will have heard of the Paris catacombs, while those in Rome have featured in Hollywood blockbusters such as *Indiana Jones and the Last Crusade* (1989). Odessa's labyrinth, meanwhile, always manages to avoid the spotlight – despite the fact that these tunnels run to a total length that is more than three times those of Paris and Rome combined; indeed, greater than the distance from Odessa to Paris itself.

Another key factor is the process of fetishization. The catacombs beneath Paris are famously littered with human bones and daubed with bright or macabre graffiti, and serve as a counter-cultural meeting place for the city's self-designated *cataphiles*. In Rome, the tone of the catacombs is defined by ornate altarpieces built from human skulls, mummified bodies and the bejewelled skeletons of saints. Such *memento mori* serve to shape the mythos of the tunnels, as well as directing the experience of those who descend into the darkness.

The Odessa catacombs are bare and their history is one of concealment. What evidence there is of humanity – poems scrawled on walls in Cyrillic script, the remains of military encampments – survives in the form of occasional landmarks, rather than a structured environment. Contemporary explorers do not dictate the tone of this place; rather, their marks, litter and debris are swallowed in time by the darkness itself. These crumbling limestone walls have a habit of eating up graffiti; even the most deeply etched marks, the most indelible paints, will in time fall to dust.

The mythology of these catacombs, too, forms a narrative of inhospitality. There are folk tales of lost treasures that have lured seekers to their deaths beneath Odessa, and of the 'White Hunter', the spirit of a lost mercenary that is said to roam the labyrinth. Legends even tell of a subterranean god, a vengeful deity that imprisons those who would seek to steal its treasures. In a shifting labyrinth such as this, where rockfalls and subsidence create an ever-changing topology so that even frequent explorers must choose different routes from one visit to the next, such deification proves a poetic metaphor for nature's autonomy.

While those other European catacombs may be perceived as dark and morbid places, as dungeons or as oubliettes, they are at least *human* places. The Odessa catacombs, in comparison, are a *nowhere*. Skulls and bones may be unsettling, but there is ultimately nothing more terrifying than the emptiness of a void.

On the last night of 2004 a group of local youths descended into Odessa's catacombs to celebrate the new year. In the ensuing revelry, however, they lost count of their own number and a girl, Masha, was left behind in the tunnels. Later – that is, almost three years later – coroners recovering the corpse would speculate that Masha had spent three days alive in the darkness before finally dying from dehydration. So much for *memento mortis*; perhaps *oblivisci mortis* is a better term for the capacity of these catacombs to swallow all traces of life, to digest even death itself within their timeless depths.

REFUSE

Human-built underworlds are no longer solely urban phenomena. The techniques and technology used to excavate below city streets have also afforded the possibility of spatial submersion in more rural areas, where gold, seeds, servers and secrets are being sunk. It is also where we now put much of our waste.

The underground, according to David Pike, has long functioned as a place where the 'ruins of things, places, people, techniques and ideas end up both figuratively and literally'. As 'garbage dumps and landfills of the world', the underground as a site of refuse is a fundamental tenet of capitalism: constant accumulation requires a place to dump the waste left behind, preferably buried and therefore out of sight and mind.[1] The notion of hidden waste has its origins in the classical *mundus*, a shadowy place underneath the centre of Roman towns: a pit where trash and filth of every kind was dumped, whether public rubbish, the bodies of condemned criminals or newborn babies whose fathers had been disinclined to raise them. As the philosopher Henri Lefebvre (1901–1991) remarked, the *mundus* was not only an accursed place, but also one that 'connected the city, the space above ground, land-as-soil and land-as-territory, to the hidden, clandestine, subterranean spaces which were those of fertility and death, of the beginning and the end, of birth and burial'. Later translated by Christians into the consecrated ground of cemeteries, the *mundus* was, at root, an ambiguous space that was also a site of the 'greatest foulness and the greatest purity, life and death, fertility and destruction, horror and fascination'.[2]

The rapid growth of cities during the nineteenth century challenged the essential ambiguity of the *mundus*: with the planning and construction of vast citywide sewer systems in both London and Paris in the 1850s and 1860s, waste was separated into its usable and non-usable components, and the latter expelled from the city limits. Widely adopted from then on in towns and cities across the world – including Boston, Washington, DC, and New York – these sewer networks effectively created a new kind of *mundus*: a space entirely removed from the city, where waste could be effectively consigned to oblivion. Yet, despite the development of increasingly sophisticated ways of treating sewage from the 1880s onwards, there was nevertheless always a residue, whether toxic sludge that was dumped far out at sea or, more recently, poisonous ash that remains when human excrement is incinerated.[3] And yet, despite our desires to consign refuse and waste to the realm of the unseen, there has remained an anonymous fascination with it. Residents of nineteenth-century Paris – many enticed by photographs of the city's sewers (one of the first underground places to be photographed) – visited them to take boat rides down the underground sewerage channels.[4] Today tours of sewers are still offered in Paris, Vienna, Brighton and Tokyo, among other places.

Perhaps no form of waste demonstrates the illusion of extermination better than that left over from nuclear fission. With an almost unimaginable longevity (up to a million years in some cases), nuclear waste reinvigorates the essential meaning of the *mundus*, which was, according to Lefebvre, a 'void' at the centre of the world; indeed, as Martin Heidegger pointed out, *mundus* was one of the Latin words for 'the whole of creation'.[5] The spaces that contain nuclear waste, no matter how deeply buried, nevertheless constitute a 'whole' beyond human understanding – a void that presents a challenge to the very foundation of the more familiar worlds that we construct above ground. Our fascination with that relationship of course causes other problems, since humans, insatiably interested in the remains, seek them out against all common sense.

Into the Vortex: Brighton Sewers
Bradley L. Garrett

Brighton was not far behind London in the construction of a robust and aesthetically striking sewer system in the Victorian era. In the mid-1860s, in the midst of the engineering feat plotted by Sir Joseph Bazalgette (1819–1891) to harness London's rivers into the world's most complicated and ornate series of sewerage channels, officials in Brighton thought the construction of a similar (but infinitely simpler) system to transport waste from houses to the sea was nothing short

Overleaf
The vertical outfall of Eddie's Vortex.

of a modern necessity. London-by-the-Sea was not to be outshone by its older sibling.

The mortar between the millions of hand-laid bricks that make up the sewer colloquially known as COTS (The Colossus of the South) was made from sand from the town's beach. The construction stripped the seafront and left the beaches in their current state – covered in pebbles. And, as in London, the nineteenth-century brickwork that makes up COTS – enveloped in dead sea creatures – is still in public use today. Standing on Brighton pier looking west, outside the entrance to the arcade, one can look down into a jutting stone jetty and see something rather remarkable: a grille of rusting iron bars guarding the outlet to COTS. The stacked-stone groyne is in fact a hollow sewer outfall. As they ping off their holiday snaps, perching over the serene sea with the pier's whirling, whirring carnival rides in the background, very few tourists are aware that they are standing on top of a still functioning 150-year-old sewer designed to jettison raw effluent into the sea in the event of a faecal emergency. In non-critical situations, however, sewage never makes it this far; instead it is transported to a pumping station at Peacehaven that is disguised as an ornate Victorian railway station. Only in Brighton, the capital of weird Britain.

In the 1990s a decision was made (this time ahead of London) to upgrade the Victorian system. A tunnel-boring machine similar to the one that ripped through the English Channel to create the Chunnel was dropped into a large excavation on the seafront and, in a short space of time, Lower COTS was excavated: a massive (and decidedly less interesting) cement pipe, built to accommodate storm water and Upper COTS overflow. The pipe was dug out 30 metres (98 ft) below street level, far deeper than would have been practicable in the nineteenth century, and right under Brighton's most famous asset – its shingle beach. Digging at this depth also allowed the use of one of Brighton's greatest infrastructural assets: a gently sloping topography that facilitates gravity-fed flow. In Brighton, everything stops at the beach.

But how are the systems connected, you might ask, one being below the other? The answer lies in the photograph shown here: a 20-metre (66-ft) vertical pipe, a unique piece of sewer engineering known as Eddie's Vortex. The run-off rolling down the Victorian bricks of Upper COTS, just below the surface of the street, converges into a terrifying whirlpool where it is flung into the air in a spiral of storm water, spilling down into Lower COTS in an endless stream. Standing in the middle of the ring of water at the bottom, it is difficult not to imagine it as a Star Trek transporter pod, ready to beam a hapless space explorer on to some desolate planet populated by angry aliens.

Southern Water, the current custodian of this unique public space, conducts regular tours of COTS. Indeed, Brighton is the only place in Britain where members of the public can tour the Victorian infrastructure beneath their feet, and if you find yourself there you should most certainly take the opportunity to see the old system. For those of you looking for a more hands-on experience, a manhole in Victoria Gardens and 30 metres (98 ft) of rope will get you into Lower COTS through Eddie's Vortex, although I'd suggest you bring a waterproof poncho if you want to stand in the transporter.

Waste and Work: New York City Sewers
David L. Pike

The iconic New York underground space is not the sewer but the Subway, symbol of modernity for the first half of the twentieth century and image of its failures in the second half. As in most world cities, however, it is the waterworks that actually constitute the oldest, most extensive and costly component of the subterranean infrastructure. The sewerage system grew out of New York's native network of streams, covered over as they became polluted by industry and incorporated into the drainage system, which, for all of Manhattan and a greater part of the other boroughs, combines waste removal and storm drainage in a single network.[6] Construction is ongoing: the first of the aqueducts to bring water into the city dates from the first half of the nineteenth century; the construction of Tunnel No. 3, the largest public works endeavour in the history of the United States, began in 1970 and is scheduled for completion in 2020. New York City's 9,600 kilometres (6,000 mi.) of sewerage pipes dwarf the 1,355 kilometres (842 mi.) of tracks that comprise the Subway system.[7] Blasted out of bedrock at depths of up to 305 metres (1,000 ft) and up to 7.5 metres (24 ft) in diameter, the water tunnels are of a scale that far exceeds the imagery of everyday life that characterizes the quotidian spaces of the Subway.

Nothing could be more mundane than the purpose of the tunnels – providing water to the city and removing waste from it – but that purpose cuts to the heart of the metropolis. An outbreak of cholera in 1832 and a devastating fire two years later spurred the construction of the Croton Aqueduct. Planning for Tunnel No. 3 began in 1954, when engineers realized that it would be impossible to repair ageing Tunnels Nos 1 and 2 without being able to shut them down, prompting a number of both plausible and apocalyptic scenarios based on the breakdown of these tunnels before the new one could be completed.[8]

Apocalyptic sewer ooze in *Ghostbusters II* (1989).

The sewers have also played their part in other kinds of apocalyptic fantasies, although these are primarily mythic rather than infrastructural in character. In an echo of their origins in the natural landscape, they have long been the haven of monstrous New Yorkers, from alligators and CHUDS (Cannibalistic Humanoid Underground Dwellers) to the Teenage Mutant Ninja Turtles and Marvel Comics' Morlocks, monstrous mutants in the X-Men world, too grotesque to pass as human, who have established a secret community deep underground.[9] Water here distinguishes the monstrous from the everyday, as in this comparison by a sandhog (New York tunnel worker) of his job to that of Art Carney's character in the 1950s sitcom *The Honeymooners*: 'Norton was a sewer worker. We build tunnels, he cleaned them. We're miners.'[10] Water enters sandhog narratives as a threatening, destabilizing force, as in the explosion under the East River that kills one character and establishes the lifelong relationships of the others in Colum McCann's *This Side of Brightness* (1998), or the free-flowing alcohol that enables the city's racist and violent id to emerge above ground in Jimmy Breslin's epic drama *Table Money* (1986) or Thomas Kelly's *Payback* (1997).[11]

Where sandhog novels explore exclusion and inequality in the realist terms of working-class experience, sewer narratives imagine the same social categories in the pulp exaggerations of fantasy. Both forms flourished in the 1980s, when the economic and political policies of the Reagan administration exacerbated social division and made nuclear apocalypse a probable scenario. But where sandhog fiction imagines the underground as a racially and ethnically blind space (formed in 1903, the sandhog union, Local 147, was the first integrated union in the country), sewer fantasies stress the failure of the democratic imagination. Epitomized by Travis Bickle's dream in *Taxi Driver* (1976) of a 'real rain' that would 'wash all this scum off the street' and down into the sewers, and sprawled across the dark vision of a Manhattan counting down to Armageddon in Alan Moore and Dave Gibbons's *Watchmen* (1986–7), the New York sewer embodies the scale of social dysfunction and the power of the dispossessed while admitting that the cause and the solution of these problems persist in the real world above.[12]

The sewers of New York continue to figure prominently in visual spectacle, but the focus of cultural attention in the twenty-first century has shifted from the human element to the infrastructural. For urban historians as well as place hackers (to borrow Bradley Garrett's evocative term), these great public works are the reminder not only of heroic labour in the past but also of a will to invest in a future that would benefit all the city's inhabitants. That this material trace of public works persists today is cause for optimism; that it can be accessed only illegally provides an equally pessimistic image of dwindling public space in the new century.

Lost Undergrounds: Atlantic Avenue Tunnel, New York
Julia Solis

The Atlantic Avenue Tunnel in Brooklyn, New York, has spent more time as a myth and mystery than as a functioning train tunnel. Since its closure more than 150 years ago, the tunnel has intrigued historians and fuelled the public imagination. It is certainly one of the most curious sites in underground New York.

The tunnel was built in 1844 as part of a plan to connect Boston and New York. At the time, Brooklyn was a new but rapidly growing city across the East River from New York, connected to Manhattan only via ferries. The Brooklyn and Jamaica Railroad Company (later replaced by the Long Island Rail Road) planned to connect a ferry stop in Brooklyn to a railway hub in Queens, and from there run services all the way to Boston. After laying tracks along Atlantic Avenue from the riverfront terminal, the company began regular operations with small passenger trains in 1836.

Steam locomotives were still a novelty, and not yet powerful enough to handle the steep uphill gradient beyond the ferry terminal. The small trains had to be pulled up by reluctant horses, causing the animals great distress and leading to vociferous complaints from the shopkeepers along Atlantic Avenue – not just about the noise but also about the smoke spewing from the steam engines, which made regular business on this main thoroughfare unbearable.

To remedy the situation, the railway company constructed an arched brick tunnel wide enough for two train tracks and about 760 metres (2,500 ft) long. Vents were installed along the tunnel roof – fenced in by railings on the street – to prevent the passage from filling with black smoke. On the opening day, a short train ran back and forth through the tunnel fifty times, carrying cheerful Brooklynites and barrels of cider for refreshment. Since it carried trains beneath a city street as early as 1844, it is considered by some to be the world's first subway tunnel.

However, this underground project failed to placate the property owners on Atlantic Avenue, who worried about the continued pollution along what was becoming an important business street. Steam locomotives were banned from the city of Brooklyn in 1859, and the tunnel closed in 1861. Under the new Tunnel Act, its ownership passed from the railway company to the city of Brooklyn. The tracks were dismantled, the portals sealed and the road above smoothed over to eliminate any traces of the tunnel's existence. It did not take long for the public to forget that it was ever there.

The subject would certainly come up on occasion. Walt Whitman famously commemorated the last days of the tunnel in a poem, and occasionally a Brooklyn newspaper would publish rumours about shady transactions beneath Atlantic Avenue. One article from 1896 relayed gossip about the underground passage being a haven for moonshiners, bandits and murderers. Already it was clear that there was only scant general knowledge of the tunnel's exact dimensions, access points

The abandoned Atlantic Avenue Tunnel, New York.

and function. There was a rumour that the riverfront end of the tunnel – which was sealed off from the main passage by a thick masonry wall – still harboured the last locomotive, resting on the tracks.

If the sealed tunnel was indeed being used illegally as a smugglers' cove or a mushroom farm, it was not clear how anyone could access it. The ventilation shafts had been filled in, so the only other entry points would seem to be via secret passages constructed from adjacent cellars, but no one had a clear idea as to where these would be. An inspector from the city's engineering department drilled through the tunnel roof in 1916, expecting to discover poisonous gas, counterfeiters and giant rodents, but found it silent and empty. Over the years the tunnel has become an urban legend, forgotten by most of the city's populace.

In 1980 an engineering student, intrigued by a radio story alluding to the lost tunnel, found a blueprint in the city archives that showed a possible manhole entrance. With the aid of a utility crew, the student climbed into the cavity below the street and managed to crawl towards the top of the former archway at the eastern end of the tunnel. The tunnel itself turned out to be completely intact, and the space was opened up for occasional tours once the entryway from the manhole was cleared and a stairway into the tunnel installed. However, the section that might contain the old locomotive remained untouched, blocked off by an enormous brick wall.

For thirty years the only way to gain access to the tunnel was through the original manhole on the busy intersection of Atlantic Avenue and Court Street. Unfortunately, New York's fire department, after issuing warnings about the lack of an emergency exit, lobbied for the closure of the site due to safety concerns. And so, in December 2010, the tunnel was sealed up once more.

However, it is unlikely that Brooklyn will ever forget about the tunnel again, not least because of the rumoured lost locomotive. In 2011 engineering consultants hired for a documentary by National Geographic investigated the riverfront section of the tunnel with a magnetometer and found a 6-metre (20-ft) metallic 'anomaly'. So far, the city has resisted plans for any official excavation of the site, claiming that it would be too disruptive to traffic. So, instead of becoming a historic artefact, the locomotive remains an object of speculation, fuelling the imagination of anyone interested in the tunnel's rich past. Some 150 years after its closure, the tunnel continues to hold its mystery.

Repressed Wastes: London's Sewers
David L. Pike

When the journalist and critic John Hollingshead published *Underground London* in 1862, the adjective of his title referred almost exclusively to the city's sewerage network. Written in the aftermath of the 'Great Stink' of 1858, when the River Thames was saturated with sewage, Hollingshead's book looked back at the 'romantic' mythology and variety of the old sewerage network and forward to the 'scientific' rationalization of the system that would emerge from the work completed in 1875 by Joseph Bazalgette, chief engineer of the Metropolitan Board of Works. The main components of the new sewer system were an interceptor tunnel feeding into the Main Drainage System east of the city at Crossness (opened in 1865) and the embankment replacing the former mudflats along the Thames (finished in 1870). Declared one of the 'Seven Industrial Wonders of the World' by the BBC in 2003, the thousands of kilometres and millions of bricks of the Victorian sewerage network remain the backbone of the city's drainage system to date.[13] However, the system today is overloaded, leading to increased overflow discharges into the Thames.[14] Current infrastructural improvements being carried out by Thames Water include the Thames Tideway Tunnel, an enormous collector sewer running for roughly 25 kilometres (15 1/2 mi.) long, running parallel to or under the Thames to intercept the 34 'most polluting sewer outflows' before they reach the river.[15] Recently approved, construction began in 2015 and is scheduled for completion in 2023 at a cost of around £5 billion ($75 billion), although critics note that the plan will eliminate far more public green space than Bazalgette's embankment.[16]

In early modern London, drainage had been in the open air and lent itself to numerous journalistic and literary accounts of literal and figurative corruption. By 1834 some 114 closed sewers had been built, a third of them after 1824. Schemes of urban renewal, such as John Nash's cut of Regent Street through the West End (1814–25), included drainage tunnels under their new streets.[17] These bricked-over conduits and the city's polluted rivers (such as the Effra, which became the tunnel pictured here) were fertile ground for the Victorian 'appetite for the wonderful in connection with the sewer', for mystery and adventure in fiction, sensational scenes on the stage, and for the unique occupations of toshing (scavenging in the tunnels) and mudlarking (foraging on the mudflats and sewer outlets along the Thames) recorded with such wonder by Henry Mayhew and others as emblems of the fantastic variety of London life.[18] Although filthy and disease-ridden, the tunnels were also associated with the vibrancy of a city that was seen to be vanishing at the onset of regularizing modernity. While Hollingshead welcomed the prospect of a salubrious city promised by the drainage works, the exuberance of his description of 'blood-sewers' beneath the meat markets, 'boiling sewers' like 'hot springs' and sewers harbouring watercress and 'edible fungi' suggests how powerfully the mythology still worked on him and his readers.[19]

Since the heroic feat of engineering achieved by Bazalgette and his workmen, the London sewer has fascinated for its combination of the strange, the atavistic and the organic with the technological, the controlled and the sanitary. Unlike many other European networks, the London sewers have never been opened to the public, although recently Thames Water has begun offering annual tours of the magnificent Abbey Mills Pumping Station and part of one of the outfall sewers. The rhetoric of reportage has changed little from a century earlier: wonder at the engineering, admiration of the sangfroid of the flushers and horror at the organic matter, most sensationally in reports of the 15-tonne ball of congealed fat discovered blocking a tunnel below Kingston upon Thames in 2013.[20]

Meanwhile, for the first time since the late nineteenth century, the London sewers have begun to catch up with the Tube as a fictional setting in popular culture.[21] Although some of these novels and films are set in the middle decades of the nineteenth century and some are set in a version of the present day, nearly all include some measure of the fantastic and a dash of criminal low life.[22] They play in varying degrees on the tension in the sewer space between organic nature controlled and organic nature turned monstrous and repulsive. Unlike imagery of the Tube, which is usually rooted in questions of everyday life, sewer settings tend to introduce elements of myth and mystery, a simultaneous dream and nightmare vision that continues to find a place for everything repressed by the ordinary world above.

Burying Incomprehensible Horror: Yucca Mountain Nuclear Storage
Bradley L. Garrett

It was not until the early nineteenth century that Egyptian hieroglyphics began to be decoded. It was soon found that many Egyptian tombs had dire warnings about opening them etched on to their exterior surfaces. The Egyptologist Zahi Hawass quotes one of these as saying: 'Cursed be those who disturb the rest of a Pharaoh.

Depiction of a proposed subterranean layer in the Yucca Mountain facility.

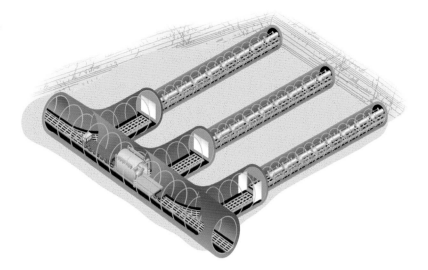

They that shall break the seal of this tomb shall meet death by a disease that no doctor can diagnose.'[23] Of course, today few tombs can be found that have not been looted by people who ignored such inscriptions.

The possibility of a replay of precisely this sort of scenario has fuelled much debate around the Yucca Mountain Nuclear Waste Facility: a 'nuclear graveyard expected to exist many millennia into and perhaps *beyond* human history'.[24] The facility, which was to be excavated 120 metres (395 ft) into the side of a mountain range 160 kilometres (100 mi.) northwest of Las Vegas, Nevada, is on sacred Western Shoshone and Western Paiute land that was subjected to regular nuclear weapons testing by the United States government during the Cold War.[25] The storage facility, as planned, would have made the relationship between this place and nuclear technology even more intimate, once 70,000 tonnes of spent uranium rods and liquid waste of the most toxic variety have been carefully arranged 300 metres (985 ft) below the surface of the mountain.[26] The contents of Yucca Mountain were expected to tranquilly emit radiation for between 10,000 and one million years.

Yucca Mountain has been a fascinating, terrifying and expensive (its estimated cost was $1.7 billion, around £1 billion) prospect from the moment it was proposed in 1987 until the project's federal funding was withdrawn over ongoing litigation in 2010. The reason for the expense was obvious: extensive studies had to be carried out into the impact on various resources under environmental protection laws. Consideration had to be given to the depth of groundwater (370 m/1,200 ft below the waste) and the amount of moisture that might percolate into the sealed canisters. To complicate matters further, two geological fault lines on the site had to be strategically bypassed. Once the massive, U-shaped tunnels had been excavated and a decision made about what to store the waste materials in (12,000 steel canisters), engineers next worried about the future unknowns: the level of subterranean humidity (which could cause the canisters to corrode) once the sarcophagus was sealed, and how the whole complex would be affected by future variables including climate change, which could raise water-table levels closer to the sealed repository.

For all the difficulties, the United States government surely would have preferred a focus on these technical and logistic issues, because at the same time cultural commentators, Native American tribes and social scientists were refusing to allow it off the hook on the bigger question: namely, reconciling the fact that this was all taking place on sacred land in the context of trying to conceptualize 'unimaginable and incomprehensible timescales of hazard' beyond anything anyone had ever had to deal with before.[27]

The most volatile element in this entire plan was, of course, future humans, because any species irresponsible enough to create this sort of waste would also probably be irresponsible enough to crowbar the waste site open out of pure curiosity, just as we did with those Egyptian tombs. Anthropologists, archaeologists, sociologists and others argued heatedly over how to warn future humans of the dangers of the site. Among the proposals were a granite monolith inscribed with warnings in myriad languages; 48 standing stones evenly spaced throughout the landscape; a large-scale depiction of Edvard Munch's painting *The Scream*; a series of intimidating roadblocks; a group of large buried magnets (to give the site a 'unique radar signature'); randomly distributed underground markers; and, finally and more straightforwardly, a permanent visitor's centre.[28] The most promising proposal, perhaps, was that all documentation, discussion and visible material remains of the site be obliterated completely, in the hope that thousands of years from now no one would ever know the place existed and therefore no one would go looking for it.

The plans for Yucca Mountain, after millions of dollars of investment in research and construction, were halted by the Obama administration in 2010. For some, its 'failure', and its current status as a subterranean ruin of an aborted future, is a victory for rationality; for others, the mothballed remains are an indication of the inability to make necessary decisions in the deeply polarized political climate of the United States.

MEMORY

Sigmund Freud has argued that the city, like the mind, is a palimpsest where 'earlier phases of development are absorbed into the later ones, for which they supplied the material'.[1] Imagined as a series of layers that, if excavated (even mentally), would reveal the city's chronological development, Freud's equation of mind and city is a persuasive one. But is the city really like the mind, with a 'buried' unconscious that awaits uncovering? Freud's palimpsest is perhaps most enticing where material remains have been completely erased. To what degree then are the buried layers of the city comprised more of memory than of material?

Often the erasure that prompts a more immaterial memory of underground space is intensely political. Problematic but pervasive buried pasts can be located in Berlin during National Socialism and in the troubled colonial history of Cape Town. Berlin stands somewhat uniquely as a city where the memory of a collective traumatic past has been not only preserved but also commemorated and made visible. Less politically charged are the mnemonic associations of the hundreds of caves beneath Nottingham, which are nevertheless contestable, since they are currently being developed as tourist attractions. By contrast, in Hong Kong urban memory has a different kind of presence, one that is coded, digitized and stored safely underground for constant retrieval, perhaps the antithesis of underground waste. Memory is played out or obscured in different ways through the various socio-political entanglements of cities.

Surface buildings and monuments that are difficult to 'erase' settle into the soil matrix to become future sites for archaeology. Their sheer material permanence – easier to efface than destroy – suggests that the model of the city as palimpsest is more the exception than the rule. Even the digital histories that are now stored in underground data centres point to the almost universal desire to preserve our virtual lives in perpetuity in 'safe' physical spaces beneath the earth's surface. As such, the relationship between the underground and memory might be posited in more nuanced terms. In the philosopher Michel Serres' evocative words, memory 'percolates' and flows 'in a chaotic and turbulent manner'.[2] In this reading, the urban underground is not a series of layers waiting to be deciphered as a geologist might uncover the passage of deep time through rock strata; rather, its spaces create a series of pleated memories that are still bound up with the city and inform its present and future change. Some of the most interesting underground memories are those that are provoked unbidden.[3]

Sinking Histories: Berlin's S- and U-Bahn Tunnels
Samuel Merrill

Berlin is built on sand and water. The city's earliest nuclei grew on the silt islands, sandbanks and confluences of the River Spree during the twelfth and thirteenth centuries. For many years these settlements clung to the edges of a swampy marshland, until Berlin became the seat of the Hohenzollern dynasty in the early fifteenth century and Dutch expertise was eventually harnessed to drain the area. More than four centuries later, in 1882, a former watercourse provided the route for one of the earliest stretches of what would later become the S-Bahn. Thereafter, the S-Bahn's network was mostly extended above or on the surface, with the exception of the North–South tunnel and its six centrally located subterranean stations constructed between 1934 and 1939. The engineers responsible for these stations had to deal with the same problem that had faced the creation of the city's first U-Bahn stations in 1902, namely, the combination of unstable subsoil with a high water table. Those first U-Bahn stations, like the majority of the rest of today's network, were built just below the surface using a cut-and-cover method in conjunction with elaborate pumping mechanisms that lowered the water level during construction.

Besides shaping Berlin's transport networks, the local geology provides a poignant metaphor for the city's twentieth-century history: 'Many men of power have built monuments to themselves on this sand. The monuments topple, the power-handlers vanish, the sand remains. It is political quicksand.'[4] These shifting sands saw the city serve as, in turn, the capital of the German Empire, the Weimar Republic and the

Third Reich before becoming an epicentre of Cold War divisions and more recently the fulcrum of today's unified Germany. Each of these periods has left its mark on the city's surface and in its fabric, but below ground, in the infrastructure of the S- and U-Bahn, some of Berlin's darker memories have been occluded partly because of the necessity to maintain the everyday provision of public transport beneath and across the city. These transport networks can thus be considered landscapes of buried memories – material manifestations of the city's collective unconscious with the potential to give rise to uncanny remembrances – replete with places of physically and psychologically repressed narratives.[5]

This is particularly true of the National Socialist period and the little-known events that, had they unfolded on the surface, might have commanded greater attention given the city's propensity for working through its negative past. Take, for example, the limited historical awareness and lack of commemoration of the nineteen construction workers killed during the S-Bahn tunnel's construction in 1935, when Berlin's sands shifted uncontrollably, close to the Brandenburg Gate, on what was then called Hermann-Göring-Strasse.[6] The cause of the accident, the rush to complete the project in time for Hitler's Olympic spectacle in 1936, pre-empted its consequences, the martyrdom of the

The war-damaged North-South S-Bahn tunnel in 1946, Berlin.

victims by way of a militarized state funeral and the public display of their coffins draped with swastikas. The immediate plan to erect a memorial at Potsdamer Platz station was never fulfilled. Even if it had been, it is unlikely that the memorial would still be in place today, given the changes in Germany's politics of memory.

Alternatively, consider the unresolved memory related to the flooding of the S- and U-Bahn during the final days of the Battle of Berlin in April–May 1945. A lack of historical consensus about the causes of the flood and uncertainty about the number of victims inhibited memorial efforts that were already complicated by the delicate discourse surrounding German civilian suffering under Nazi rule. Whether a Nazi scorched-earth order or the Red Army was responsible may never be ascertained beyond doubt.[7] Given that the subterranean networks doubled as emergency field hospitals, military command posts and civilian shelters, the post-war authorities prepared themselves to retrieve 10,000 corpses from the tunnels. Sensational press reports fuelled the myth of thousands dead, although only around fifty bodies were retrieved as the water was pumped out.[8]

The flood has since been reflected through multiple filmic lenses that promulgate myth and historical inaccuracy. The Russian-made film series *Liberation* (1970 and 1971) depicts a heroic subterranean battle and Soviet soldiers rescuing women and children as the waters quickly subsume a U-Bahn station that is unlikely to have been so severely affected by the flood. The German-made *Downfall* (2004), meanwhile, makes no reference to the flood; instead, the same U-Bahn station features only as part of the route taken by the remainder of Hitler's entourage as they temporarily evade capture by travelling beneath the city's surface. These buried memories thus fortify the cultural framing of subterranean space as a site of danger, and specifically reinforce the idea that Germany's underworlds may be the realm of lingering and hidden Nazi threats.[9]

Bunker Art:
Christian and Karen Boros Collection, Berlin
Sasha Engelmann and Harriet Hawkins

'If there was a fire . . .'. The art collector and advertising mogul Christian Boros ponders the question, sitting on a concrete slab in his penthouse . . . on top of a bunker. Behind him, slightly out of focus, is a pill painting by Damien Hirst, and a large portrait of Kate Moss by Wolfgang Tillmans. In a corner is a red fan sculpture by Olafur

Overleaf
Exterior wall of the former bunker now housing the Christian Boros collection, Berlin.

Eliasson. Boros says: 'I would take an [Elizabeth] Peyton in each hand and run.'[10]

The Boros Collection, or what Berliners call the Boros Bunker, is a former air-raid shelter built in 1942 by the architect Karl Bonatz, which now houses exhibitions of contemporary artworks in the collection of Christian and Karen Boros. The bunker squats next to Oranienburger Tor station in Berlin's Mitte district, and appears either pale grey or warm beige, depending on the shade of the sky. Its design is symmetrical and labyrinthine: the concrete walls, in some places up to 2 metres (6 1/2 ft) thick, wrap the core of the building in stony envelopes with narrow passages and hallways in between. There are no windows. The 120 rooms on three levels have low ceilings, crawl spaces and strange features including narrow air vents, trapdoors and spyholes. There is more concrete than air. The bunker is above ground, but once one is inside, the building's mass is palpable: one has the sensation of being folded and pressed from all sides.

Originally constructed to shelter passengers on the Reichsbahn (Imperial Railway), the bunker was used in 1945 as a prison by the Russian Red Army, and a decade later to store exotic fruit sent by Fidel Castro (hence its other nickname, 'Banana Bunker'). In the 1990s it was rented by an arts company, which sublet the space for techno, fantasy, S&M and fetish parties, earning the bunker the reputation of being the 'hardest club in the world'.[11] When the Berlin city government got wind of these activities, the parties stopped and the building was put on the market. In 2003 Christian Boros and his wife, Karen, then living in the Rhine Valley, were looking for a space to house their growing collection of contemporary art. After viewing a hospital and a railway station, they settled on the bunker.

To say that the Boroses turned the bunker into a gallery would be to miss the point. It is not a gallery, but a context that wraps artworks as though they are unusual specimens. Today one can visit the Boros Collection by booking a tour at weekends. In a marked departure from the rapid schedules of galleries and museums, the 'shows' at the Boros Collection last for four years. Moreover, there are no curators: the collectors choose the artworks from a stock of 700 pieces and recent acquisitions. Individual rooms are assigned, but the display of each piece is entirely up to the artist. In the show of 2012–15, Tomás Saraceno painted the walls of his room white, setting the black strands of his webbed *Flying Garden/Air-Port-City* in stark relief. Ai Weiwei's *Tree*, a monstrous construction of found camphor-wood pieces joined with steel bolts, appeared to brace itself and push against the concrete surrounds. Many artists choose to work with the oddities of the bunker's walls. Klara Lidén's *Teenage Room* made use of a knee-level trapdoor as an entrance (and exit) to a room with a macabre bunk bed; and Awst & Walther placed a bronze arrow on a wall directly opposite a small spyhole in the exterior of the building, in *Line of Fire*.

The Boros Bunker is host to countless traces of its past uses and inhabitants: a black stripe near the ceiling snakes into the stairwell; a sharp corner is worn smooth, perhaps by hands; there is a series of depressions where a row of toilets used to stand. But the presence of such marks highlights the redaction of many more. A small room formerly used as a prison cell now houses Alicja Kwade's *Bordsteinjuwelen-Miami* (2007): a series of asphalt pieces in the shape of diamonds. In this tiny room the texture of the walls is variable, so that one imagines the wear possibly caused by other objects, or by a person sitting in the corner. Black writing forms scattered constellations. While many accounts remark on the numerous traces in the bunker, the walls give us a different impression. We suspect that continued human use is the condition for the persistence of these marks: left to their own devices, the layers of concrete would shed all evidence of human occupation, like so many leaves or scales.

Perhaps the most unnerving experience in the bunker is the pervasive smell of popcorn on the third floor, a perception that is confirmed, after several minutes on the tour, by Michael Sailstorfer's *Popcorn Machine*, popping one kernel at a time on to a massive heap. Before this point in the tour, each room feels like its own world, a self-contained experiment. Even the very loud ringing of a bell (Thomas Zipp's *Ghost without a Body*) or the resonance of a keyboard (Zipp, *Untitled*) do not travel beyond their immediate environs, a fact that offers a lesson in interference patterns: in the hallways and hollows of the bunker, scent travels further than sound. It is no doubt a phenomenological insight that, through the melding of experience and history, brings the Boros Bunker's past lives into sensual contact with the present.

Bedrock Memories: Nottingham's Caves
Paul Dobraszczyk

In 2011 and 2012 the Nottingham Caves Survey worked to map the city's 540-plus man-made caves that have been cut into the city's natural sandstone bedrock since at least the medieval period.[12] Building on the work of the British Geological Survey in the 1980s, the new Survey has produced a 'full measured record of the caves in three dimensions', using a 3D laser scanner. As part of the longer-term

Three-dimensional map of part of the cave complex under Nottingham.

Caves of Nottingham Regeneration Project, the Survey has also formed the starting point for a 'fresh' approach to the city's underground, promoting the caves as a tourist attraction and a 'unique historical resource'.[13]

The hundreds of caves have served (and continue to serve) a wide variety of functions: some are currently used for commercial purposes (many are pub cellars), while others are part of the City of Caves tourist site beneath Nottingham's seventeenth-century castle. The rest include former dungeons, cesspits, tanneries, malt kilns, tunnels, wine cellars, sand mines, air-raid shelters, dovecotes and, perhaps most unlikely of all, a bowling alley. There is also a plethora of domestic caves, such as Lenton Hermitage, Thomas Herbert's caves and the Peel Street caves, and during the survey of 2011–12 the archaeologists canvassed Nottingham residents for access to caves under their homes. Indeed, the Survey was also interested in any space that featured cuts into natural sandstone, going beyond their strict definition of what constituted a cave. Its purpose was to attempt to establish the complex connectivity of man-made interventions in Nottingham's sandstone bedrock, the ways in which the underground of the city had itself, over time, been carved and hewn to become intertwined with the urban world above. That these domestic underworlds have persisted for so long suggests the accretion of unique forms of historical memory in Nottingham, something that the Survey and the Regeneration Project are clearly seeking to uncover and exploit in their plans for the caves. Yet such an approach has the potential to result in a homogenizing of those memories into a 'heritage' tourist attraction, where their sheer multiplicity will be smoothed over in favour of a reductive, but visitor-friendly, attraction.

Perhaps in response to this possibility, the *Sidelong* project, set up by the artist Jo Dacombe and the curator Laura-Jade Klee in 2012, has sought to imbue Nottingham's caves with different kinds of historical memory. Through the interactive art event 'A Walk through the Underworld', held in September 2013, the duo led a series of curated walks around some of the caves, walks that were 'rooted in place, identity, community and the power of imagination'.[14] Through a combination of storytelling and installation artworks, the walks imbued the caves with an imaginative charge that drew on the city's historical mythologies (such as the legend of Robin Hood) as well as more subjective 'relics', including 'cave myths sound recordings', a 'cryptic text scroll' and a 'cave beast leaflet'.[15] Such imaginative readings of underground spaces and the historical memories they evoke do not necessarily conflict with a heritage-led approach (indeed, the *Sidelong* project was in part supported by the Nottingham Caves Survey), but they do highlight the fact that underground memory is a contested subject: it is both extraordinarily open and heterogeneous, but can also be manipulated in ways that diminish rather than celebrate that openness.

Remembering the Map: Prestwich Memorial, Cape Town
Kim Gurney

The first sight of the Prestwich Memorial complex in Cape Town's trendy De Waterkant precinct gives an indication of the dichotomies to come. In its public square is a rainbow-coloured arch that reads 'It's beautiful here', while next to it a homeless man sits on a bench sorting through a black refuse bag. Inside the Memorial building an understated portal marks the stark transition from a bustling coffee shop and an exhibition of information boards to the quiet of the underground. Through this hip-height portal, a narrow sloping passage leads down between high walls to a formidable double-volume door that blocks the entrance to an ossuary. Behind the grille of the door are row upon row of timber shelves holding numbered archival boxes containing the skeletal remains of about 2,500 slaves and members of the colonial lower classes.

These remains were collected mostly from unmarked graves, which were discovered in 2003 during the development of the Green Point

Interior of the Prestwich
Memorial, Cape Town.

area of the city, formerly District One. In the early Colonial period
of the seventeenth century, this area was a burial ground for Christians
as well as for slaves and the dispossessed Khoisan, who were often
interred in unmarked graves. In the 1820s the area was subdivided
and sold. In the later apartheid years, forced disinterments added
to its fraught history. In the early twenty-first century, after much
debate, the Prestwich Memorial was built near the excavation site; no
anthropometric studies of the human remains were allowed and the fate
of the bones is still contentious, as comments from visitors suggest:
'Nobody should be on display', one has written; another adds: 'I think
only pictures should suffice.' Many are positive, however: 'This makes
me think differently', says one.

The question of who has the right to represent the dead is a difficult
one to answer. Some suggest that we should all own the stories about
the dead; it is projects that are disengaged that fail.[16] But in the case
of the Prestwich Memorial there is more at stake: 'The surfacing
of the dead is a moment of irruption of what has sunk from sight.'
The dead are a form of haunted archaeology: 'To listen to bones, to
discover remnants and remains, to revisit the archive – these are acts

of mourning, of emplacing memory, of making the city and the nation a haunt, and of claiming one's right to inhabit the postcolonial city.'[17]

Cape Town's municipal authority, which now looks after the Memorial, generally keeps the ossuary secure, opening it up only under certain conditions. The principal function of the ossuary, it says, is to give a final resting place to those who were once buried in unmarked graves, and to restore some dignity to their remains while also offering visitors a historical view of Cape Town's origins. The curator was present during my visit and I was granted access to the ossuary itself. I walked through the vast door and past the rows of boxes. The atmosphere was subdued, the noise of the traffic above softened in the underground space.

The boxes themselves, which line the walls, are marked with identifiers but otherwise each is the same. The vaulted ceiling is pierced with small coffin-shaped skylights that are replicated in the passageway outside. Through an elongated side window a fragment of the animated outside world can be seen passing by. The passage inside the ossuary is oddly angled: it descends towards the centre and the effect is immersive. Around the corner, it ascends once more towards the exit door. I pause at the U-turn to gather my thoughts; a backing track of patrons in the Memorial's 'Truth'-branded coffee shop above filters through the ossuary's thick walls.

As I leave the Memorial, I take in the everyday street scene before me, its inhabitants oblivious to the bones down below. The Memorial's external brick walls are covered with an outer skin of Malmesbury shale stone from the city's nearby waterfront excavations, an architectural reflection of how cemetery boundary walls were built in the past. In the depths, however, there is no singular narrative of these remains; rather, that liminal space is poised ambiguously between remembrance and forgetting.

Underground Clouds: Hong Kong Data Centres
Carlos López Galviz

An adequate planning policy framework, an Underground Development Programme Fund and a Cavern Ordnance will contribute to turning Hong Kong into Asia's pre-eminent World City. Or so says the feasibility study 'Enhanced Use of Underground Space in Hong Kong' by Arup, one of the largest civil engineering companies in the world and jointly responsible for such iconic projects as the Centre Pompidou in Paris, the National Aquatics Center in Beijing and Heathrow's

Terminal 5 in London. The study, which was commissioned in 2012 by Hong Kong's municipal authorities, mapped five different sites that might become 'strategic cavern areas', namely Lion Rock, Mount Davis, Tuen Mun, Sha Tin and Lantau Island: 'A strategic area is defined as being greater than 20 hectares [50 acres] . . . and having the ability to accommodate multiple cavern sites.'

The idea behind the sites is that they will provide a range of services – governmental in the first instance, but later extending to different industries, commerce and housing – in a city where land is scarce, and available sites for tall buildings have largely reached their limit. For this, the Hong Kong authorities can draw on experience elsewhere: in Norway, the Gjøvik Olympic Cavern Hall and the Oset Water Treatment facilities in Oslo; the Itåkeskus Swimming Hall in Finland; the extensive underground pedestrian network and malls in Montreal, Canada; the underground ammunition facility in Singapore (completed in 2008); Helsinki's 'Underground Master Plan', introduced in 2009; and the 'non-binding zoning plans' of Arnhem and Zwolle in The Netherlands, which divide the underground into three layers of development, comprising buildings, transport and groundwater resources respectively.

Data – big or otherwise – is central to any world city. The Hong Kong authorities have experimented with large data centres using

An illustration from the environmental assessment for a proposed data centre in Hong Kong.

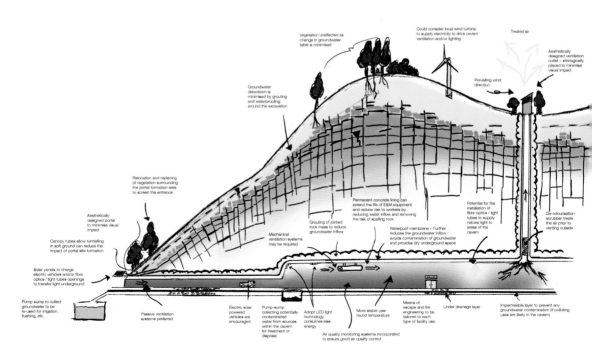

former factory buildings as part of their attempts to attract IT businesses to the city. Large, safe and reliable data centres would only complement and benefit from the important number of banks, law firms, insurance companies and other financial agencies that have a foot in Hong Kong. Underground data centres offer something that similar facilities above ground cannot: a nearly sealed environment (seemingly) closed off to intruders, keeping data safe from natural disaster or terrorist attack.

Successful precedents include Green Mountain in Norway and SubTropolis and Cavern Technologies in Kansas. Hong Kong might soon be the Asian hub for companies such as LightEdge Solutions, a cloud service provider and consulting company that has $58 million invested in SubTropolis. Information vital to our everyday lives – the blog you keep, say; the photos you have just uploaded on to a social media site – is built on the perceived immateriality of 'clouds'. Clouds, we are told, travel with us, or at least with our devices.

But, as underground data centres develop in Hong Kong and elsewhere, we might also think about the links between clouds and underground spaces: at one end of the spectrum is the idea of immediate and omnipresent access to all the information we need; at the other a cool, safe, allegedly indestructible server, stored somewhere remote, buried underground, inaccessible to all save the keyholder. Such developments prompt us to ponder what is safe where, and whether rain would ever reach Cloud-polis.

Mirror of History: Berlin's Water Tower
Matthew Gandy

Just one street from the popular bars and restaurants of Kollwitzplatz, in Berlin's former DDR district of Prenzlauer Berg, is a striking water tower. The curious brick rotunda, dating from 1877, looms over the streets with its many pairs of eye-like windows. The tower, with its network of outbuildings and underground chambers, forms part of Berlin's modern water infrastructure network, which gradually replaced thousands of wells and pumps dotted across the city.[18] Beginning in the 1850s, the communal street-level aspects of social interaction with water were progressively displaced by a series of technological networks including underground engineering projects to supply water that gradually culminated in the plumbed interior spaces of modern apartments: it was only in the case of massive disruption of infrastructure, towards the end of the Second World War, that the

Water tower in the former DDR district of Prenzlauer Berg, Berlin.

shattered shell of Berlin fell back on earlier pumps and other precarious sources of water.

Although the water-tower complex was designed for a very specific purpose, at different moments in history various parts have been turned over to other uses. In 1916, for example, one of the machine houses was used as a kitchen to help tackle wartime poverty and malnutrition. Between February and June 1933 one of the machine halls and the underground vaults were used as torture chambers by the SS, and a nearby building was converted into the first concentration camp of the Nazi era, the thick brick walls serving to deaden the sound of the violence within.[19] In June 1933 the machine hall where many of these atrocities had taken place was converted into an SS dining room and lounge before its demolition in 1935 to make way for a park that opened in May 1937. In 1946, in the wake of wartime destruction, much of the land around the tower was used for food production, and one of the buildings was turned into a kindergarten (which remains to this day).

In 1952 the water tower lost its functional role and the site became an architectural curio and technological relic. During the DDR era it served as a youth hangout or oblique backdrop to parades: it features, for example, in the street photos of Gerd Danigel and Jürgen Hohmuth.

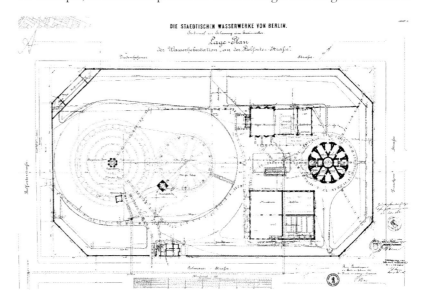

'The Municipal Waterworks of Berlin', site plan.

In one of Danigel's photographs from 1983, the tower seems to dwarf the crowd below with their banners and placards celebrating the DDR as they make their way through one of the areas of the city that was most opposed to the Honecker regime. After the city's reunification in 1990 the underground chambers became a space for cultural experimentation, including alternative theatre and sound art. The buildings were a focal point of the Singuhr Hörgalerie ('listening gallery'), attracting thousands of visitors, as part of a European network for acoustic investigation. And, more recently, the former workers' apartments in the tower have been converted into luxury flats.

In its oscillation between the hydro-social rationalization of the bacteriological city and the corporeal terror of Nazism through the appropriation of its hidden spaces, the water-tower complex illustrates the Janus face of modernity. The structure's post-utilitarian appropriation as moribund hangout after the 1950s and realm of cultural experimentation in the 1990s, and finally its transformation into luxury residences in the 2000s, further illustrate the chameleon-like malleability of technological spaces under their transition to late modernity.

The water tower also poses interesting questions about the relationship between above and below, and between the seen and the unseen, since its underground structures and connections are far larger than what can be seen from the city streets. The tower forms only a small element of a large network of vaults that extends beneath what is now a small urban park. In this sense the tower forms a kind of outgrowth from the hyphal networks spreading from beneath these visible structures. This hydrological installation is not only a cultural palimpsest but also an architectonic excrescence emanating from the hidden spatio-corporeal dynamics of modernity. Above all, the tower poses the problem of memory and the stratigraphic dimension of urban history: only in 1981 was a plaque installed to indicate that atrocities had been committed on the site, and there is now a children's playground in the space once occupied by the former machine house.

GHOSTS

A particular manifestation of those often unwanted or unexpected underground memories are ghosts: phantasmagoric apparitions that confirm the ongoing relevance of the past in the present.[1] As many horror stories demonstrate, underground spaces are the pervasive haunts of spectres, ghosts and demons. Ghosts are no less real than the tangible, material spaces from which they arise, not only to those who 'witness' their fleeting appearance, but also to the narratives of space that become part of most cities' collective meaning.[2] Every city has its ghosts, it seems, and many of these reside beneath the surface, as if the subterranean were itself their natural habitat.

A number of contributions in this book speak of spectres of one kind or another in urban undergrounds, whether ghosts of the dead in catacombs; 'ghost' Tube stations under London; the ghosts of defunct political regimes in Prague and Plovdiv; or hackneyed ghost tours in Edinburgh's underground vaults. Many of these ghosts inhabit underground spaces of temporal juxtaposition, where processes of modernization have detached them from the movement of time around them. Even as the entire city might open itself up at any time to the countless ghosts of its former inhabitants, the underground nevertheless seems to hold those ghosts more strongly – and more viscerally – than the world above, perhaps because of our perception of its capacity to encapsulate memory.

Just as the relationship between memory and the urban underground is often centred on traumatic events in collective history, so ghosts often lead to the recognition – usually on a more personal level – of loss, trauma and injustice in the life of a city. That these hauntings seem indelibly associated with the material spaces of the underground demonstrates the strong link between physical and mental space in urban life. The philosopher Henri Lefebvre has argued that these kinds of representation ultimately stem from ancient magico-religious practices, ones that may have been largely extinguished in the above-ground city but which nevertheless persist, both materially and mentally, in 'the realm of the dead'.[3] Even as many urban underground spaces take on the appearance of their contemporary counterparts above ground (whether railway stations or shopping centres), they may still harbour the ghosts of the unquiet dead who refuse to be expelled.

'To be sure, many of the living want a fate after death different from their lot in life: the necropolis is crowded with big-game hunters, mezzo-sopranos, bankers, violinists, duchesses, courtesans, generals – more than the living city ever contained.' Marco Polo thus describes the city of Eusapia to the Chinese ruler Kublai Khan in Italo Calvino's *Invisible Cities*.[4] Eusapia is a city in which 'to enjoy life and flee care', a fact made possible by its twin city below, where the dead live. Every so often the 'hooded brothers', the only ones who are allowed passage between the two, comment on changes that have been made below to those above. Their stories mirror but also connect changes between the two cities so that 'there is no longer any way of knowing who is alive and who is dead.'[5]

Haunted Spaces: Edinburgh's Medieval Vaults
Paul Dobraszczyk

Some of Edinburgh's most popular and enduring tourist attractions are the numerous ghost tours offered by competing companies, such as Auld Reekie and Mercat. With their round-the-clock trips leaving from outside Tron Kirk on the city's famous Royal Mile, these companies provide an unashamedly kitsch take on the ghost-story horror genre. Auld Reekie, for example, offers five different tours on the interrelated themes of ghosts, torture, the occult and terror.[6] With some reservations (and accompanied by my heavily pregnant wife), I opted for the company's more innocuous-sounding 'Original Underground Tour', which offered a visit to the vaults beneath the city's South Bridge.

The peculiar topography of Edinburgh – a series of steep ridges, valleys and craggy outcrops including Castle Rock – coupled with its long history as a defensive stronghold, has produced a veritable honeycomb of underground spaces beneath the city's streets and tightly packed tenement buildings. The construction of the Flodden Wall around the city, after a disastrous defeat by the English armies in 1513,

led to an extraordinarily dense cityscape of narrow closes and high
tenement buildings that were hollowed out underground into countless
cellars to maximize inhabitable space.[7] In the eighteenth and early
nineteenth century this extremely dense urban fabric was transformed
once again with the building of the city's five giant arched bridges,
which effectively levelled Edinburgh's hilly topography across the gaps
between the hills, and the infilling of the land between. Built from 1765
to 1833, the bridges created Edinburgh's unique architectural character:
a vertical urban landscape of high garrets and low cellars and vaults.[8]
The newly stratified city quickly developed its now quintessential
Victorian image of a place of extreme social division and urban squalor,
its tenement buildings becoming microcosms of society as a whole.
Early social reformers, such as George Bell, described the conditions
of those living at the bottom of the city's social scale, the countless
vaults under otherwise respectable tenements overcrowded with
destitute families, many of them Irish immigrants after that country's
calamitous famine of 1845–52.

Today very little of this Victorian subterranean world remains,
much of it having been cleared by either destructive fires or slum
demolition in the late nineteenth century. However, some of the vaults
under South Bridge (1785–7) are still used by such venues as Whistle
Binkies, the Bare Story and Bannermans as alternative nightclubs or
for storage. Behind these places of entertainment, moreover, other
tunnels and vaults still exist in their original form, and these were
opened to the public in 1994, quickly gaining notoriety for ghost
sightings and other occult phenomena, which tourist agencies such
as Auld Reekie capitalized on. Now considered to be one of the most
haunted spaces in Britain, the South Bridge vaults have provoked
dozens of reports of spectral apparitions and ghostly sounds, including
sightings of several resident spirits: the Imp, the Watcher and the
McKenzie poltergeist, whose arrival in 1995 seems to have displaced
the first two. As documented in the BBC television series *I Believe in
Ghosts* (2010), unexplained voices were recorded in one of the chambers
in the vaults after the eponymous ghost-hunter (and former *Eastenders*
soap star) inadvisably spent the night there.[9]

As might be expected, my visit to the vaults under South Bridge
proved fruitless in terms of paranormal sightings, but it was
nevertheless an unsettling and strange experience. First, the vaults
are accessed by climbing stairs *upwards* into a Victorian tenement
building, going against one's expectations of the spatial orientation
of the underground. Indeed, the South Bridge vaults seem to be within
the building itself, rather than below it, in some strange, disconnected
spatial realm. Second, the vaults themselves felt squalid and

Passageway in
Edinburgh's
medieval vaults.

claustrophobic, and flash photography revealed them (in retrospect) to be decaying spaces littered with the grubby accruals of the ghost tour: decrepit mannequins and other paint-stained props. Even the laughably kitsch torture chamber felt peculiarly chilling once armed with the knowledge that one of the vaults had been used for a time by a modern-day coven of Scottish witches as a place of worship.[10]

It is easy to dismiss urban ghost tours such as those of Edinburgh's vaults as just one more example of the commodification of city spaces in the postmodern era, or part of the recent growth in so-called dark tourism.[11] Yet, as the geographer Steve Pile reminds us, stories of urban ghosts, no matter how outlandish or clichéd they might appear, can 'introduce a haunting effect that permits an emotional recognition of . . . loss, trauma and injustice' in the history of a city.[12] Because underground spaces like the Edinburgh vaults have a tendency to be preserved as remnants of a city's past – petrified and detached from urban modernization – they are often perceived as bearing the traces of that past. Even if they are grafted on to clichéd narratives or commodified spectacles (as is the case in Edinburgh), these spectral presences are nevertheless an important part of the real city – that is, the city of the unquiet dead whose voices seemingly refuse to be stilled.

Visiting the Dead: London's Victorian Catacombs
Paul Dobraszczyk

Catacombs are underground structures built of brick or stone, in which coffins are housed in recesses in galleries. In the nineteenth century ten cemeteries in London were constructed with catacombs: the first at Kensal Green in 1832, and others following at West Norwood in 1839; Highgate, Abney Park, Brompton and Nunhead in 1840; and Tower Hamlets, City of London, Saint Mary's and New Southgate in the 1840s and 1850s. These catacombs provide an important insight into Victorian attitudes not just towards underground space and death but also to the rapidly changing urban fabric of London.[13]

The oldest precedent for the catacombs of London is those built in Rome, most famously by the early Christians in the second and third centuries. However, the most recent influential catacombs were those in Paris, which were established in 1786 when, in response to the overcrowding of the city's cemeteries, the bones of the dead in the Cemetery of the Innocents were moved to what had formerly been underground quarries under the Left Bank of the Seine (see essay 'As Above, So Below'). Thereafter catacombs became an important element of urban sanitary reform, and ossuaries were constructed in many cities, including Naples, Vienna and, more recently, under the Cathedral of Our Lady of the Angels in Los Angeles. Some of these catacombs made use of existing underground spaces, as in Paris and Naples, while others were incorporated into new cemeteries and churches.

London's catacombs were built according to a uniform grid plan. The galleries were constructed with brick arches, the standard architectural form of Victorian London; at West Norwood and Kensal Green, these arches were divided into insets recesses, with deep cuts at their ends to let in light from above. Within the individual arches, various arrangements were possible for the coffins, the most frequent being a division of the space into separate loculi, one for each coffin, inserted lengthwise into the recesses to save space. Some of the arches were (and still are) reserved for single families; some are still empty, having never been used.

An important feature of several of the London catacombs was a cast-iron hydraulic lift, or catafalque, by which coffins would be mechanically lowered from the chapel above to the catacombs below. The cumbersome lifting mechanism of the catafalque would have been

Coffins in the catacombs at West Norwood Cemetery, London.

concealed by the coffin drapery, giving the mourners the illusion of a miraculous descent into the underworld, in effect a piece of pure theatre that combined up-to-date technology with ancient myth. The space of the catacomb gave the appearance of a regulated, even automated, process enacted within an inorganic man-made environment of brick, lead and iron, with the lead-lined coffins giving the impression of an incorruptible body, even if this was far from the reality (most of the coffins are now badly decayed and infested with woodworm). Yet, even today, you can still buy a space to inter yourself (or your entire family) in the West Norwood catacombs.

The London catacombs, like those in Paris, were also once open to the public. Family members and curiosity seekers regularly descended into their spaces to revisit the dead – a practice obviously not possible with traditional methods of burial. This subterranean visit transported visitors to another world, albeit one strictly controlled by modern technology. Today most of London's catacombs have been sealed off; only Kensal Green and Highgate (and, to a lesser extent, West Norwood) offer regular opportunities to those who still want to visit London's dead.

Temporal Disjunctions: Abandoned London Underground
Bradley L. Garrett

The London Underground ('Tube'), like the sewers, hovers on the edge of dereliction in a state of necessary neglect despite the slick and efficient facade presented to casual travellers. Hidden in the shadows of Tube tunnels, London has the largest number of ghost stations of any subterranean transit system in the world, owing to the intense pressure of space and a contorted series of changes in the private ownership of the various lines over the course of 150 years.[14] However, there is much discussion about what constitutes a 'ghost station', embedded in academic debates about the ambiguities between materiality, memory and history.[15] At the high end of estimates, there are forty stations in the London Underground that were built and subsequently taken out of use. At the low end, there are fourteen complete abandoned stations in the system. Information about these changes, and the current locations of derelict places within the Tube, can be found in post-war rebuilding plans, Transport for London worker track maps and two books, Joe Brown's *London Railway Atlas* (2009) and *London's Disused Underground Stations* by J. E. Connor (2008).

A sign in Down Street station reminds interlopers that they are venturing into off-limits territory.

Many stations have been knocked down, reclad to become new stations or simply left to rot after being abandoned. Some stations were simply constructed too close to each other, and stopped being used or were never used at all. Others had a more dramatic ending. St Mary's station in Whitechapel, for instance, was levelled by a German air raid in 1941, although the platforms remain intact underground. Some, like Marlborough Road in Holloway and City Road in Islington, no longer have platforms. In other instances, such as at Holborn and Charing Cross, one platform is live, another disused.

Down Street station is a particularly interesting example. The station is between Green Park and Hyde Park Corner on the Piccadilly line, and opened in 1907. Since it was only about 500 metres (550 yd) from Hyde Park Corner, few people used it. Apart from Aldwych, it was the least profitable station in the system, and it closed in 1932. It had a second life as home to the Railway Executive Committee and then as a War Cabinet for Winston Churchill.[16] Brompton Road is also captivating. Like Down Street, it fell derelict owing to disuse, but it is one of the most intact, with its original oxblood glazed faience tiles hand-picked by famous London architect Leslie Green and original wooden handrails in the stairwells, covered in decades'-worth of dust.[17]

The best-known station in the system is Aldwych, originally called Strand. The station, which finally ceased operation in 1994, was used (as were many others) as an air-raid shelter during the Second World War. During German bombing raids it also housed objects from the British

Museum, including the Elgin Marbles. One of the most interesting things about it, however, is that there is a Northern line train dating from 1972, sitting awkwardly on the Piccadilly line track, permanently ensconced there for filming purposes.

British Museum is the station most steeped in mystery. It closed in 1933 and access is no longer possible from street level, as the ticket offices have been demolished and a branch of Nationwide Building Society erected on top. London mythology suggests that the spirit of a dead Egyptian pharaoh, escaped from the British Museum, haunts the station. The only way to gain access today is to walk the tracks of the Central line from Holborn or Tottenham Court Road stations, or stop a train mid-tunnel.

Despite a large amount of public interest in London's abandoned Tube stations, most remain derelict and unused. Stations such as Aldwych, as well as the derelict platforms at Charing Cross, have been used as film sets in the horror film *Creep* (2004) and the James Bond film *Skyfall* (2012). British Museum station appeared in Neil Gaiman's TV series *Neverwhere* (1996), and it and Aldwych make an appearance in the video games *Broken Sword: The Smoking Mirror* and *Tomb Raider III* respectively. The latter station is also sometimes open for public tours. Transport for London maintains the abandoned Jubilee line platforms at Charing Cross specifically for use by film and television companies (which can use Charing Cross for a contemporary look and Aldwych for a period style), a fact that confuses the notion of these stations as 'abandoned'.

In 2005 a London banker, Ajit Chambers, founded The Old London Underground Company, an organization with a mission to purchase and redevelop London's disused Tube stations into bars, restaurants and houses, but it has so far been unsuccessful. In 2014 Brompton Road station was sold to Dmitry Firtash, a Ukrainian billionnaire arrested on bribery charges the same year, for £53 million as part of a plan to convert the site into flats.[18]

Adopting the Dead: Fontanelle Cemetery, Naples
Julia Solis

Inside ancient quarry caves in Naples, the dead are revealing their secrets. Piles of anonymous skulls and bones line the halls of this old cemetery; for decades, locals would come here to communicate with the deceased by adopting and caring for their remains. Fontanelle cemetery in this ancient Italian city is not just a stunning ossuary but was also the site of a unique devotional cult that lasted until a few decades ago.

The cemetery is located inside an old tuff quarry on via Fontanelle in the Sanità district of Naples, an area that was historically used for Roman and Christian catacombs. The name 'Fontanelle' refers to the many local underground springs that helped to create access for the extraction of tuff as a building material for the city. As a result, the hillsides are riddled with vast caves that are still being used for storage, small-scale manufacturing or car repairs. Starting in the seventeenth century, when the Fontanelle caves were still outside the city boundary, enormous underground spaces were used as mass graves for corpses that would no longer fit into the city's church cemeteries.

During the plague of 1656, which wiped out two-thirds of Naples' residents, the caves received enormous numbers of bodies – more than 200,000 plague victims found their final resting places here. Other corpses, usually those of the lower classes, would later join them; they were often interred in a church graveyard during daytime hours and transferred to the mass cemetery that same night, a practice that was not widely advertised. A series of floods in the late eighteenth century swept some of the bodies in the front sections of the caves into the city streets, causing havoc and requiring the assistance of the community for their reburial. For a while, some nearby residents would not leave their houses during heavy rains for fear of encountering their dead relatives. Many more bodies were piled in after a cholera outbreak in 1837, after which the cemetery was abandoned, if only temporarily.

In 1872 the priest Don Gaetano Barbati decided to clean up the main space, which covers an area of 4,650 square metres (50,000 sq. ft). Bones were exhumed and stacked in neat piles against the walls, topped by rows of skulls. Since this was increasingly being recognized as a sacred site, a church – that of Maria Santissima del Carmine – was built at the entrance to the caves. The ossuary would continue to accommodate bones found in other churchyards until the 1930s.

It was not long after the cemetery was cleaned up that people began to visit and form relationships with some of the human remains. Many people took pity on the dead and incorporated them into their prayers as if they were their own relatives. Occasionally a dead person would appear to a visitor in a dream, ask for prayers to be said in his or her name and reveal where his or her skull was. The new caretaker would then find it, clean it and care for it, perhaps bringing a pillow for it to rest on or a case to house it. People even began to build shrines for their adopted skulls. For a while, a street market sprang up outside the church, where visitors could buy candles, flowers, wires and tin to fashion the cases for the remains.

Adopted skulls in
the catacombs of the
Fontanelle cemetery,
Naples.

As the caretakers prayed for the owners of the skulls in order
to ease their transition into the afterlife, they asked for some help in
return: for the soul to protect a recently dead family member; for good
luck at a wedding; or to help with fertility problems. The skulls would
be cleaned and watched for signs of sweat (condensing moisture), which
indicated that the soul would grant the favour being asked of it. It is
said that one particular skull in the rear section of the ossuary sweats
more than the others; to this day – according to the current caretakers –
it is still being sought out by women who want help conceiving a child.

The cemetery became a place where bodies were assembled
according not to identity but to aesthetics, where skulls served as
communication portals between this world and the purifying, fiery
landscapes of Purgatory. No wonder the skulls were sweating, especially
since one of their most desired tasks became the prediction of winning
lottery numbers. Since the national lottery was held on Saturdays,
people flooded to the cemetery caves on Fridays to polish 'their' skulls
and ask to have the winning numbers revealed to them in dreams.

These fetishist rituals left Catholic Church leaders aghast, but it was
not until 1969 that the city's cardinal ordered the cemetery to be closed
to put a stop to these practices. Apart from occasional tourist visits, the
bones are now allowed to rest in peace. In the early twenty-first century
the city made some efforts to restore the deteriorating space and open
it back up to the public. It can now be visited by appointment but
adoptions, alas, are no longer allowed.

Communist Ghosts: Plovdiv Seismological Lab
Anna Plyushteva

In all but a handful of cases, seismological labs are located in remote,
sparsely populated areas, where there is less background 'noise'.
Being away from the vibrations of cities and major roads allows a
seismographic facility to pick up very weak signals, including those
made by either very minor or very distant earthquakes. Yet such
locations have marked disadvantages when it comes to the logistics
of research and educational work. In this context, the seismological
laboratory located in the centre of Plovdiv (Bulgaria's second-largest
city) was always going to be exceptional. Unfortunately, on more than
one occasion history got in the way.

Plovdiv's ancient city centre, built thousands of years ago on seven
rocky hills, offered an unusual solution to the seismological lab dilemma.
Since the start of the Cold War, tunnels had been dug through the solid
syenite of Plovdiv's hills to serve as shelters and military headquarters
in times of crisis, including a potential nuclear war. A sense of
imminent disaster thus pervaded these humid tunnels from the start,
but after a tragic earthquake in neighbouring Romania in 1977 claimed
1,578 victims, the somewhat vague nuclear threat coming from the
West was replaced by a much more specific fear: that of cataclysms
in the earth's crust.

In the late 1980s (when Bulgaria was under Communist governance)
a seismological lab was given rooms in one of the tunnels under
Plovdiv's hills. Back then a close friend of my parents worked there.
As a geophysicist, she was responsible for monitoring the data and
changing the tape onto which the seismograph's stylus records seismic
waves, producing something that strongly resembles a cardiogram.
My parents sometimes visited the tunnel lab with her: through an
inconspicuous door hidden amid thick vegetation; along a dry and well-
lit tunnel into the heart of the hill; past six or seven locked rooms with
thick metal doors, ready to keep out the radiation from an American
bomb; to the last two rooms, which were open and full of laboratory
equipment. This part of the vast underground space was doing useful
work in the present, and not in a potentially dramatic future. Or was it?
In 2014 I interviewed a local geophysicist, who spoke of the hopes and
disappointments of seismology in the late twentieth century, and the
ways in which they had shaped the fate of the Plovdiv lab:

> Back then, we all thought that a method for predicting
> earthquakes was a few years away. After the big Romanian
> earthquake, we got all these resources, because [the

government] wanted us to be able to tell where and when the next earthquake would be. The hope we would be able to avoid the human cost of natural disasters was what made the lab so important to the politicians.

But political backing and funding dwindled as hope faded for the imminent invention of a method of prediction. Soon afterwards came the 1990s, and big changes swept through Eastern Europe. By that point the old equipment from the lab had been moved into a basement, in anticipation of the receipt of state-of-the art Soviet equipment. However, after 1991 the Soviet Union was no more, and the new equipment never arrived. Thereafter the tunnel of the seismological lab stood empty, awaiting a new identity. Plovdiv was meanwhile shedding its Communist identity: street names (previously named after Communist heroes) were changed and factories closed, and thousands of people left the city. Some of Plovdiv's underground tunnels became bars and restaurants; one is still used as the training facility of the Civil Defence Agency. Knowing that the former seismological lab had experienced no such reincarnations, I was not sure what to expect during a visit to the site in 2014.

'We'll have to stop by the Municipality to get the keys. They had to go into the tunnel yesterday to pick up some old furniture. The former

Interior of the Plovdiv seismological laboratory.

seismological lab is at the very end of the corridor and, to be honest, I haven't even peeked in for years', the engineer from the Civil Defence Agency said as we walked quickly towards the entrance of the tunnel during a summer thunderstorm.

When he unlocked the door to the tunnel, it seemed at first that rainwater had been seeping in: the tunnel's floor was under half a metre of water, as far in as I could see. 'The Municipality's workers have damaged the mains, it seems.' My host looked uncomfortable as he rushed to shut off the water. We took off our shoes and walked through the water towards the heart of the hill and what remained of the old seismological lab.

Thinking about earthquakes made walking through the grim, flooded tunnel an unsettling experience. Turning light bulbs on to the crackling sounds of old wiring while knee-deep in water only added to the sense of apprehension. At the same time, feeling fearful seemed perfectly appropriate in this space, which owed its existence to an era riddled with anxieties. Finally we entered the lab: old equipment that even in the 1990s had been too tattered to move to the new location; a radio twice my age; a barely standing chair. All around us lingered the presence of timeworn political and scientific agendas – the ghosts of unfulfilled promises to prevent disaster.[19]

Orpheus in the Air-raid Shelter: Underground Theatre, Prague
Petr Gibas

Orpheus (*Orfeus* in Czech), a small independent theatre company from Prague, descended into the underground not in quest of Eurydice, but out of necessity. Without a permanent place to perform, 'we had to take whatever there was', says Radim Vašinka, the founder and long-term director of the company, 'and there was nothing else', except for a decommissioned air-raid shelter in the basement of an ordinary apartment block. In this space, the everyday fears of the Communist Cold War era collided with the struggles of a post-Communist avant-garde theatre company.

The fear of war under state socialism appeared in many forms and in many places in the city, from the large-scale nuclear shelter constructed in the metro to the everyday civil defence shelter no. 0105 0055, the one that would eventually house a theatre. Built between 1953 and 1955, at the peak of Stalinism in Czechoslovakia and during the Korean War, this small air-raid shelter (with a volume of 413 cu. m/14,585 cu. ft) was prepared to house up to 120 people in the event of a supposedly imminent war. It was equipped with three dry toilets, a shower, two washbasins, a large boiler, electricity and water. Built from brick and concrete, the shelter could be assembled in between two and six hours and kept in operation for 24 hours at a time.[20] Yet behind these dry facts a real space was hidden, one that was filled with past imaginings of threatening futures. Indeed, Prague and many other cities in the former Czechoslovakia are still full of spaces like this shelter. Once underground materializations of fear, they now lie dormant under buildings and hills.

The Orpheus theatre company was founded in 1968, the momentous year that precipitated the 'Thaw': the melting of the Communist Party's firm grip on the everyday life of the Czechoslovak citizens and the rise of widespread engagement with politics and the country's future. Through this process of 'normalization', the Orpheus theatre survived. In 1972 intoxicated officials from the Russian embassy attended the company's performance of *Tea* by Šárka Smazalová, a young and

Part of the underground theatre in a former air-raid shelter, Prague.

talented poet, only to denounce it as seditious, leading to the closure of the company and its re-emergence underground.

The Orpheus theatre took up residence in the air-raid shelter soon after it was decomissioned in 1995. The Cold War was ending and with it the fear of imminent nuclear war. The Orpheus theatre company thus moved its new performance space from the metaphorical to the literal underground. In recent years the shelter has been sold to private owners, but the theatre has remained in the space by securing municipal funding and providing an alternative to the now dominant capitalist regime of entertainment in Prague, as exemplified by the nearby multi-purpose business and entertainment district built in the 1990s.

Today the company is struggling to survive. As in the ancient myth, Orpheus has not found peace in its underground space. After all, the story both of the shelter and of the theatre company mirrors the (geo)politics of the precarious times under state socialism and its successor, capitalism.

FEAR

One of the most primal, and enduring, associations of the underground is fear, namely the fear of death. That the dead are generally hidden deep below ground provides a spatial locus for an entire sub-genre of horror fiction, from *Dracula* (1897) to *World War Z* (2006). Fear also drives responses to the conceptual underground, where we perceive uncontrollable forces (from disease to ghosts to magma) that threaten to rise up to the surface and wreak havoc. Whether the tomb or the id, control of the underground requires a panoply of rituals of appeasement: practices that admit the demonic forces (albeit within strictly defined limits) into the world above in order to limit or direct their power. The Maya of Central America famously sacrificed many human lives to appease the lords of Xibalba, the underworld.

Perhaps the most salient underground spaces resulting from fear are those that respond to human-made threat. On the one hand, underground spaces are closely guarded, and they have often been places where violence has emerged: from Guy Fawkes's Gunpowder Plot of 1605 (focused on the undercroft of the Palace of Westminster) to the Tokyo subway gas attacks in 1995 and the 7/7 bombings on the London Underground. On the other hand, entire underground complexes have been created to assuage fears about violence coming from above, particularly that arising from conventional aerial warfare or a future nuclear conflagration.

Indeed, fear of destruction from above has resulted in a proliferation of bunker architecture that has increasingly come to define large parts of the global urban underground, forming an important aspect of what the urbanist Steven Graham has termed the 'new military urbanism'.[1] The cultural theorist Paul Virilio, in his account of the Nazi-built Atlantic

Wall, argues that bunkers signify the move underground in modern warfare, where the advance of aerial bombing forced a retreat 'into the very thickness of the planet' for protection. According to Virilio, the function of the bunker is to ensure survival, to be a shelter during the critical period of war, and then to allow the survivors to 'resurrect' themselves to the surface.[2] Yet bunkers and shelters also give us a powerful sense of the kind of force that is mobilized by fear (whether seen in the infrastructure that will house 1 per cent of the population of a city like Shanghai following a hypothetical nuclear attack, or in the repurposing of the 'concrete mushrooms' of Albania's heritage) – one that is political and reorientated towards a future that differs substantially from that envisioned in the 1970s.

By being a form of materialized fear, the underground demonstrates the breaking down of conventional territorial boundaries and the bleak prospect of the total annihilation of urban areas above ground, a reality for many towns and cities in Germany and Japan towards the end of the Second World War. Even as the prospect of long-term survival underground in the event of a nuclear conflagration has become largely discredited, the desire for a bunker of one's own remains, whether demonstrated in the apocalyptic narratives of films like *The Road* (2009) or *Take Shelter* (2012), or in the upsurge in the number of mainstream American suburbanites preparing themselves and their homes for Armageddon.[3]

Striving Underground: Stockholm's Atomic Bomb Defences

Samuel Merrill

During the 1950s and 1960s Sweden was occasionally referred to as 'the nation that strives underground', reflecting a Cold War civil defence model, dating from the late 1930s, that relied partly on the widespread provision of subterranean bunkers and shelters.[4] The combination of a large population and a geology dominated by gneiss and granite meant that this strategy was arguably most complicated in the country's capital, and largest city, Stockholm.

In 1943 the Pionen bunker was built beneath 30 metres (100 ft) of Stockholm's granite escarpment in the central area of the city's Södermalm district (known as the White Mountain). It was constructed to function as one of the city's control centres, from where the first responses to a nuclear attack would be coordinated in cooperation with a network of other similar facilities built across the country. The underground expansion of Stockholm continued in the 1950s and 1960s as the authorities simultaneously tackled the city's shortage of civilian shelters and car-parking facilities. Between 1952 and 1957 a huge three-storey civilian shelter with room for 20,000 people was built under the Katarina Mountain, also in Södermalm. This shelter was part of what the international press labelled 'Operation Granite', an ambitious subterranean building programme that also led to the construction of bunkers to house most of the Swedish Navy and Air Force. In 1953 members of the international press were invited to visit Stockholm's 'underground city' in order to demonstrate to the world how well-prepared the country was for nuclear war.[5] Six years later, a public information film called *Vi går under jorden* (Let's Go Underground) helped to prepare the Swedish population for an underground existence, while 'Operation Granite' gained further international exposure when it featured on the British current-affairs

Data centre in the former Pionen bunker, 30 metres (100 ft) below the Södermalm district in Stockholm.

television programme *Panorama*.[6] The *Panorama* correspondent closed his report with the rather mocking words:

> Sweden isn't a great power preparing against a war with herself at the burning centre. She trains for a war she's kept out of for nearly 150 years. But if by any chance she should have to meet a sudden attack or find herself caught up in the fringe effects of a hydrogen bomb war, why then she intends to survive, if she can – an oyster with a hard shell – and in a world where no one knows all the answers at least this can be said, she's made a start on finding a characteristic one of her own.

In the mid-1960s the construction of underground shelters in Stockholm continued, as illustrated by the completion of the Klara civilian shelter in the city's Norrmalm district. By this time Sweden had approximately 43,000 shelters, which collectively could house around three million people, almost half of the country's population. Even in the 1980s the country's budget for civil defence per capita dwarfed those of the Soviet Union, Britain, France and the USA, and was exceeded only by that of another neutral country, Switzerland.[7]

In the late 1990s most of these facilities were decommissioned, and those that didn't already have dual purposes, for example as car garages, were leased out to third parties. In 2007 the Pionen bunker was leased to the Swedish Internet service provider Bahnhof, which enlarged it by blasting out an additional 4,000 cubic metres (141,000 cu. ft) of space in order to use it as a data centre. Bahnhof also contracted the architect Albert France-Lanord to redesign the bunker's interior. The futuristic result, in which a 'floating' conference room and a suspended glass corridor provide centrepieces, drew inspiration from the film sets of 1970s James Bond movies. This, with its temporary use by Julian Assange to store the WikiLeaks files, made Pionen for a time 'the most famous . . . and stylish' data centre in the world and led to a flood of Internet coverage.[8] Obsolete Cold War architecture thus found new life and exposure thanks to the most successful of Cold War technologies, the Internet, the origin of which, like Sweden's subterranean atomic bomb defences, was linked to the necessity to plan decentralized command-and-control networks that would function in a post-nuclear scenario.[9] While Bahnhof's choice of location was mostly motivated by market conditions, publicity value and the sheer fun of doing it, it is still poetic to consider that in today's world, where the threats of nuclear attack have been increasingly replaced by those associated with cyber warfare, these underground spaces, as Pionen proves, can still provide protection, albeit now for information rather than human beings.[10]

Sheltered Lives: Shanghai Civil Defence Shelters

Carlos López Galviz

'There's nobody in.'

'That's fine, I'd like to have a look at the space, if that's okay?' And so in we went, stamp on our wrists. It was Friday night, end of summer, in the French Concession area of Shanghai. The Shelter is one of the highlights of Shanghai's nightlife. 'Don't go there before eleven', several friends had advised. 'It's after midnight that the fun really starts.'

'At least two more hours to go, then', I said to my colleague, having confirmed that it was only a few minutes past ten. We were the only customers. Four DJs and one barman stared at us as we ordered our drinks.

The place is a maze of sorts. As we descended the stairs from the entrance (a door in the side of a building), we came to a winding tunnel that led to a central hall where the bar, the DJ station, a couple of sofas, big loudspeakers and the six of us stood, in expectation of what the night might bring. At first sight, it has all the ingredients of a 'gritty' bar: bare walls, dark, damp, the odd red light, smoke. Through the hall you can walk into a corridor connecting two wider spaces on either side. Colours and textures change here, if only slightly: cement walls give way to brown and golden mosaic tiles covering the vaulted ceiling on both sides.

The construction of underground civil defence shelters was part of a comprehensive response to mounting tension between China and the USSR in the 1960s, a response that included the potential use of other underground spaces, such as mines and those housing transportation networks. In cities, shelters often took the form of vaulted tunnels built by local associations at neighbourhood and district level. More elaborate and generally deeper structures were built with the support of metropolitan and national bodies to house hospitals, energy plants and other facilities of prime importance in the event of nuclear attack. For the most part, tunnels were excavated by hand. Burrowing underground and building shelters was perhaps one way of channelling the anxieties caused by the prospect of war. Entire networks were built across China, including an underground city in Beijing, allegedly 32 kilometres (20 mi.) in extent. The civil defence programme continues: Shanghai's newest bunker was completed in 2006 and can accommodate around 200,000 people for fifteen days. Reports by the Chinese government in 2009 spoke of a 5,000-kilometre (3,100-mi.) Underground Great Wall.

A large number of tunnels and shelters in Shanghai have been repurposed as alternative venues and facilities, including as wine cellars,

A 21st-century socialite in The Shelter, Shanghai.

underwear shops and art galleries. A report of 2012 stated: 'There are now more than 6,000 of these facilities throughout the city with "civil defense" signs' – a significant number for a population of 23 million.[11] However, only 5–6 per cent of the tunnels are usable, because of limited ventilation and a dearth of water and electricity mains. Most underground shelters were never used and remain abandoned or, at best, overlooked, except in the French Concession, where it is precisely the overlooked and abandoned spaces that have become fashionable venues.

Socialites – once mostly foreigners – are now a crowd of self-fashioned yuppies, a good number of them Chinese, some remarkably skilled routine dancers. One of the club's owners says it is the Shelter's policy to 'kick people out before old ladies walking their dogs in the morning start bumping into drunk people'.[12] I did see an unattended dog, but no sign of any old ladies. It was the mixed impressions of socialites rather than the social history of the shelter that jumped out of its walls.

Remote Shelter: Andersgrotta, Norway
Henriette Hafsaas-Tsakos

In 1862 a church was built on the headland between two smaller inlets in Varangerfjord on the northeastern fringe of Norway, an area known as Finnmark; the church was named Kirkenes ('church on the headland'). Iron ore was discovered at nearby Bjørnevatn in 1865, but mining industries in Norway were mainly developed after the union with Sweden was dissolved in 1905. In 1906 the company A. S. Sydvaranger constructed a railway line between the mines and Kirkenes (for the area came to be named after the church), where processing facilities and a harbour for shipping were built. The export of iron started in 1910. Although the first two ships loaded with iron sank, the demand for the metal was so high that the company expanded. Germany was the main importer of iron ore from Kirkenes, and on the outbreak of war in 1914, all contracts and sales were annulled. When the war ended, limits were imposed on the amount of iron ore that Germany could import, and A. S. Sydvaranger was issued with a quota. Despite these restrictions and the depression of the 1930s, Kirkenes continued to grow, rising to a population of around 7,000 by 1940, when the Germans occupied Finnmark after the outbreak of the Second World War.

Kirkenes became an important strategic site for the German Wehrmacht during the war, since it was the northernmost settlement in the occupied territories and less than 150 kilometres (95 mi.) from the important town of Murmansk in the Soviet Union. Murmansk was the only harbour that was ice-free year-round in the northern part of the Soviet Union and the terminus station of the Karelian railway to Petrozavodsk near Leningrad. In both world wars, Murmansk was a key strategic hub for the transportation of military supplies. Germany attacked the Soviet Union on both a northern and a southern front in June 1941. Before the attack, Kirkenes had been transformed into a fortified garrison town quartering, at any given time, almost 100,000 of the half a million soldiers fighting on the Murmansk front. However, at Litsa River – only 50 kilometres (30 mi.) from Murmansk – the German offensive came to a halt. The Red Army forced the Germans to retreat after more than three years of fighting in extremely difficult terrain and hostile weather conditions. During this period, Kirkenes became a primary target for the Soviet air force; it was bombarded 328 times during the Second World War, making it one of the most frequently bombarded towns in that period.

The Norwegian engineer Anders Elvebakk took the initiative to construct an underground bomb shelter for the civilian population in the autumn of 1941, and the shelter bears his name. The subterranean tunnels were dug in the Haganesfjell – a small hill in the centre of the town – and they had three entrances. The main tunnel was about 250 metres (820 ft) long and was excavated straight through the hill from the harbour-side to the town centre. In the middle of the shelter was a large room, which was connected to the most populated parts of the town by means of smaller tunnels. Above the tunnels sat more than 7 metres (23 ft) of solid rock.

The shelter was ready for use on 20 January 1944, and it replaced the cellars that were hitherto used by the civilian population. Inside the shelter were benches placed along the walls for the first comers, but the majority of the evacuated people – numbering several thousand – had to stand. In its bombing raids, the Soviet Air Force concentrated its firepower on strategic targets, but since the Germans had built their barracks in between civilian houses, many homes were also destroyed.

The worst attack took place on 4 July 1944, when 140 houses were reduced to ashes. Most residents of Kirkenes spent four hours in the bomb shelter while their homes were being levelled. Despite the brutality of the attack, no civilians were killed. At this point, most of the town had been destroyed, and the people moved to the nearby settlement of Bjørnevatn. On 10 October it became clear that the Germans were going to retreat, using, as they did, the scorched-earth tactic by burning everything not already destroyed by the Soviet bombs. Meanwhile, more than 1,000 civilians took refuge in a tunnel 500 metres (1,640 ft) deep in the mines at Bjørnevatn. There they survived for ten days while the Red Army and the Germans were fighting on the surface. On 24 October 1944 a train carriage full of explosives was detonated by the Germans inside the opening of the tunnel, but the resulting blast did not affect the people sheltering deep inside, and the entrance to the mine did not collapse. This was the last act of terror by the Germans before the Red Army liberated Kirkenes, the first town to be liberated in Norway. With few houses left standing in Kirkenes, Andersgrotta was used as the location for the negotiations between the Red Army and representatives of the town. The first civil council for more than four years was held in the bomb shelter on the same day.

In the centre of Kirkenes, just above the bomb shelter, stands a monument to the soldiers of the Red Army. Erected in 1952, it was originally intended to depict a soldier with his foot crushing an eagle – the most prominent symbol of Nazi Germany. When Norway became a member of NATO in 1949, the eagle – also the state symbol of its principal ally, the USA – was removed, to avoid the symbolism being misconstrued in the light of the ensuing Cold War. In the final monument, the soldier is simply resting his foot on a piece of rock.

Andersgrotta functioned as a bomb shelter until the beginning of the 1980s, and is now open to the public as a tourist attraction. Visiting it today provides a powerful impression of how cold and raw this subterranean shelter must have been; more unfathomable but no less powerful is the sense of terror the people must have felt when they crowded together in its sheltering spaces as the bombs were falling on their homes above.

Defence of the Nation: National Redoubt, Switzerland
David L. Pike

As I was taking the photograph of an entrance to one of the defence networks beneath the Swiss Alps that accompanies this article, a man drove up and told me that I was breaking the law by doing so. Rather than arrest me, however, he invited me to his home, offered me lunch and plied me with pamphlets and books describing the parts of the subterranean defence network that I was legally allowed to know about. This combination of secrecy and openness is fully characteristic of the Swiss attitude towards its military and civil defence networks, as the essayist John McPhee suggested in his book *La Place de la Concorde Suisse* (1984): "'About this we don't talk,' a colonel on the general staff said to me one day. 'Don't ask me about it. But keep your eyes open. You may see something.'"[13] Among the most extensive such networks in the world, the 'Gruyère' (affectionately named after holey French cheese) was able to shelter the entire Swiss army in the event of an invasion, and the nation was able to shelter all of its civilian population beneath its buildings, towns and highways. Although regularly debated in the Swiss parliament, the construction of shelters continues to be required by law for all new Swiss buildings.

The defining moment of Switzerland's identity as a fortified nation crystallized around a geographic amplification, the conception of the 'Réduit national' or 'Alpenreduit', the national redoubt proposed by General Henri Guisan in 1940. Guisan made the radical decision to

Entrance to the Second World War shelter under Andersgrotta, Norway.

'reduce' the defence of Switzerland to a fortified enclave defined by its topography, and to concede the loss of the central plateau in order to create, in effect, 'the largest fortress in Europe'.[14] By blocking passage from the north as well as from the south, the redoubt would function as a double Maginot Line. Excavating deep within the mountains themselves would create a networked shelter-fortress capable of garrisoning the entire army. How much of the retreating civilian population would also have been brought into this enormous fortress is still being debated, and it is an important question, since the strategy of withdrawal necessitated the sacrifice of the *Mittelland*, the central plain where most of the Swiss population lives, works, farms and produces.

As the Cold War drew on into the early 1960s, the redoubt was supplemented by legislation for a shelter and militia system diffused throughout the nation. The redoubt remained the focal point of the myth of national defence and a deterrent to any land invasion, whether or not accompanied by atomic, biological or chemical weapons, but the broader goal of civil defence became survival wherever one was. This could range from elaborate private shelters in individual homes to the world's largest nuclear shelter, in the Sonnenberg Tunnel near Lucerne (now demolished), with a capacity of 20,000 people, and fully equipped with sleeping quarters, doors 1.5 metres (5 ft) thick, sophisticated air filters, a prison and everything the army would need to conduct the defence of the nation from within its confines.[15] Until the end of the Cold War, attitudes towards the shelter system were starkly divided between a militaristic right and a pacifist left, with eminent writers such as Friedrich Dürrenmatt and Max Frisch coming out strongly against the whole conception of a shelter society, and Igaal Niddam, Jean-Marc Lovay and Jean-Luc Delarue producing novels and films that used the idea of shelter as a conceptual framework for a satirical critique of Swiss society.

Because so much of the shelter network remains active, there has so far been less active redevelopment of the Swiss underground for tourism or creative reuse than in other formerly heavily fortified areas such as Albania, Germany, the United States or the Kinmen and Matsu islands in the Taiwan Strait. In 2009 the conceptual artists Frank and Patrik Riklin and Daniel Charbonnier opened the budget Zero Star Hotel in a former bunker in Teufen, Switzerland. While the built environment of the redoubt remains among the most active in the world, its political underpinnings have been cited by the American moral philosopher Elaine Scarry as 'one of the few pieces of evidence we have that the right of exit (as well as the "right to exist") is still imaginable in the nuclear age'.[16] Indeed, Scarry argues that emergency preparedness is, in fact, a fundamental component of organized society,

Entrance to Switzerland's
National Redoubt,
in the Alps.

and one that pre-dates democracy. Having outlived its Cold War identity, the Swiss underground suggests a different way to approach the ruins of bunker architecture that persist across the world.

Undergrounds at War:
London's Second World War Bunkers
Paul Dobraszczyk

Underground spaces take on heightened significance during times of crisis above ground, particularly periods of war. When cities are threatened by destruction, subterranean spaces are mobilized as places of shelter, secrecy and production. During the Blitz in London, from 1940 to 1941, the normal associations of the city's underground – darkness, danger and death – were dramatically reversed. In this period, the workaday Tube was inundated with large numbers of people seeking shelter and a safe place to sleep. At the same time, new tunnels were dug beneath the city to house munitions workers, including a series of bunkers beneath the Tube's Northern line, while the government built underground rooms to house its war operations, and church crypts, vaults and even empty coffins were used as temporary places of shelter.[17]

The Cabinet War Rooms – now a popular tourist attraction – were built under the Treasury in Whitehall in 1939 and remained in operation throughout the Second World War.[18] They were in fact the successors of another set of war rooms, in Dollis Hill, northwest London, which were codenamed Paddock and still open for public visits twice a year.[19] Paddock was abandoned in 1939 in favour of more central sites, including the abandoned Tube station at Down Street (see essay 'Temporal Disjunctions'), but it remains, even after seventy years, in its original state. In contrast to the comfortable experience of touring the Cabinet War Rooms – complete with their underground café – visiting Paddock is disconcerting. It has stood empty for more than half a century: stalactites now hang from the ceilings; piles of rubbish and mud fill the once pristine rooms; the furnishings are rotting and metal rusts unchecked. Without the reassuring narrative provided for visitors to the Cabinet War Rooms, the spaces of Paddock take on a nightmarish, uncanny quality. Rooms originally designed to house equipment now stand empty, their oddly shaped spaces receding into darkness, while relics from the intervening years – 1970s Coca-Cola bottles and fire extinguishers – speak of other stories of illicit exploration. As much as a frozen past, the spaces and

'Paddock': Winston Churchill's alternative war rooms beneath Dollis Hill, London.

relics of Paddock suggest an abandoned future, a place that has yet to become what it was once meant to be.

In fact, with their curious temporal quality, the underground spaces at Paddock feel more akin to those that have characterized the post-apocalyptic imagination in cinema and television since the Second World War. Paddock's spaces seem to speak of a disaster that is yet to happen, in which even underground spaces would be no longer safe from ruin. Post-apocalyptic films such as *Threads* (1984), *Day of the Dead* (1985) and *The Road* (2009) provide differing causes of annihilation – respectively nuclear war, zombies and an unidentified cosmic strike – but they all suggest that bunkers might be used as a means of surviving apocalyptic destruction. However, in all these pessimistic visions of the future, the underground as place of safety is eventually overwhelmed by either the sheer force of the apocalyptic destruction above or social breakdown below. Experiencing the decaying spaces of Paddock reminds us forcefully that the underground is not a secure refuge, a place inviolate to ruin; rather, in contrast to Paddock's sanitized counterparts under Whitehall, their abandoned future shows us what becomes of such hubris.

Tortoises, Oranges and Giant Tunnels: Bunkers, Albania
David L. Pike

It is difficult to imagine a more extensive bunkering than that which occurred in Albania over a ten-year period from the mid-1970s. The long-serving dictator Enver Hoxha planned the construction of 750,000 bunkers, about one for every four of the country's inhabitants at the time; estimates of the number actually built range from around 100,000 to the full three-quarters of a million. They were made in three sizes: *Qander zjarri* or 'single fire', colloquially known as 'tortoises' or 'concrete mushrooms', which were pillbox bunkers just big enough for a single person with a gun, shaped like an igloo, and made of granite-based concrete reinforced with thirteen layers of steel; *Pike zjarri* or 'fire points', colloquially known as 'oranges', which were artillery bunkers large enough to hold about a dozen individuals, assembled from concrete wedges gathered together into a dome; and larger, speciality bunkers in the mountains, used to store munitions and house larger forces, and often connected by tunnels. These last (most of which incorporated earlier fortifications, such as the Soviet-built hidden submarine base in the Porto Palermo bay or the Chinese-designed

or that Rio and Gaza have gradually come to reflect one another.[10]

In addition to specialized training complexes in remote locations, full-scale military exercises also now take place in the vast subterranean realms beneath US cities. One occurred beneath Chicago in 2004. This was motivated by then current efforts to control the elaborate bunkers and tunnels beneath Baghdad and by perceived threats of urban terrorists to infrastructures such as subterranean railways (as well as by wider clandestine activities, such as urban exploration). As in all areas of the 'war on terror' and its descendants, the tactics, strategy and discourse of national security in the 'hot' zones of colonial frontiers and counter-insurgency overlap unerringly with the securitization of the metropole at the heart of empire.

Such tunnels, which can be superbly engineered and surprisingly elaborate, allow surreptitious or proscribed movements, migration and economies to survive or even flourish, despite intensifying surface and above-surface surveillance and the proliferation of aggressively fenced ground-level borders. Trans-border tunnel complexes represent, in many ways, what Bryan Finoki has called 'dark places . . . united in a landscape solidarity against the "immanent domains" of [a] transnational corporatism'.[11] While the surface world is organized around 'free trade' for corporate commodities, it increasingly confines or proscribes the mobility of other flows as well as of excluded masses of poor non-citizens.

A robot with a snake-like shape, designed to explore and map smaller tunnels and pipes.

It follows that, rather than being viewed as geopolitical lines on a map seen from above – as on traditional maps or Google Earth images – international borderlands must instead be viewed as three-dimensional domains linked intimately to above-ground scrutiny as well as clandestine, subterranean flow and circulation. Through subterranean tunnels, as Finoki puts it, the 'limits of power are undone by the primordial urge to human ingenuity persistent in its crudest form, in its naked right to move freely beyond all constraints and survive, snoop, escape, evade, profit.' Indeed, such tunnels work to render the above-ground discourses of perfect, militarized control as an ineffective post-9/11 'security theatre' – a series of architectural fallacies and lucrative military-industrial fantasies, organized by politicians and contractors to symbolize projects deemed to 'protect' vulnerable national identity against some demonized, external or racialized Other.[12]

Surface-level walls also disguise the social complexity of the tunnels below. Tunnel worlds are represented by wall-building political elites as being necessarily criminal and nefarious even though, very often – as in Gaza – they merely sustain the basic needs of human life in places where the militarization of surface borders and above-surface airspace works to make these all but impossible. Tunnels thus grow in parallel with the criminalization of migration, deepening trade blockages, foreign occupation or colonization, and bi-national corruption. We did not hear of 'baby medicine' tunnels beneath the walls around Gaza, only of 'terrorist' or 'smuggling' tunnels.

Once again, as so often in history, the linguistic and theological constructs of verticality mean that those circulations and people driven into the subterranean realms are easy to demonize, animalize and project as targets that require violent destruction. By driving migration, refugee and labour flows underground, it becomes much easier to represent them as intrinsically demonic or feral.

Sent Down: Oxford's Prison Tunnels
Paul Dobraszczyk

The extraordinary survival that is the series of tunnels connecting Oxford's courthouse building with its former prison shows just how the symbolic can infuse the utilitarian. Constructed in 1841 with the court itself, these strange spaces constitute one of only two examples in the United Kingdom, the other being under Castlereagh Prison in Northern Ireland, which was built in the late eighteenth century and from which derives the phrase 'to send down', meaning to convict and sentence to imprisonment. Just as in Castlereagh, in the Oxford courthouse the convicted prisoner would descend wooden steps in front of the assembled crowd, disappearing into a narrow brick-lined tunnel (now used for storage), then passing through a holding area – with its public convenience – and through an iron gate before descending again into a more forbidding tunnel, which would have led to the receiving area of the prison. The Oxford tunnel was last used in the early 1980s, most famously for the 'sending down' in 1983 of Donald Neilson (1936–2011), the notorious 'Black Panther' who committed many violent armed robberies and murders in the 1970s.[13]

While it is clear that the tunnels connecting Oxford's courthouse and prison were conceived as functional spaces – simply an efficient

and secure means of transporting prisoners from one space to another – they nevertheless have symbolic meaning as well. The convicted criminal would descend before the eyes of the court, literally cast down by the judge into the symbolic hell of prison; both the iron gates and two levels of descent reinforced the notion of 'going down' into an infernal region. Today the tunnel is blocked up, a dead end. In the mid-1990s the prison was converted into a luxury hotel, and the function and symbolism of the tunnels have been altered ever since. Yet a few court employees still work in the offices between the two tunnels, the squeaky, rusted hinges of one of the tunnel's doors sometimes suggesting the ghostly presence of unquiet prisoners.

Indeed, the former prison is thought to be one of the most haunted places in England. The history of the prison, which is in the grounds of the eleventh-century castle, stretches much further back than the Victorian courthouse and its tunnels. Together with the castle's crypt, the prison has come to be seen as a place replete with spectres; something that the tourist agency Oxford Castle Unlocked exploits in its regular ghosts tours of the crypt, complete with moody lighting, sound effects and guides dressed up as figures from the past.[14] Yet at the same time, with its recent transformation into a Malmaison hotel, the prison has become a place of luxury, one that has commodified (and thoroughly sanitized) its former spaces of incarceration. Now surrounded by cafés, restaurants and the Oxford Castle tourist attraction, the former prison sits within a landscape of conspicuous consumption and commodified leisure, one that eschews any reference to the prison's spectral spaces below ground. To acknowledge the ghosts of victims of the past is one thing; to recognize those of the perpetrators of crime is quite another.

Under Control: Metro, Santiago de Chile
Dhan Zunino Singh

I used Line 1 of the Santiago Metro for the first time in 2000. Built in 1975, it gave the impression of a simple and efficient system, emphasized by its streamlined 1970s functionalist style. In contrast with the bustle and noise of the Buenos Aires Underground, Santiago's exuded a calm atmosphere produced by the sonorous effect of its trains' pneumatic tyres. Spacious stations and a relatively small number of passengers also enhanced this effect.

However, significant changes in Santiago's transport infrastructure have recently taken place: the city's new public transport system

Passageway linking the Oxford courthouse and former prison.

(Transantiago), introduced in 2007, has the city's metro at its core. Today the trains, despite their high frequency, are full of passengers. What caught my attention in 2013 were the guards standing at the edge of the platforms, controlling the flow of passengers – a symptom of the increased need for order as the number of riders swells. Now, according to most residents of Santiago, inconvenience and discomfort are usual in their daily journeys.

In July 2013 I had the privilege of viewing the system from its control centre. I spent some time exploring one of the metro's stations before meeting the colleagues with whom the visit had been arranged. My movements were more erratic than normal: I walked along the platform, taking photographs, and stood for several minutes looking at the details of the station. The control centre itself was at the top of a high building. Designed by a Chilean architect – who was guiding the tour – the office seemed like the futuristic NASA control centre that features in numerous Hollywood films. All the different control levels (circulation and surveillance) create a centralized and unified coordination of the metro. Each row of screens deals with a particular area of control (trains, signals, power, information and passengers), and these screens form a fan shape at the apex of which is the director's chair – from where the chief surveys everything.

In the control centre, the lived experience of the metro vanishes into a virtual representation of lights and lines, codes and calculations. Here, I felt one could obtain a complete representation of the underground system in its entirety (in contrast to our fragmented experience of it in everyday life). Yet, despite the ubiquity of CCTV cameras and screens, the complexity of passenger circulation was difficult to capture as a whole. Surveillance here goes beyond crime control; rather, it concerns controlling circulation: one camera zoomed in on a young man who did not board a train (an action that immediately

Santiago Metro
control centre, 2013.

turned him into a suspect). I immediately recalled my earlier movements in the station and realized: 'Not to circulate makes you a target of surveillance.' Our guide explained that it was important to detect and prevent potential suicides. Indeed, suicide is seen as more troublesome for the metro than robbery, because it causes significant delays and incurs enormous costs to the authorities.

My visit to the control centre helped me to understand the power of the idea of circulation and, in turn, the perils of blockage. If movement ceases, the system dies. Being outside, the control centre provided a better understanding of the underground railway as a network that can extend (socially and materially) beyond the subterranean space. The travel experience shapes our idea that this transport infrastructure is entirely localized under the ground, but, as with power stations for example, there are elements of the underground system that facilitate mobility but are not visible to the passenger. Despite its isolated location, the Santiago Metro control centre – outside the underground spaces of the metro itself – is at the very heart of the system.

Crossing Borders: Tijuana and San Diego
Carlos López Galviz

> We do not yet have full control of the border. I am determined to change that.
> George W. Bush, 15 May 2006[15]

The USA–Mexico border, 3,100 kilometres (nearly 2,000 mi.) long, is one of the most frequently crossed international borders, with about 350 million legal crossings every year. Recent counts of illegal tunnels across the border put the number at around 170, more than half of them built in Arizona and California.[16] The San Diego Tunnel Task Force discovered one of the most elaborate tunnels in 2013: over 3.2 kilometres (2 mi.) long, 1.2 metres (4 ft) high, 90 centimetres (3 ft) wide, and linking two warehouses, one near Tijuana airport, the other in San Diego. The tunnel has lighting, ventilation and an electric rail system. According to the San Diego authorities, it was never used.

News reports from recent years seem to agree that such tunnels point to a change of tactics by the drug cartels, which are willing to invest in infrastructure to bypass a fence that has 'become higher, stronger and more extensive' following the US Secure Fence Act of 2006, to which former president George W. Bush's high-profile speech

Overleaf
A stark representation of the US–Mexico border at Tijuana.

on immigration was a preamble. The fence is a byword for an impressive system of surveillance and enforcement that draws on a 21,000-strong agent force (that is, across all borders, including the border with Mexico), a range of vehicles (all-terrain, unmanned aerial and conventional SUVs) and ever more sophisticated sensors and cameras.

Local residents and ranch owners along the border are less impressed, however. From their properties, they often see groups of around twenty men, women and children, on their way to the dream of a better life. A number of them die in the harshness of the desert; others are caught. Only a minority 'succeed', entering a life of illegality with all the anxieties and everyday challenges that such an existence brings.

The inefficacy of the border control has prompted some action of the kind led by Glenn Spencer, chairman of American Border Patrol, a non-governmental organization 'that monitors the border on a regular basis – mostly by air. It has three aircraft, each designed for a specialized mission.' One of their functions is to 'gather intelligence' to counter the effects of the American people being 'sacrificed on the altar of globalism' as a result of weak border control.[17] Their role is that of surveyors – watchdogs who share the information they collect with the border authorities in the hope of instigating effective action.

Tunnels challenge control at the USA–Mexico border and elsewhere. Tunnelling is one of the methods that Joaquín Guzmán Loera, leader of the Sinaloa Cartel, used to evade the several attempts to seize him after his infamous escape from prison in 2001. One of the findings after his recapture in February 2014 was an elaborate system of tunnels connecting several houses to the sewers in Culiacán, Sinaloa. It was the tunnels that had frustrated the combined efforts of US and Mexican intelligence for more than thirteen years, or so their stories claim.

Tunnels are also symptoms: that is, ways in which traffic, legal and otherwise, bridges borders, bringing people into contact with others whether they are illegal migrants, drug smugglers or border patrol forces. The motivation behind the construction of tunnels differs, as do the mechanisms to control the very functions they serve. They show determination either to instil control or to deflect it.

Golfers at the Fort Brown golf course in Texas, bordering the Rio Grande, come across a sign that reads: 'Do not hit golf balls into Mexico.' Another sign next to it, more prominent, in red, might read: 'Fragile. Underground workers.'

Pathet Lao soldiers perform a training drill in a cave during a visit by delegates from the Organization of Solidarity with the People of Asia, Africa and Latin America (OSPAAL), thought to have taken place in the late 1960s.

the support of the North Vietnamese Army and the Viet Cong. When the US covert aerial bombing campaign began in 1964, these forces moved their headquarters to the cave network beneath Viengxay (known until 1970 simply as the 'special zone'). What had previously been a sparsely inhabited area experienced rapid underground urbanization as a subterranean city was created through the expansion of existing voids in the limestone. Some 23,000 people lived in the caves for nine years, many venturing into the open only to farm during the night. Such a troglodyte existence was necessary because their adversaries carried out a bombing mission on average every eight minutes during the conflict, resulting in the release of an estimated 2.1 million tons of ordnance on the country, more than the US had dropped during the Second World War.[4]

The cave complex was thus developed to provide as much infrastructure as possible, to allow the opposition leaders, soldiers and their families as well as many local residents to live underground. Some caves housed homes and offices, while others acted as supply centres, factories, workshops and barracks. Perhaps most impressive were those caves used as a school, hospital and auditorium. When the Americans began to withdraw from Vietnam a ceasefire was brokered, at which point some of the opposition leaders returned to the capital, Vientiane, to join a coalition government. Others remained in Viengxay and built new homes in front of their caves, while the inflated population led to the first example of socialist town planning in the country.[5]

The town was given the name Viengxay, which means 'city of victory', during the early 1970s as a reflection of the opposition's successes, which eventually resulted in the Pathet Lao establishing a new government, the Lao People's Democratic Republic (LPDR) in 1975. Thereafter the remainder of Viengxay's political leadership also relocated to Vientiane to join the governing Lao People's Revolutionary Party, which still leads the country today. Viengxay remained in use as a military training base, and, more controversially, a re-education camp was established nearby, but the caves were vacated and the general area marked as off limits to visitors from outside.

This changed during the late 1990s, when some of the caves were opened to tourists and the government of the LPDR began to use its heritage, history and memory explicitly as a means of political legitimization.[6] The caves have since become key motifs of Laos's revolutionary and heroic past, and on state-sponsored tours they are officially framed as 'the birthplace' of the socialist republic in ways that resonate unwittingly with the metaphorical parallels between caves and wombs.[7] In 2005 the caves were heritage-listed by the Lao government, which began cooperating with the SNV Netherlands Development Organisation and Deakin University in Australia to develop a heritage-based 'pro-poor tourism' strategy that framed Viengxay as the 'hidden city'.[8]

These efforts have not been without problems or compromise. For example, unexploded ordnance has the potential to disrupt tourism and heritage strategies as it has elsewhere in the country, and presents an altogether more dangerous material memory that can kill and injure more than forty years after the end of the conflict.[9] Meanwhile, foreign partners have had to tolerate the Lao PDR's partial interpretation of the past, most evidently in relation to the area's post-conflict re-education camp, in order to continue pursuing the efforts that they hope will benefit the area's rural poor.[10] In the poorest province of one of Asia's least economically developed countries, where 74.6 per cent of the populace lives below the national poverty line, such efforts are crucial. But with growing yet sustainable tourism, positive local perception and increasing international interest these efforts look likely to bear fruit in the coming years.[11] For the population of Viengxay, it seems, the future as much as the past is to be found underground.

Defensible Spaces:
The Underground Cities of Kinmen and Matsu
David L. Pike

In 1949 Chiang Kai-shek's Kuomintang troops retreated in defeat to the Kinmen islands. On 25 October some 10,000 Communist soldiers crossed the 2 kilometres (1 1/4 mi.) from mainland China in fishing boats. They were repelled after a fierce and bloody battle, and Taiwan (officially the Republic of China, or ROC) has held the islands ever since. They were soon transformed into a front-line defence, often termed a 'mini-Maginot Line', that protected the island of Taiwan across the Taiwan Strait. The ROC also occupied the islands of the Matsu archipelago, 150 kilometres (93 mi.) up the coast, off the Min Chiang estuary. Military bases capacious enough for the 100,000-plus troops (a full third of the ROC's total force at its peak) were built, almost entirely underground, both along the flatter Kinmen beaches and rugged Matsu coast and beneath the mountainous interiors.

    The islands became a Cold War hotspot during the sustained bombing of 1958 (as many as 10,000 people were killed in a single

Part of the Chinese artist Cai Guo-Qiang's *Bunker Museum of Contemporary Art,* 2004, installed in a former bunker on Kinmen, Taiwan.

day in August; over 30,000 shells were fired in under two hours, and a total of half a million over six months). President Eisenhower sent the Seventh Fleet to patrol the strait in support of its close ally's resistance against the People's Republic of China (PRC). Escalation was narrowly avoided, but PRC and ROC troops continued to shell each other until the end of the 1970s, although the exchange eventually became ritualized to the degree that the two sides would alternate shelling days, both resting on Sundays, and the contents of the shells were more likely to be propaganda leaflets than explosives.

In 1992, when the PRC's possession of mid-range missiles capable of striking Taiwanese targets directly had negated the strategic importance of the islands, they were finally returned to civilian government. The military mostly pulled out of Matsu in 1996, but it still maintains a significant presence on Kinmen.

Although tensions rose in 1996 and have done so at varying times since, the primary function of the islands in the relationship between the two governments has transmuted from military to economic symbolism. In 2001 the 'mini three links' (shipping, post and air travel) were established between the islands and nearby mainland ports, permitting, for the first time, travel between Taiwan and the mainland PRC. A roaring smuggling trade was largely shut down, but travel was heavily skewed in favour of the Taiwanese, who benefited from their government's far more liberal travel policy. Meanwhile, the Taiwanese invested money in the removal of landmines and provided economic support to islands with very little natural means of self-support. After tension eased with the election of the pro-unification candidate Ma Ying-jeou, serious discussions began in 2008 over the construction of a 10-kilometre (6-mi.) bridge linking Kinmen with Xiamen, an idea that dated back to 2004.

These islands are among the most heavily fortified territories in the world, both in number (more than 100 tunnels seam the 29 sq. km/11 sq. mi. of the Matsu archipelago's 36 islands) and in scale (Taiwu Mountain in central Kinmen boasts an auditorium with a capacity of 1,000, and tunnels on both islands are large enough to hide naval forces and to drive tanks through). It is not an exaggeration to say that Kinmen (132 sq. km/51 sq. mi.) and Matsu (12 sq. km/4 1/2 sq. mi.) were effectively transformed into underground cities. Bereft of typical urban amenities, their militarized and spartan form of urbanism echoed that depicted in much speculative fiction dealing with anti-nuclear bunkers and Cold War super-shelters. The adaptive reuse of these enduring features of the landscape elucidates many of the meanings attached to these underground spaces. Fortresses and tunnels have been transformed into parks and monuments, visited by busloads of ROC and PRC tourists, and complete with mannequins staging daily activities, explanatory maps and plaques, and activity rooms for younger visitors to colour in tracings of wind lions, the local protective deity. The studio of Maestro Wu produces world-class knives from the high-grade steel used in the hundreds of thousands of propaganda shells that were launched across the bay by PRC guns. Elsewhere, shell casings can be found in guard-rails, perimeter fences, benches and playgrounds, taking the expression 'swords into ploughshares' literally to assert that the deadly war of the past has been overcome and turned to peaceful ends.

Kinmen and Matsu are also famous for their local liquor, and distilleries on both islands have transformed nearby tunnels into cold storage for their wares. Underground brothels were the other distinctly urban vice long indulged on the islands. Back in 1991, the Chinese artist Cai Guo-Qiang played on this history when he proposed transforming the still active bunkers into 'love hotels'. Cai was also responsible for the *Bunker Museum of Contemporary Art* (2004), an installation of work by eighteen artists in decommissioned Kinmen bunkers that displayed a combination of anti-war sentiment, historical reckoning and ideas for making some kind of positive artistic, religious or cultural meaning from the inorganic relics of the Cold War.[12] And while Kinmen is rapidly expanding its newly legitimized role as a trading fulcrum between the PRC and the ROC, the residents of the more isolated Matsu voted in 2012 to allow a casino and a resort to be developed on the two largest islands. No doubt the casino, too, will take advantage of the subterranean heritage of its site as it designs its own artificial paradise.

Ideology and Fear: Prague Metro
Petr Gibas

Prague's metro is an underground transport complex with about 59 kilometres (36 1/2 mi.) of track and with 57 stations on three lines. To understand and appreciate its complexity, we must first learn about its historical context. The first proposal to build a metro system in Prague was allegedly made in 1898 by a wealthy entrepreneur, but it was not until the end of the 1950s that the debate crystallized into serious intention.[13] This was the time of what would become known as the 'Thaw' – a post-Stalinist loosening of the grip of the Communist Party over its citizens, the easing of censorship, a boom in technological advancement and the ascent of consumption.

In 1964 the decision was finally made to build an underground railway, and a celebratory start of the excavation works was made in 1969. Yet during this period the reforms of the 1960s were dramatically curtailed, especially during and after the military invasion of Czechoslovakia by the Soviet Army in the summer of 1968. The invasion marked the beginning of what was termed 'normalization': the return – politically and socially – to the firm rule of the Communist Party. Political experimentation with socialism was over. It was in this context that the Prague Metro was ceremonially opened on 9 May 1974, the national holiday that marked the liberation of Prague by the Red Army from Nazi occupation and the end of the Second World War. The event carried important political symbolism at the time.

Socialism can be understood as a modernist project promising a better collective future through increased social equality. During the period of 'normalization', this took the form of a narrative of technological progress. In that respect the Prague Metro was used by the Communists as a testimony to the technological advances made possible by the socialist order and the help of the USSR,

Entrance to a tunnel
of the Prague Metro.

advances that promised to move its citizens towards a bright future. Throughout normalization, the metro was referred to as the 'edifice of the Czechoslovak-Soviet cooperation' and the expression of the never-ending friendship between the two nations. As such, the metro was infused with ideological meaning that was embodied in its spaces by means of decoration and artworks, such as the mosaics and statuary at Cosmonauts station.

Normalization also coincided with the climax of the Cold War. The fear of nuclear war with the 'imperialist West' had an impact on the metro, which was also built to act as a shelter for 200,000 people in the event of a nuclear conflagration. In addition, hospitals, warehouses, air filters, morgues and airlocks were scattered throughout the underground system. Indeed, the very reason why the metro was built so deep underground was its capacity to resist a nuclear blast. This 'metro protective system' remains mysterious, and the documents related to its construction are still classified as secret. Yet it is a secret that anyone riding the metro can get a glimpse of: the blast-proof airlocks and hermetically sealable doors stand conspicuously alongside mosaics, statues and reliefs that represent the ideology as well as the fears of life under socialism.

Intractable Histories: Moscow's Secret River
Darmon Richter

Moscow is a city of layers. It is built on old stones and spilled blood, and has grown out of fire and flood and age-old secrets. Most notorious among the latter are the city's subterranean realms, places like the legendary lost library of Ivan the Terrible and the closely guarded military/government transport network known as 'Metro-2'.

In recent years a growing subset of Muscovites have dedicated themselves to exploring the city's lost, forgotten or otherwise restricted lower levels. Known as 'diggers', these contemporary urban explorers have been investigating Moscow's secrets since the 1980s; their alleged discoveries range from Soviet-era military installations to the shrines of secret underground cults, as well as a system of tunnels that many claim descends as deep as twelve storeys beneath the capital.[14] While some of these reports seem to tread the threshold of fantasy, the Neglinnaya River – commonly known by its diminutive, Neglinka – is a well-documented landmark of the Moscow underworld.

In 1495, when the Kremlin was completed, the Neglinka formed a natural moat curving around its western flank. The river flowed from

Overleaf
The Neglinnaya River
beneath Moscow.

the north of Moscow, through the city and out into the larger Moskva River to the south. As a moat, however, the Neglinka proved far from effective: it did not repel the Crimean Tatars, who sacked Moscow in 1571; and it offered no defence against the Polish–Lithuanian Commonwealth, which defeated Russia in the Battle of Klushino in 1610 before marching on the capital and holding it under siege for two years.[15] Moreover, the broad floodplains of the Neglinka halted all construction west of the Kremlin.

The river was at first dammed to control its flow, creating interconnected ponds that spanned the city; for a time these served the developing capital as bathing pools, by turning watermills and by aiding firefighters. As the city continued to grow, however, the Neglinka – once perceived as a tactical advantage – became the enemy of progress. In 1792 work began to redirect the river into a masonry canal, but by the early nineteenth century that canal had grown so foul that steps were taken to hide it from sight altogether. The first Neglinnaya Tunnel was built between 1817 and 1819, in the vicinity of present-day Teatralnaya Square. This tunnel at first served as a sewer as well; for seventy years it channelled foul water into the Moskva, until dedicated sewers were constructed in 1887. In time the Neglinka was lost to Moscow: it was built over, buried and forgotten altogether.

Today this subterranean waterway flows for 7.5 kilometres (4 1/2 mi.) beneath the city, to meet the Moskva River just south of the Kremlin, where it is discharged through outflows under the Bolshoy Kamenny Bridge, and to the east, beneath the Bolshoy Moskvoretsky Bridge. Although the Neglinka is removed from sight, however, there are access points along the entire length of its course. Lift a manhole cover on Tsvetnoy Boulevard or peer beneath the metal lids that pepper the park on Sadovaya-Samotechnaya; only a leap of courage separates one from the murky, timeless flow of the Neglinnaya far below.

Crossing that threshold is the hardest part – to descend from buzzing city streets into those damp, cobwebbed shafts, hand over hand down rusted rungs into a labyrinth of dripping stone. Down there the sounds of traffic recede, to be replaced by a new ambience: the endless rush of water through pipes, the drip, drip, drip of condensation from the walls.

While Moscow above has exploded in size and density – today it is a sprawling metropolis of eleven million people – the Neglinka has changed very little since the turn of the nineteenth century. The history of these tunnels is plain to see, written into the very walls themselves. Moscow suffered catastrophic floods in 1965 and 1973, and both occasions prompted the construction of new, larger channels. These renovations stand out in brutal form as vast concrete pipes built to Soviet scale. They also add contrast to the older sections, including the passages of crumbling masonry that mark the site of the original Neglinnaya Tunnel. The Moscow Diggers claim to have made gruesome discoveries: human skulls hidden in side tunnels, along with rusted weapons and jewellery.[16]

The Diggers were not the first, however, to embrace such a fascination with Moscow's hidden river. Vladimir Gilyarovsky, an early twentieth-century journalist, chronicled the shifting regimes and shared his memories of pre-revolutionary Russia, but also, less famously, was an accomplished urban explorer, being 'the first journalist who dared descend into the Neglinka, where he found incredible quantities of dirt . . . and dead bodies'.[17] In more than 800 years Moscow has earned noble accolades such as 'The Hero City' and 'The Third Rome', but beneath its pavements, the Neglinka remembers every dirty secret.

Reverse Modernization: Saw Mill River, New York City
Caroline Bâcle

From the moment our film crew drove into Yonkers in December 2010, we knew this inner suburb of New York City had reached a critical point. Once a booming industrial town – the mecca for hat and furniture production, not to mention the infamous Otis elevator – it took a slow and painful beating throughout the twentieth century, when many of its businesses relocated to cheaper parts of the world. By 2010 Yonkers had long been a hub for derelict buildings and 'For Rent' signs. But things were about to change.

My crew and I were making a documentary film that would tell the stories of six waterways buried under six cities around the world.[18] One of these was the Saw Mill River. Once known as the Nepperhan (a Native American word meaning 'sparkling waters'), the Saw Mill runs 30.5 kilometres (19 mi.) through New York State before flowing into the Hudson River. According to Ann-Marie Mitroff from Groundwork Hudson Valley, it was Henry Hudson himself who stumbled upon the junction of the Saw Mill and the river that bears his name. There he found a beautiful bay stocked with fish, and a source of water power. This place would eventually become Yonkers.

In the nineteenth century the Saw Mill River was the key to Yonkers' development, but in the process the river was canalized, polluted and eventually regarded as a danger to public health. Rivers all over the United States were treated in this way: 'Everybody thought this was a lousy, stinky little river,' said Mitroff. In the 1920s, like so many other urban rivers, the Saw Mill was buried and covered with a car park.

There it would remain for ninety years, becoming an object of fascination for historians and urban explorers alike. In the 1980s two residents of Yonkers, Bob and Andy, were even inspired to paddle their canoes into the flume that kept the Saw Mill River under the city. 'This was in an adventure phase', said Bob. 'Any river that no one else had paddled, we gave it a shot.' Thus was born the dream to return the river to what it had been.

To survive de-industrialization, Yonkers has had to find a way to reinvent itself. As Mitroff put it: 'People have really been waiting for things to happen in the downtown. [But] it's really hard to get people to invest for new things around a parking lot.' Yet, on 15 December 2010, 'Groundbreaking Day' saw the start of the year-long process that would transform the car park into a green space and bring a section of the Saw Mill River back to the surface. The new park – designed by the City of Yonkers and Groundwork Hudson Valley in collaboration with Project for Public Spaces – is a critical part of the city's $3 billion redevelopment plan, and was made possible by years of community lobbying and political backing, federal and state money, and Yonkers' own investment of millions of dollars of future tax revenue. Environmental groups pledged to restore habitats for fish and fauna around this 'daylighted' section of the river. 'Some people call it a full circle. We're trying to re-mimic the things that work well in nature,'

'Daylighted' section of the Saw Mill River, New York.

said Mitroff on Groundbreaking Day. Bob put it another way: 'I think nature is going to revitalize Yonkers. The power of nature is going to generate the power of people in this area.'

And so it has. A few years after its completion, Van Der Donck Park is not only the new home for a surprisingly vast array of fish and fauna, but also hosts music, arts and science events in what is now one of the main gathering places in the city. 'What's totally cool is how much the park has gotten into people's psyches. People stare, smile, taking time from their day to enjoy the river. It just acts like a magnet', says Mitroff. At the same time, the city is seeing a direct impact on its economy; the abandoned properties around this magnet are also being transformed into new commercial and residential buildings.

Our crew filmed each stage of this remarkable revitalization project. Yet for Yonkers, it's just the beginning. The city plans to 'daylight' other sections of the Saw Mill in the downtown area, with the goal of exposing a total of six blocks of the river in coming years.

The trend of bringing back unseen nature – what was once pushed away from the urban landscape – is a growing phenomenon, not just in Yonkers but around the world. As Mitroff says:

> Our lost rivers and other lost natural resources, in their rebirth, can save our cities and make them sustainable and liveable again. Nature is a powerful ally and needs to be unleashed again in these very dense post-industrial cities. Reconnecting people to their rivers is magic.

Remaindered Flows: The Irk Culvert, Manchester
Paul Dobraszczyk

The River Irk in Manchester's city centre was culverted in several stages from the mid-1840s to the 1900s, principally because of the periodic expansion of the city's Victoria railway station. The culverting of urban watercourses in the nineteenth century was not only a pragmatic response to the need to create more space to build on, but also part of a process that regulated and separated 'nature' in the city. Rivers were thus 'lost' as cities were modernized, becoming part of just that confined and hidden nature that is written into the very discourse of modernization.

Today, those who wish to explore alternative memories of the ruined Irk have to negotiate the space of the culvert itself. Like many urban river culverts, the Irk's is deliberately hostile to

Overleaf
Former wooden cattle bridge preserved in the Irk culvert under Victoria railway station, Manchester.

would-be explorers. Its entrance – seen from the steps that descend into Manchester's gentrified Green Quarter from Cheetham Hill Road – is a forbidding black hole, into which the fast-flowing river rushes over a weir 2 metres (6 1/2 ft) high. As documented by Manchester's community of urban explorers, getting into that black hole is difficult even at the driest of times: it involves wading in chest-high murky water before descending the slippery weir into complete darkness. Flanking the river before it disappears are the shiny new skyscrapers of the Green Quarter, a characteristic (if extreme) juxtaposition of high technology and 'low' nature in the post-industrial city.

Once inside the culvert, the space seems to grow – the arch with its 6-metre (20-ft) span seen at the entrance now supported on immensely high brick walls – while the noise of the rushing water is magnified by the cavernous space. The river still has a fearsome quality: a smell that makes one light-headed (dangerous, as all urban explorers know); a furious velocity; and, as if in testimony to that, a channel lined with tree branches, shopping trolleys, car tyres and other forms of urban detritus that the river has brought here over the years. Such accumulated ruin is counterbalanced by what has been preserved – a bricked-up arched space in one of the walls that was once used as a chute for depositing dead cattle on to boats; the half-ruined remains of a brick-and-stone bridge that once linked buildings in Chetham's College and which dates from the 1820s; and, perhaps most extraordinary of all, an intact wooden bridge suspended between the walls of the culvert. For hundreds of years, this bridge – now bricked up inside and used as a utility tunnel – carried cattle from the fields on the north side of the Irk to the markets in Shudehill, and it probably dates, at least in part, from about 1650, when Manchester was little more than a large village clustered around the medieval Collegiate Church (a cathedral since 1847).

For this bridge to have survived so long after its original function was extinguished is testament to its power as a petrified ruin. It is paradoxically the ruin of the river (and its subsequent banishment) that has preserved this ancient relic intact; out of sight (and mind) it has been allowed to escape the relentless modernization that has dominated the development of Manchester's urban fabric from the late eighteenth century to the present day. If urban modernity requires the city to develop by a process of creative destruction – or deliberate ruination and rebuilding – then this preserved ruin directly challenges that process. Its continuing existence speaks rather of the residue of modernity, or of the ruins that do not yield to modernity because they continue to serve it in some unforeseen way. Indeed, modernization in cities like Manchester always leaves remainders – leftover spaces and architectural vestiges that suffuse the present with the ruins of the past. Confronting such remainders provides a necessary check on classifications that try to fix the understanding of place, as seen in the anodyne heritage-driven re-creation of the lost River Irk in the new Cathedral Gardens. Perhaps the name given to the Irk culvert by urban explorers – Optimus Prime, after a character from the *Transformers* franchise – is more than a rather infantile pseudonym; for the culvert has indeed transformed the river and its entombed ruins into something mythic, something that offers rich layers of meaning to the city above.

RENDERINGS

Because they are often unseen and invisible, underground spaces are rich sites for the telling of stories and the projection of ideas, desires and imaginings. According to the philosopher Henri Lefebvre, the creative appropriation of space is in itself a practice that resists the simultaneous fragmentation and homogenization of urban space under the dominant capitalist model of production and consumption. For Lefebvre, the creative appropriation of urban space tends to 'destroy the appearance of solidity' of the built environment, instead replacing this image of 'immobility' with 'a complex of mobilities, a nexus of in and out conduits'.[1] This image of the city is not based on the dominant principles that guide urban planning and governance, but rather intimately linked with the human body; here, the city is perceived as a living being.

The rendering of imaginative responses to the underground – whether in visual or verbal imagery – has a long history that intensified in the nineteenth century, when urban subterranean realms began to be exploited in the name of modernization. As the cultural historian Rosalind Williams outlines, the new urban underground spaces created by industrial technology – tunnels, sewers, railways, water reservoirs, subways, vaults – were often pictured as Sublime, drawing on an aesthetic trope that had originally been applied to natural spectacles such as caves and caverns.[2] Seeing – and picturing – the technological underground in this way invested it with an imaginative meaning that enriched and sometimes contradicted its basis in rational engineering, and this is illustrated by photographs of underground constructions, where the sublime spectacle created by the new spaces is often emphasized.

The Sublime mode left a legacy of imagery that has continued to inform contemporary renderings of the underground, such as James Turrell's

Roden Crater and Michael Heizer's *Levitated Mass*. Meanwhile, urban explorers are reinvesting the mundane spaces of urban infrastructure with a sense of the Sublime originally seen in nineteenth-century photographs of these spaces, such as those taken of the Paris sewers by Nadar. Something that is worth mentioning here, however briefly, is the 'vertical' or 'spherical' dimension of Nadar's work. Nadar took photographs of Paris from a hot-air balloon, where the challenge was making still images from a moving vessel, and deep in the Paris sewers, where the technical challenge of the lack of light meant stillness was crucial. Time, space and the vertical were central themes of nineteenth-century photography, as they are now.

What these renderings provide is a reading of the urban underground that relates it directly to the human body and to the stories that the very intervention of creating an image might tell. The stories might be invested with a strong sense of history, or be equally fictive ones, as are those rendered in films such as *The Third Man* (1949), *Alligator* (1980), *Mimic* (1997) and *Creep* (2004). The intertwining of the real and imaginary in renderings of the urban underground forms an important aspect of how these spaces are perceived by city-dwellers. At the same time, the undergrounds of the imagination might also bring us closer to recognizing our place in the universe: for example, by waiting eighteen years for the moon to reach its zenith and to be visible in all its splendour only from open-sky chambers buried underground in the 'wild' Arizona desert.

Subterranean Sublimes: Roden Crater, Arizona
Harriet Hawkins and Sasha Engelmann

Drive 80 kilometres (50 mi.) north-northeast across the desert from the city of Flagstaff, Arizona, and you will come across Roden Crater. Rising above the desert scrub and grass, the 400,000-year-old volcanic cinder cone resembles its swarm of neighbours in the San Francisco Volcanic Field. Inside this particular red-and-black cone, however, the artist James Turrell has, since 1974, been conducting a geomorphological project of epic proportions.[3] In an ongoing feat of aesthetic engineering, Turrell has moved more than 1.3 million cubic tons of earth to shape the crater bowl and form twenty underground tunnels and chambers. Transporting Land Art's practices of sculpting the earth's surface underground, Turrell is creating sites of subterranean experience that invite

James Turrell, *Roden Crater*, 1974–, Arizona, as seen on Google Earth.

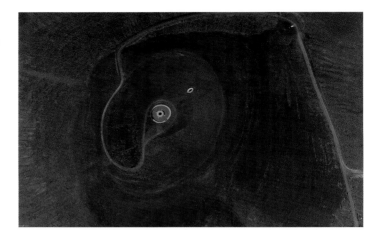

viewers, in the artist's words, to 'feel geologic time' and 'encounter celestial events'.[4]

The geography of Turrell's subterranean network maps the volcano's ancient morphology. Formed in the mid- to late Pleistocene, it has a complex physiognomy bequeathed by its dramatic past: a compound red cone, sitting within an older black cone formed from millennia of pyroclastic flows, and a secondary vent or fumarole populating its northeastern flank. Following the form of this geological history, Turrell's undergrounds situate us above subterranean strata and deep, molten masses, but they also seek, by way of vents, oculi and notches cut into rocky walls and ceilings, to link the below with the above, charging these subterranean spaces with light and energy from the sun, Moon, stars and planets.

It may be unfinished and inaccessible to the public, but we can construct an imaginary journey through the spaces of Turrell's *Roden Crater*, guided by the painstaking plans, prints, etchings and models that the artist has created to steer his project.[5] Entering the cone through an entrance on the northeastern flank, we are led through a sequence of tunnels and rock-hewn staircases to four cardinal chambers. A dimly lit tunnel that rises at an incline of 15 degrees leads viewers to a luminous point, delivering them after 315 metres (1,035 ft), blinking, out into the desert sun on the crater floor. Here, in an effect Turrell terms 'celestial vaulting', the sky appears to be domed over the crater, pulled down towards the surface of the earth, which in turn curves upwards to meet it.

Following another tunnel, the solo visitor (Turrell prefers that one experience his works alone) might find herself in the north chamber. Carved into the lava scarp, the 18-metre-diameter (60-ft) chamber, like its southern twin, is sculpted to showcase celestial luminous range, from solar light at high noon to the almost imperceptible light from the North Star and the planets. Set into the centre of the roof is a camera obscura: by day clouds are projected on to a disc in the centre of the chamber floor; by night (and in season) the planets will appear. By contrast, the rectilinear eastern chamber is powered solely by the sun. The sequence of wall slits suffuses the space with changing light, most striking at sunrise. This shifts at sunset to the west space, which stages the setting sun and the 'rise' of night across the desert.

Turrell's underground spaces are collaborative efforts, their construction speaking across art and science and echoing down the centuries, enrolling a cast of engineers and astronomers alongside the ghosts of ancient architects. The chambers, lit by shafts of light from long tunnels, are reminiscent of Neolithic passage graves, while the rectilinear spaces echo in their form those of kiva, the underground ritual sites built by the ancient Pueblo peoples, Native Americans who once inhabited the Arizonan desert.

Turrell's key collaborators are, however, inhuman: rock, celestial bodies, light and environmental sound combine to create both atmospheres of ambient illumination and architectural stages for 'image events' that showcase celestial rhythms of diurnal, centennial and millennial extent. Perhaps the most dramatic subterranean stage for these celestial performances is the sequence of five spaces fashioned within the fumaroles. Once filled with pressurized gas and steam, these spaces will funnel ambient sound and changing light effects. Most dramatically, every 18.6 years the moon, at its southernmost declension, will pass over the tunnel's aperture, casting its image 3 metres (10 ft) in diameter, with intricate detail of craters and seas, on to the wall of the innermost space. The culmination of this quintet of cavities is a vast chamber open to the sky. At its centre a reflective pool forms a surface within which to see moonlight, but also, Turrell imagines, an aqueous volume within which to immerse yourself to experience, sonically, radio waves from deep space emitted by quasars and Seyfert galaxies.

Turrell's subterranean spaces are sites of the Sublime. Linking the down below ineffably with the up above, they create vertical imaginaries that situate us at the edge of geologic time and celestial space. Puncturing the earth's crust and taking us below its surface become a way to intensify perceptual experience, to collapse time and space, as we are invited to contemplate both the molten subterranean that extends for miles beneath our feet and the intergalactic space-times that stretch beyond our comprehension. Turrell's underground spaces may not be beneath cities, but the subterranean experiences they offer are fit for all our times and spaces, simultaneously enlarging our perception of the cosmos and reducing our sense of our importance within it.

Remaindered Spaces: Manchester's Air-raid Shelters
Paul Dobraszczyk

Many of Manchester's underground spaces have left traces of former modes of habitation that endure to this day. Friedrich Engels described a whole subsection of the city's population living in dark and dirty cellars in the 1840s, and a century later many of their descendants would have taken refuge in one of the city's hundreds of air-raid shelters, particularly during the so-called Manchester Blitz – three successive nights of intensive bombardment by the Luftwaffe in the run-up to Christmas 1940 that left hundreds of buildings in the city centre either in ruins or severely damaged. As documented exhaustively by Keith Warrender, these air-raid shelters – which numbered at least 1,185 – ranged from single basements and large cellars to entire underground complexes, such as the Victoria Arches and the Manchester and Salford Junction Canal tunnel.[6]

Until recent maintenance work forced them to suspend visits, the tourist agency Manchester Walks offered regular tours, entitled 'Underground Manchester', of the former air-raid shelters in the canal tunnel that promised to give visitors a unique experience of the 'damp, dank and dismal' world and 'vast chasmic chambers' under the city, spaces that supposedly provided aromas 'of the dark recesses of the planet'.[7] From my experience in London, 'official' tours of this kind promise much in their alluring descriptions but usually deliver very little in terms of actual subterranean space, so beset are they by stringent safety regulations and fear of litigation were someone to get hurt while exploring. At first the Underground Manchester tour seemed to fit the pattern: a long ramble through the city's streets, during which the guide talked about Manchester's underground and revealed portals to the subterranean now sealed off and inaccessible, such as the bunker-like entrance to the Guardian Exchange tunnels, built as a nuclear shelter in the 1950s near the city's iconic Town Hall. Halfway through the tour, however, things took a dramatic turn as the party of 35, mainly elderly, visitors descended a 24-metre (80-ft) staircase beneath the Great Northern entertainment complex, an ultra-modern, innocuous-looking building inside what was previously the gargantuan Great Northern Railway warehouse, a late Victorian building that handled industrial quantities of raw cotton until its closure in the 1970s.

At the bottom of the stairs we entered the tunnel of the former Manchester and Salford Junction Canal, which ran from the warehouse on Deansgate to Grape Street, near what for many years was Granada Studios (site of the famous set for the long-running television soap

Graffiti on a wall inside the former air-raid shelters under Deansgate, Manchester.

Coronation Street). The 5-metre-high (17-ft) tunnel of the former canal still visibly sweats and drips, as if in memory of its former function, fogging camera lenses immediately and making photography difficult. Sparsely lit, this fetid space was where thousands of Mancunians would have sheltered for sometimes weeks on end during the German bombing raids of 1940 and 1941. Hung on the wall are the remains of the official instructions to these reluctant troglodytes, rules of behaviour in this most unusual of environments, now almost illegible after years of gentle scouring by the humid atmosphere. In fact, the first underground space we entered on the tour – the former trans-shipment dock of the canal – was but a portal into an extraordinary and mysterious subterranean world, shrouded in darkness, slippery underfoot and filled with rubble from the Blitz and the ruins of both the former canal – the trans-shipment dock, wagon hoist and hoist shafts – and the tunnel as air-raid shelter, including the wardens' lookouts, first-aid posts, toilet booths and faded signage. That we were allowed to enter these spaces was remarkable enough, and they felt every bit as wild and alien as other underground spaces that are usually shut off from public view. With hostile indifference to my high-specification camera, the cavernous spaces appeared and reappeared in phantasmagoric spectacles of sublime architecture, including a giant brick arch spanning the upper reaches of one of the caverns as if holding together the substructure of the city itself.

The characteristic architectural brickwork of Victorian Manchester – seen in the city's countless mills, warehouses, railway viaducts and streets of terraced housing – take on more elemental forms in these spaces below ground, the arches seemingly merging with the substructure of the city itself, its former bedrock turned to bedbrick. Even if the canal tunnel was built many years after Manchester began to industrialize, its half-ruined forms now seem much older than they really are, perhaps because these spaces have remained largely untouched since they were closed as a shelter in 1948.[8] Indeed, the archaic and sublime quality of these subterranean brick spaces sits uneasily alongside the knowledge that they once sheltered many hundreds of anxious wartime residents (in contrast to the rather more homely chalk tunnels of the Chislehurst Caves in south London, also used to shelter thousands during the Blitz).[9] In fact, one anonymous artist – perhaps even one of the unfortunate wartime shelterers, or a later infiltrator – has scrawled an image of the Devil on one of the brick walls, as if representing the infernal being best suited to dwell in this nightmarish world. If the Victorians modernized cities like Manchester by remaking their subterranean spaces, they also created, through those very spaces, a world that seems archaic and atavistic. This space is an underground of spectres, ghosts and demons: an urban space that is no less real than the tangible, material ruins from which these ghosts arise.

Under Construction: Buenos Aires Subte

Dhan Zunino Singh

The cut-and-cover method used for the construction of the first
underground line in Buenos Aires in 1913 made such a strong visual
impression that on the eve of the building of the second line, in 1928,
the newspaper *El Mundo* stated: 'For the second time porteños [Buenos
Aires inhabitants] will see the spectacle of the disembowelled city
[*la ciudad destripada*].'[10] The phrase 'disembowelled city' is a powerful
metaphor for the upheaval that accompanied the construction of the
underground railway. The verb *destripar* (to disembowel) alludes to the
fact that the excavation of the city's streets by machines and workers
was perceived as a violent gutting. This metaphor expressed the tension
between the instrumental use of the underground space and other sacred
meanings of it, as illustrated by the following impression: 'The bowel of
Buenos Aires will not [be] peaceful anymore . . . we dig the planet which
has the honour to house us . . . turning it into a sort of flute.'[11]

At the same time, the term 'spectacle' describes the visual impact
of the excavation works, with their enormous open trenches, exposed
cables and pipes, scaffolding, spoil carts and multitudes of workers
digging with picks. Unlike the exclusive opening ceremonies that

Construction
of Line A in 1911.

marked the completion of the underground railway, the construction process was witnessed by everyone. This vivid experience of the spectacular spatial transformation of the city's underground was reinforced by images in newspapers, popular magazines and official brochures. Before construction, images of the proposed underground railway were scarce. Press accounts generally concerned debates and plans, and did not include images of the new underground, or even plans of its proposed route. During construction, however, the city's illustrated press played a significant role in shaping public impressions of urban modernization, their images (usually photographs) reinforcing text that celebrated the underground railway as indicative of a progressive metropolis.

Overall, these photographs served the double function of documentation and representation. On the one hand, they created a visual equivalent of information contained in municipal records or technical journals; on the other, they signified the re-creation of a lived experience beyond documentation alone. Moreover, the photographs reveal the interplay of at least two viewpoints of underground construction: one from above, the other from below. Views from above – often from a 'bird's-eye' perspective – showed an urban landscape of creative destruction; those from below – the 'mole's-eye' view – revealed the inner space of the city. Rather than the expansive, totalizing view from above, the photographs showing the underground spaces themselves are fragmentary, immersed in the claustrophobic spaces under construction. In these photographs, the workers' faces become blurred from lack of light and, even though flash photography was used, the spaces still appear shrouded in darkness. In this sense, photography enhanced the mysterious aura of the tunnels under construction, endowing them with a sense of the Sublime that reminds us of the dramatic etchings of Piranesi. The new underground spaces of Buenos Aires were the embodiment at once of a moment of 'creative destruction' and of a new technological order.

Cinematic Space: Vienna's Sewers and *The Third Man*
Paul Dobraszczyk

The prevailing image of Vienna is one of a city of pleasure: the opera, waltzes, refined luxury. Yet, like all modern cities, Vienna has an underside: real underground spaces that allow the city to function smoothly, from its austere yet efficient underground railway to its invisible system of late nineteenth-century sewers. Vienna's sewers transcend their obscured everyday domain largely thanks to one defining representation: Carol Reed's film *The Third Man* (1949), with a script by Graham Greene. Like all Greene's work, *The Third Man* explores human depths – unconscious motives, criminality, personal treachery and death – which are symbolized by, and return through, the ultra-rationalized spaces of the Vienna sewers just after the Second World War.[12] It is there, in a celebrated sequence in the film, that the black marketer Harry Lime is cornered and finally shot by his one-time friend, the American Holly Martins.

Throughout the film, the Vienna we know today is barely recognizable; the city is battle-worn, barely more than a collection of ruins controlled by disparate groups of foreign occupiers: the Allied powers, who have divided up the city into four zones. Meanwhile, below ground, the city's sewers appear to be the province of Lime, who escapes the Allied zones by navigating the tunnels between them, seemingly at will. Yet when Lime is finally captured, the sewers are shown to be just as tightly controlled as the city above ground, with the four Allied powers uniting in an orchestrated display of military cooperation. As David Pike has observed, in the militarized world of post-war Vienna the sewers in *The Third Man* are posited as the last refuge for human sentiment, albeit one that is filthy and degrading and leads inevitably to death and the loss of moral certainty.[13] Here, the underground represents both shelter and death, or womb and tomb, the two principal, if contradictory, ways in which the underground has been, and continues to be, consistently imagined.

Today, with the help of Vienna's sewer authority, the Third Man tourist agency has cashed in on the film's reputation and opened up – to paying visitors – the section of the city's sewers that was actually used in the film. As advertised on the company's website, the sewer tour conflates *The Third Man* with the history and development of Vienna's sewer system, offering what it describes as an 'immersive' tourist experience that includes, in addition to the sewer tour, a visit to the Third Man Museum and a walk that encompasses the above-ground locations used in the film: a journey that enables the tourist to 'travel through time'.[14]

The sewer tour places emphasis on the idea of the tourist re-enacting scenes from the film. Descending through the lotus-like manhole used by Harry Lime in his attempted escape, one enters the same murky world he inhabited. Here, a montage from *The Third Man* and another film charting the history of Vienna's sewer system is projected on to the walls of the sewers, sounds appear from unexpected crevices and strategic lighting gives added drama to the spaces. It is a themed excursion into the underworld, one that could be accused

Overleaf
The river Wien
beneath Vienna.

of hollowing out both the originality of the film and the imaginative appeal of the sewer spaces themselves.

Yet, in reality, the raw brutality of the sewers – their grotesque stenches, hostile geometry and foul rushing flows – wins out. In one space, chocolate-coloured water merges before one's eyes into clean water in a mesmerizing display of slowly shifting eddies and whirlpools; in another, labyrinthine passages confuse in their topographical strangeness (as they do so powerfully in the film); while the submerged river Wien – used by Lime to move swiftly and unnoticed between the city's four occupied zones – is revealed as an astonishing, high-vaulted cavern, receding seemingly infinitely into the darkness. Here, accompanied by appropriately spectacular lighting and ominous sound, patches of graffiti can be made out along the walls of the tunnel. They are signs of the present-day successors of Harry Lime, those who yearn for freedom of movement and a brief respite from the oppressive rationality of the world above.

Remaking the Map: Golden Acre, Cape Town
Kim Gurney

Cape Town's landmark Golden Acre – an underground shopping centre – was built during the 1970s to solve a mobility problem for pedestrians. 'It remade a broken puzzle', according to its architect, Louis Karol. The building, in effect, is a vital interface between adjacent public transport hubs and the centre of the city. Today, twenty years into democracy, it still serves that purpose but tells a very different tale. Its four tiers once catered, in stratified fashion, to an apartheid society: upper floors served an exclusive and privileged white elite favouring private transport, while lower floors catered to mostly black customers, who entered the precinct via public transport with far less money to spend. Today the entire building is frequented by a confident and diverse middle class quite literally on the move. Standing in the concourse on any given day offers a snapshot of a newly democratic, post-apartheid country finding its feet.

The building seems to fold in on itself, like an origami sculpture. Its light-filled vaulted, striped ceilings headline a series of interlocking volumes connected at varied angles with escalators and stairwells, descending about 6 metres (20 ft) underground into basement levels. The feeling inside is more of a railway station than a shopping centre; and Golden Acre does indeed function as a transit hub, adjacent as it is to major rail, bus and taxi nuclei, as well as an underground connecting

The remains of Wagenaar's Reservoir, built in 1663, preserved inside the Golden Acre shopping mall, Cape Town.

point to the central business district. Here, pedestrians can pass through neon-lit underground passages emblazoned with consumer advertising and shops selling wares to duck underneath multi-lane highways above their heads. These self-same highways are the *raison d'être* of the Golden Acre, according to Karol. We meet at his office in nearby Woodstock, where he flips straight to a map of central Cape Town. As he explains, the post-war construction of three motorways to alleviate traffic jams 'massacred' the city centre, creating a mobility problem for pedestrians. Of the Golden Acre, he says, 'whereas Cape Town had been shredded, we connected parts of the puzzle together – and that has been [its] success.'

The subterranean passageways of Golden Acre were in turn enabled by the existence of the Strand Concourse, an adjoining underground shopping precinct created by the Cape Town municipal authorities in the late 1960s. This underground space required raising a section of Adderley Street by about 1.5 metres (5 ft), which in fact inspired the Acre's design solution. As Karol explains: 'I realized if I raised the piazza of Golden Acre about a metre or so, I could slip in another level of commercial and that suddenly made it viable.'

In the 1980s Karol was also appointed to design the Cape Sun Hotel, adjacent to Golden Acre and connected to it by another level of underground shops. The network of underground passages functioned well until 'the scourge' of regional shopping centres appeared. According to Karol, 'they had a dramatic effect all over the world on high-street shopping and a terrible detrimental effect on city-centre shopping . . . The underground started dying.' While the Cape Sun Hotel was forced to close its higher-end shopping centre, Golden Acre continued to prosper with a different retail mix.

Golden Acre has retained its appeal in contemporary Cape Town, as has its history. During its construction in 1975, excavation work uncovered the remains of the Wagenaar's Reservoir, built in 1663, which supplied passing ships with fresh water when the Cape was a colonial trading station. Golden Acre is actually sited on what was Cape Town's original shoreline, before land reclamation began in the 1930s. The building contains some of these historical traces, including a section of a brick channel that used to drain the reservoir, now on display in one of the centre's underground passages. These material artefacts serve to juxtapose the city's trading past with its present incarnation. Yet, even as an explanatory plaque declares that 'these ruins are the oldest remaining Dutch structures in South Africa', shoppers entering the adjacent SportScene and Heroes Footwear barely stop and notice.

As I try to find my way out of this convoluted underground mall and back to the surface, I take the subway route that passes under

Adderley Street and discover another example of the meeting of the old and the new: a contemporary bright-red post box standing next to a messaging system of another kind, namely a dark grey oval 'postal stone' displayed in a glass vitrine, also discovered during the Golden Acre excavations. This stone was originally used by sailors to send messages to passing ships, and it still bears a timeworn inscription, stating in block letters (in Dutch) that the ship arrived on 8 April 1635 and left again en route to Batavia. As I leave the underground and make my way back into the sunlight, I notice two women standing at the top of the pedestrianized thoroughfare wearing sandwich boards that read: 'Gold Exchange' and 'Money for Gold'.

Encountering Undergrounds: Levitated Mass, Los Angeles
Harriet Hawkins and Sasha Engelmann

It is the perfect rock: 340 tons of diorite granite, 6.5 metres (21 ft) high, 150 million years old, blasted out of Stone Valley Quarry in Riverside County, California, and transported 170 kilometres (105 mi.) to its current resting place at the corner of Fairfax and Sixth, outside Los Angeles County Museum of Art (LACMA). Thanks to the artist Michael Heizer, this 'megalith', as it has been nicknamed, now sits poised above a 142-metre-long (465-ft) minimalist concrete trench carved out of LACMA's lawn. Deposited in perpetuity in the middle of the city, Heizer's *Levitated Mass* (2012), which was visited by a third of a million people in its first year, offers us a conversation of multiple undergrounds, manifold subterranean spaces experienced and imagined in the encounter with this piece of art.[15]

Stand on the lawn and look in one direction and you are presented with an archetypal LA scene: sunlight bleaches the trench's smooth concrete white; heat radiates visibly from the ground; and the peaks and craggy faces of Heizer's rock stand out against the blue sky, flanked by lines of palm trees. Our companions spot a plane leaving a white contrail across the aerial expanse of blue. We walk across the grass – frayed-looking in the drought – towards Heizer's site-specific sculpture sitting in its own miniature desert. Look in the other direction and this ancient rock is given a banal backdrop by lorry cabs crowding the car park, advertising hoardings marching across the skyline 'against anarchy', and a faded sign for a 99 cent store. From here *Levitated Mass* looks rather more domesticated than its transcendental name implies. Move below the surface, though, walk down into the concrete trench,

passing out of the glare of the sun beneath the rock and then back out into the light, and something happens: Heizer's perfect geological specimen appears to levitate.

The trench forms a symmetrical slash in the ground, 4.5 metres (15 ft) wide with vertical walls, with a base that slopes down towards a flat portion beneath the boulder where visitors congregate for pictures, to gaze up at the boulder above their heads, or to sit and chat in the shade. The matte concrete walls, 5.5 metres (18 ft) high at their deepest point, are designed to bear the boulder's enormous weight while remaining outside the viewer's consciousness.

Heizer's other earthy voids are often less city-bound than *Levitated Mass*. In his piece *Double Negative* (1969–70), paired raw slashes cut a ragged path 15 metres (50 ft) down into the eastern ridge of the Nevada Desert's Mormon Mesa, lining up on either side of a natural gap to create a continuous 457-metre (1,500-ft) cut in the earth.[16] Blasted and bulldozed, Heizer's negative spaces share the Land Art movement's formal vocabulary of scale, mass and process, creating in his case a sculptural language of voids, of enigmatic emptiness.

Levitated Mass, in contrast to the journey through ancient strata that navigating *Double Negative* offers its audiences, situates its viewers in a much more constrained and refined subterranean space. The trench is shallower, the walls and floor are of smooth concrete, rather than the eroded forms of desert rock, and the impulse is to look up and out, to reflect on the mass of the rock above your head or pause in your immediate experience of the trench, rather than be aware of the tonnes of earth that are restrained beyond the minimalist concrete forms.

The rock's hewn, craggy form offers a counterpoint to the subterranean trench's smooth void. Heizer spent nearly forty years seeking the perfect 'geological specimen' (in his words) for *Levitated Mass*, and then some further seven years passed and $10 million were spent in bringing the rock to LACMA. If visitors have criticized the installation for its lack of levitation, fixed as the rock is with steel plates, grout, pins and epoxy to prevent movement should an earthquake occur, other narrations of its mass movement have proven more profound. Indeed, the rock's story of surfacing has become a point of fascination and the subject of a documentary film.[17] Some 150 million years after its formation and the best part of a decade after being blasted out of the quarry, in the film the rock is seen beginning its eleven-day crawl through LA County, drawing the communities of Southern California from their beds to witness its early-morning passage through the streets and sparking large street parties across the county, including a triumphal celebration of its epic journey on its arrival at LACMA.

Michael Heizer, *Levitated Mass*, 2012, Los Angeles.

Los Angeles, the archetypal postmodern urban landscape, is a city of concrete, but also of earthquakes. Conversations about the underground in this city are not only social, but also, inevitably, geologic. Heizer's rock – a presence from the underground – brings to the surface other subterranean LAs. Visible from one end of the trench are La Brea Tar Pits, a juxtaposition that places the rock in dialogue with these ancient but still bubbling pits, and folds it together with the region's economic past and present as well as its volatile geologic condition. It is ironic that the rock, with its roughly hewn form and ragged edges, should be perfect, in contrast to the smoothly moulded concrete of the trench, with its minimalist underground of voids and negativity. Together, these two volumes develop an occupation of the underground that is both immediate and present (your experience of the trench, and its funnelling of focus towards the surface), and bound within much longer and more violent narratives of what lies beneath the city.

Cameras and Cleaning Balls: Paris Sewers
Bradley L. Garrett

Although the initial formation of sewers in Paris can be traced back to the fourteenth century, from 1853 to 1880 unprecedented subterranean construction took place under the helm of Baron Haussmann and Eugène Belgrand for Emperor Napoleon III, who ordered the construction of over 600 kilometres (370 mi.) of new sewerage tunnels, a component of sweeping changes mirrored at street level. The fervour of this urban overhaul, which included the destruction of the sordid Place du Carrousel, caused the poet Charles Baudelaire to lament that 'the form of a city / Changes more quickly, alas! / Than the human heart'.[18] From this period, metaphors of progress, efficiency, scientific knowledge and sanitization became 'entangled with wider cultural and political developments surrounding the transformation of nineteenth-century Paris' and the sewers therein.[19] The angular subterranean channels full of rushing combined-system wastewater became, for the residents of Paris, far more than a system for waste management; they were part of a package of progressive ideals made concrete beneath their very feet.

One of the celebrants of the expanding vertical city was Gaspard-Félix Tournachon, a photographer working from the 1850s to the 1870s, who sought to make a permanent record of the mechanization of the urban metabolism underneath the city. Known by his pseudonym

Nadar, he created photographs of the Paris sewers from eighteen-minute exposures using magnesium lighting, perhaps the world's first underground photos; he was also one of the first to take aerial photos from a hot-air balloon.[20] His ambitious attempts at long-exposure photography, which included human mannequins in frame for architectural scale in the underground, adeptly coordinated the new aesthetic sensibilities afforded by still-camera technology with the overhaul of urban infrastructure. The photographs, along with tours of the new sewers during the International Exposition of 1867, enthralled many citizens and certainly contributed to the sewers becoming popular tourist destinations, where boat rides were offered down the stream of the combined system. The mystique of the new sewers was further bolstered by a description in Victor Hugo's novel *Les Misérables* (1862): 'Paris has another Paris under herself; a Paris of sewers; which has its streets, its crossings, its squares, its blind alleys, its arteries, and its circulation, which is slime, minus the human form.'[21] It is interesting, then, that the inclination of both Nadar and tourists of the new infrastructure was to insert that human form back into those spaces.

One of the stranger stories from the Paris sewers is that of the workers who used to unclog them by sending colossal iron *boules de curage* (cleaning balls) hurtling through the tunnels at great speed. As the website Gizmodo reports, 'The orbs, which measure 10 to 15 feet [3–4.5 m] in diameter, slam into the refuse, knock it free, and restore the flow.'[22]

The expansion of the original system has continued for the last 150 years, and today there are over 1,000 kilometres (620 mi.) of sewerage tunnels beneath Paris. One can still take a tour of them, near the Pont de l'Alma, but the rest of the system remains closed to visitors, more a component of the infrastructural imagination of the city, a memory of nineteenth-century modernization, than a contemporary destination. Unfortunately, over time people have begun to take for granted the physical, historical and metaphorical importance of the Paris sewers; now they tend to pay it proper attention only when it fails, or when they're playing *Assassin's Creed Unity*, where some of the action takes place in the dark sewers of La Ville Lumière.

Overleaf
An urban explorer stands in one of the junctions photographed by Nadar in the late 19th century.

EXPOSURE

A more literal kind of visualization of the underground occurs when it is excavated and exposed to scrutiny. In its official guise – as the discipline of archaeology – exposure of the underground serves the cause of knowledge, usually as heritage and therefore sanctioned and supported by various government-funded bodies. Archaeologists uncover the hidden strata of the city in order to see back in time, a process akin to peeling back the layers of an onion. The time they reveal is one that is stratified, with each successive layer of the underground yielding knowledge of urban history in reverse chronological order – at least in theory. Every layer has its own history and with it a range of stories, some of which overlap over time and across space.

A different form of exposure results from illicit journeys into the urban underground, namely those that can be gathered under the term 'urban exploration'. The first urban explorers were probably nineteenth-century journalists such as John Hollingshead (1827–1904), who ventured into London's underground to satisfy his insatiable 'appetite for the wonderful in connection with sewers'.[1] Bradley Garrett points to Hollingshead's adventures as a prototype for the recent – but growing – practice of urban exploration (the exploration of sewers is generally known as 'draining').[2] Today's explorers of the urban underground are drawn to sites that are normally hidden from view – sewers, tunnels and abandoned metro stations – and their exposure of these sites normally takes the form of verbal accounts alongside exquisite photographs. Less adventurous explorers can see a selection of sanctioned sites through official (and sometimes non-official) tours. A third type of exposure is geopolitical. Revealing and building beneath the ice sheet of East Antarctica is as much the promise as it is the danger of 'a city under the ice', particularly in a context whose geopolitical significance has intensified since the era of the Cold War.[3] What all these practices – excavation, exploration and exposure – have in common is their interest in the urban underground as a site of meaning whose meanings are yet to be revealed.

For the novelist Victor Hugo, the Paris sewers (and catacombs) were an exemplar of how contentious exposure of the underground might be: in levelling the social hierarchy above ground, sewers and catacombs embodied the fundamental truth of *égalité* even as it actually held little value above. For contemporary urban explorers, archaeologists and international stakeholders of Antarctica, the search for the underground might rest upon the qualities that are revealed through the personal encounter with sites where social expectations and constraints are left behind.

As Above, So Below: Paris Catacombs
David L. Pike

The term 'catacombs' in relation to Paris can refer to two underground spaces: the municipal ossuary created at the end of the eighteenth century in the city's *carrières*, the subterranean gypsum quarries beneath the Montsouris plain in southern Paris; and the much more extensive network of quarries out of which the ossuary was carved. Both spaces have a long and significant place in spatial representations of the city, the former strongly associated with the iconography of revolution, equality and order and the latter equally strongly associated with crime, subversion and the refusal of order.

The northern quarries, beneath Montmartre and the Buttes-Chaumont, have their own history, but it is the Left Bank tunnels that have persisted into the present day. Their story begins in the early modern city, when the tunnels left behind by the extraction of stone ran under the gates of Paris and were commonly used by smugglers and thieves, as well as providing grist for the mill of various urban legends. The full extent of the network came to public attention only when a series of cave-ins in the 1770s revealed the existence of a secret city beneath the familiar one above.[4] The decision to map and shore up the *carrières* dates from the formation of the Administration Générale des Carrières in 1777, contemporaneous with the debate over the state of the city's churchyards that resulted in the establishment of the municipal ossuary in 1785. Both initiatives accrued the symbolic weight of a monarchy teetering over an abyss while also partaking of a discourse of modernity that would carry through to the revolutionary government, which continued the policy of the *ancien régime* towards consolidation. At the same time, the ossuary provided a potent new metonymy for the relationship between secular and religious authorities, as it mixed the remains of all classes and degrees of person, arranged now in abstract patterns rather than distributed according to name and social position.

The ossuary quickly became a requisite city sight, although public visits were intermittently banned, ostensibly owing to claims of vandalism.[5] Accounts of visits appeared in travelogues and humorous city writing such as the broadsheet 'Green in France; or, Tom and Jerry's Rambles through Paris' (1822). The site remains a popular tourist destination today, as orderly and uneventful a traipse through the *'empire de la mort'* (as a plaque over the entrance has it) as one could ask for. So, while the catacombs proper have well served their function as the embodiment of a modern and enlightened attitude to death, the traditional frisson associated with the realm of the dead has migrated outwards into the network of quarries surrounding them.

A cataphile rests in a room of the Paris catacombs.

Nineteenth-century versions range from historical novels centred on criminal and subversive activity, such as Elie Berthet's *Les Catacombes de Paris* (1854) and Alexandre Dumas' *Les Mohicans de Paris* (1854–9), to fantastic accounts of Morlock-like creatures dwelling in the otherworld beneath the city, such as Gaston Leroux's *La Double Vie de Théophraste Longuet* (1903).[6]

The catacombs receded in popular culture during the first half of the twentieth century, but resurfaced when the tunnels were used by both Free French and German forces during the Second World War, and then more strongly during May 1968, the first period of sustained revolutionary fervour in Paris since 1870. The Situationists, one of the primary theoretical forces behind the events of 1968, positioned themselves 'in the catacombs of known culture'.[7] Chris Marker's cult science-fiction film *La Jetée* (1962) featured prisoners of war and time-travel experiments in tunnels beneath the Palais de Chaillot that had been formerly used by the Resistance. Later, the satirical film *Les Gaspards* (1973) imagined a Captain Nemo-style renegade blowing holes in the city above to protest against the destruction of old Paris to build car parks. Although (or perhaps because) unauthorized access to the tunnels has been illegal since 1955, the primary cultural presence of the catacombs since the 1970s has been through the activity of *cataphiles*, urban explorers engaged in a constant struggle over access to the space of underground Paris with the so-called *cataflics*, as the security force assigned to the catacombs is known to those trying to avoid it.

While many *cataphiles* are young men (and a few women) who get a thrill out of non-destructive clandestine activity and the documentation of their exploits on the Internet, a more ambitious heir to the Situationists revealed itself in 2004, when a functioning cinema and restaurant was discovered in a tunnel near the Palais de Chaillot, created by a once-secret group belonging to a larger organization named UX ('Urban Experience/Experiment'). Their goal was 'a typically Parisian phenomenon . . . Nostalgia for a period we didn't know. Areas "flashed" in time. The work of UX is to de-flash, to thaw, to transform.'[8] The combination of urban exploration and preservationism with old-fashioned anti-authoritarianism and pranksterism finds its perfect home in the catacombs. Like urban exploration in cities around the world, the contemporary fascination with underground Paris suggests that the nineteenth-century sub-terra is firmly established as an endangered urban space. It also reminds us of the ease with which the underground stands in for everything seen to be lacking in the 'normal', street-level city.

Cracks in the System: Antwerp Pre-metro
Alexander Moss

The excavation of subterranean space is the expression (or impression) of an imperative force for human dwelling. Where it is geographically possible, and increasingly in regions where it was formerly impossible, humans are apt to carve out spaces from the earth and yoke them to some or other more-or-less utilitarian purpose. This happens everywhere, and has happened throughout history. It follows that in areas of concentrated development, over a long time, many such structures will eventually take root, intertwining and occasionally intersecting with one another as they unfurl beneath the precincts of the everyday, street-level world. The larger and more overdetermined the city, the more complex the infrastructure that must subtend its activities. The major contemporary European megalopolises of London, Paris and Berlin are all embarrassingly rich in such architecture, with catacombs, military shelters, transport, drainage and utility systems, among others, constellating in a dizzying array, the totality of which remains empirically just beyond one's grasp. Thus sequestered in the domain of the imaginary, they become powerful narrative nebulae for the formation of urban myth. Partly responding to and partly evacuating this allure, in tandem with the increasing hegemony of the bourgeois leisure class, has emerged a novel employment of the subterranean space as an experience in itself, reified in the touristic ticket of admission that allows one simply to go and be in these places for a predetermined period of time.

From Churchill's War Rooms in London to the perennially popular Catacombs of Paris, many cities are increasingly catering to the public appetite to 'experience' underground dwellings. Although historically, and still primarily, a port city, with a relatively underdeveloped subterranean infrastructure, Antwerp has been among the more recent to have also capitalized on its underground assets, by offering tourists the opportunity to experience a small part of its extraordinary medieval and Renaissance drainage system, the Ruien, since 2005. With the logical inevitability symptomatic of capitalism's tendency to replicate the conditions of its own success, Antwerp recently extended this privilege, and has been promoting 'an experience' of its contemporary infrastructure via the opportunity to walk the '*slapende reuzenpijp*', or 'sleeping giant pipe', a major transit excavation running under the Turnhoutsebaan that had been mothballed since the 1980s. Although the construction of this abortive line extension to the Antwerp Pre-metro, from Opera to Morkhoven, had long since stalled, the 'Pegasus Plan', approved in 2004, was meant finally to press this near-finished infrastructure project into full service. For several years more, it remained in a purgatorial state. Once it came to the attention of urban explorers it began to welcome new visitors, and to share the extraordinary facts of its existence with the world again. Part of the eastern section opened to services in April 2015, closing out this strange loop, the period of historical anomaly ending in a blaze of memorial cannon-fire and a parade of 20,000 Antwerpers through its sinuous concrete tunnels.

   Notwithstanding the crowds, I hope these subterranean wanderers will find the experience as fascinating as I did when I walked down the tunnels there several years ago. Finding oneself in the (non-)non-place of a metro line that is both unfinished and abandoned is confronting; such spaces have a radical exceptionality that strips back the lies of the hyper-controlled environments of the everyday live system. The differences between these areas and the functional zones might initially seem superficial, but their cumulative effect is profound. Lacking the patina of brake-dust and sundry urban grime, the running tunnels are distinguished from the stations only in shape, every surface forming an uninterrupted panorama of cold, unfinished concrete. It is as if

A tunnel underneath Antwerp had lights, but no tracks, as of 2013.

one were wandering around in a CAD or CGI image that has suddenly been rendered in four dimensions. The spaces of the sleeping giant seem to exist in a strange tertiary zone, somewhere between and beyond the consumer zone – clean, brightly lit and complexly determined by signage and advertising – and the engineering zone – blackened, low-lit, loud, cosmetically untended. Without the regular flow of trains and passengers coursing through the system in their characteristically rhythmic patterns, the network seems at once moribund, petrified and dizzyingly alive with possibility. You can walk the running tracks and run around in the stations; you can make your way down the up tunnels and up the downs. For once, you can get a handle on the system, in its raw architectural facticity. Getting lost, as has long been recognized, can be a salutary experience, and there is no lack of opportunity to do so in a metro system completely lacking in semiotic framework. All that being said, it's still a linear system: once you reach the end, there's nowhere else to go but either out or back the way you came.

Urban Layers: Athens
Alexandros Tsakos

There are few countries in the world where archaeology plays such a prominent role as it does in Greece. Often, public works have preeminence over archaeological investigations, risking the safety of the country's rich cultural heritage. This constitutes a paradox when compared with the high degree of national pride invested in the country's archaeological discoveries. The focal point for these dilemmas is often the country's capital city, Athens.

In modern times, Athens has experienced explosive population growth, necessitating vast new infrastructure works that have impinged upon that treasured realm of archaeologists: the classical undergrounds of the capital. Yet even the situation today is nothing compared with the period in the run-up to the Olympic Games held in the city in 2004, when dozens of projects penetrated down to the foundations of the city itself.

The Athens Metro is perhaps the most high-profile of these pre-Olympic projects. The challenge of preserving the antiquities discovered during the construction of this vast new underground network was met in various ways, including the collection of archaeological data that was eventually showcased in the various stations that resulted. Perhaps the most intensive archaeological work went on at the site of the station closest to the Acropolis, under the Makriyanni district. The neighbourhood is named after General Yannis Makriyannis, who led the Greek revolution for independence in 1821. Late in life he developed a love of Greek antiquities in Athens, calling for their protection and promotion as prototypes for the values of the nation arising from its 400-year incubation under the rule of the Ottoman Empire.

Makriyanni is not the only neighbourhood with a name connected with the love of archaeological remains. On the northern side of the Acropolis, the neighbourhood of Kerameikos (meaning 'ceramic') was named after the pottery workshops that were located there in ancient times. Until recently, workshops were plentiful in that neighbourhood, and it was home to both industrial premises and working-class housing. Kerameikos has gradually become a cultural area, with many theatres built from reconstructed workshops and old houses.

Classical ruins beneath the Benaki Museum in Athens.

Museums were also opened, including one of the ten best museums of Islamic art in the world: the Benaki Museum, owned by the Benaki Foundation. Plans for the museum included underground galleries beneath the existing nineteenth-century building housing the collections, but construction was interrupted by the discovery of parts of the original fortifications of the classical city. These 5.6-metre-high (18-ft) ruins were eventually integrated into the museum, in effect providing a classical Greek foundation for an institution housing masterpieces of Islamic art from a part of the world with a long history of hostility towards Greece. In a manner of speaking, this discovery must have been a relief for the city authorities, who were surely seeking a way to anchor this 'alien' public museum in more 'Greek' terms.

Indeed, most visitors to the museum are foreigners, who tend to ignore the classical ruins contained in the building's underground spaces. These ruins are more a token to the era that preserved them, one that confirms the idea that some building materials are imbued with a sacred nature that differentiates them irrevocably from others. Yet if the Benaki Museum is to succeed as a cultural institution in the Athens of the twenty-first century, there is also a metaphorical underground that it must incorporate: not the Ottoman past or the constant threat that the Arab Islamic caliphates posed for the Byzantine Empire, but rather the marginalized legal and illegal immigrants who now live in the centre of Athens, especially in the streets directly behind the museum itself.

Secret City: Burlington, Wiltshire
Bradley L. Garrett

It was the beginning of what was to be a long, cold winter in 2009–10. We had received information that a mothballed 14-hectare (35-acre) Ministry of Defence nuclear bunker in Wiltshire had been tunnelled into from an adjacent quarry by urban explorers. We were advised that we needed to move fast if we wanted to see it and that we most certainly would want to see it, since the historical significance of the bunker was unparalleled.[9]

Burlington, known as Britain's 'Secret Underground City', had been constructed deep inside an abandoned Bath Stone quarry at the height of the Cold War and was one of the Ministry of Defence's best-kept secrets.[10] It is 1 kilometre (⅝ mile) long and 200 metres (660 ft) across, built to house 4,000 government employees and civil servants in a self-contained, radiation-proof stone sarcophagus. It was here that the British government would be rebuilt in the event of nuclear attack. Maps of the facility, which were declassified in 2004, show a telephone exchange, a Royal Air Force operations centre, offices, kitchens, a BBC studio, water-treatment facilities, a canteen, workshops, accommodation and a library supposedly full of the documents needed to reconstruct the UK government. The site had been mothballed but maintained since the 1990s (at a cost to the taxpayer of £500,000 a year) and was, by the accounts we received, full of beautifully preserved artefacts. One person had even reported a room stacked with rotary telephones, each embossed with a royal emblem, still wrapped in plastic as if sitting on a shop shelf.

We got there late and worked well into the night, checking the adjacent quarry walls by torchlight for newly dug tunnels to gain access to the bunker, finally coming to the conclusion that the only viable entrance was through an enormous red blast door that was sealed tight. Either we had been given the wrong information or the bunker had been resealed before we got there. We checked the blast door and found it had a bit of give. Peeking through the side, we could see that it was latched closed by a threaded wheel on the other side. We found two large metal bars in the quarry and wedged them into the edges of the door at top and bottom. Applying pressure to the door, we were able to move it back from the frame enough that I could get my chest through, reach up and spin the wheel on the back of the door. The wheel fell to the ground – along with the two explorers prying the door, which flew open with a rusty scream.

Inside, we found a set of electric carts, started them up and drove around the city all night long, skidding around turns, taking photographs and laughing, everyone terrified and utterly drunk on the fear. It is one of my favourite memories, tearing around that bunker. When we left, we closed the blast door at great effort, leaving the bunker almost as we had found it, the wing nut perhaps a few threads looser out of necessity.

In 2014, after a very public two-year investigation and trial, I pleaded guilty in Blackfriars Crown Court in London to removing the wing nut from the door in one of the most laughable convictions for criminal damage in recent memory. The judge, upon handing down a conditional discharge, told me: 'Dr Garrett, it's clear you have a brilliant career ahead of you and that you may have got a bit carried away in the course of this research.' At the time I was slightly upset by the comment. However, on reviewing the photos from the bunker that I took that night to write this piece, I thought: of course I got carried away, we were driving electric buggies around in a secret underground Cold War bunker! English Heritage recently expressed an interest

Overleaf
The Burlington Bunker
is so vast that it has
signposted street names.

in preserving part of the site for historic interest, and I very much hope, if the plan goes ahead, that they'll install a print of one of our photographs on an interpretation panel in there, since – like it or not – we're now a part of the bizarre history of the Burlington bunker.

Under the Ice: Polar Undergrounds
Klaus Dodds

The ice sheets, glaciers and mountains of the Antarctic and Arctic have encouraged, inspired and terrified military planners, novelists, film-makers, politicians and scientists alike.[11] They are so daunting and forbidding in their own right that it is hard enough simply to navigate, orientate and appreciate their significance. Inclement weather and remoteness combined with accident and mishap have rendered them deeply troubling spaces for human beings. The horizontal view is hard to secure, especially when faced with blizzards and 'white-outs', and flying over the polar regions is no panacea either, as machines are liable to freeze and the braiding of ice and cloud cover ensures that the 'view from above' is never trouble-free.

The view from below has always been a rather different proposition. What lies under the ice? How deep is the ice? What might be discovered there? For some, the answer to these questions requires one to be able to entertain a whole series of fantastical possibilities. Hitler's Fourth Reich might re-establish itself in Antarctica; aliens and UFOs might make the Arctic and Antarctic their 'homes'; and novels such as H. P. Lovecraft's *The Mountains of Madness* (1936) imagined a long-lost community residing in the icy world of Antarctica.

During the Cold War such questions intrigued a generation of military planners, who were convinced that the Arctic was the new geopolitical front line between the United States and the Soviet Union. They were not alone in this assumption. Films brought to life the possibility of what might lie buried beneath the Arctic, among them *The Thing from Another World* (1951), in which an unknown flying craft is discovered under the ice by a group of American soldiers stationed close to the North Pole. The film charts what happens when the ice reveals this mysterious object and the terror that is unleashed for those who investigate and confront 'The Thing'. While the alien is overcome on this occasion, the men and woman based there are left in no doubt; there could be other alien spacecraft buried in the polar ice. John Carpenter's remake, *The Thing* (1982), warms to that theme when a chance discovery of an alien craft by Norwegian Antarctic scientists

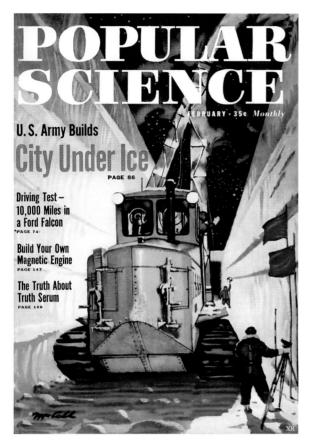

POPULAR SCIENCE

FEBRUARY · 35¢ *Monthly*

U.S. Army Builds

City Under Ice

PAGE 86

Driving Test –
10,000 Miles in
a Ford Falcon
·PAGE 74·

Build Your Own
Magnetic Engine
PAGE 147

The Truth About
Truth Serum
PAGE 106

XR

Project Iceworm:
US Army cities under
the ice, as shown on
the cover of *Popular
Science* (1960).

unleashes mayhem in their base and then in one administered by the United States.

The capacity of the ice to hide and store things was put to use most spectacularly in Greenland. Project Iceworm was an extraordinary plan to construct mobile missile launch sites under the Greenland ice sheet. Conceived in 1960, the idea was to deceive the Danish government at the time by promoting what was called 'Camp Century'. Ostensibly this was about researching the feasibility of working under the ice. The plans were extraordinary. Tunnels stretching for thousands of kilometres were to be carved out of the ice and used to deploy up to 600 nuclear missiles. Thanks to the work of glaciologists over the generations, the planners were alive to the fact that ice sheets are not stable, and so the missile launchers were to be moved fairly regularly. Over a period of six years tunnels were built, facilities established and a portable nuclear power plant hooked up. But in 1966 the project was cancelled as scientists and engineers discovered that the materiality of the ice was not something they could ever control. The ice would, it was feared, crush the tunnels, the missiles and anything else underground at the time.[12]

Speculating about what might reside under the Antarctic ice sheet has both excited and puzzled scientists. The International Geophysical Year (1957–8) marked a major turning point in the assessment of ice-sheet thickness and what might lie under ice masses. Using seismic surveys, British and American scientists discovered a great deal more about the thickness and composition of the polar ice sheets. More recent work has added to our understanding of sub-glacial lakes and 'hidden mountains'.[13] Using remote sensing and ice drilling, the Antarctic ice has been cored and probed with considerable gusto, all in the name of better understanding the East Antarctic ice sheet.

Under the ice remains a potent scientific and geopolitical force. Scientists continue to strive to increase their understanding of ice-sheet dynamics as Greenland and Antarctica sit on an environmental front line, where the fate of the ice is tied to global futures, many of which appear distinctly unwelcome – such as a world without ice.[14] Under the ice continues to inspire writers and film-makers to imagine alien and contaminated human life with the capacity to threaten human communities.

The City and the City: Underground Seattle
Paul Dobraszczyk

The idea that urban environments are comprised of layers built up over time is a commonplace one; cities are often described as 'palimpsests', where nothing is really ever erased but new structures are merely built over something else, which remains in residual form. Perhaps nowhere is the city as palimpsest embodied most literally than in the Seattle Underground, a network of passageways and basements in the downtown area that was at ground level when the city first grew up, in the nineteenth century.

Like many American cities in their early years, Seattle succumbed to a devastating fire, when on 6 June 1889 a total of 31 blocks of mainly wooden buildings were destroyed after a cabinetmaker accidentally ignited a pot of glue. Yet unusually, instead of rebuilding the city as it was before the fire, municipal leaders responded by radically changing the nature of the urban space: by regrading the streets to one or two storeys higher than the original ones (to alleviate flooding) and constructing all new buildings from fire-resistant stone or brick. The raising of Seattle's streets (by between 3.7 and 9 m/12 and 30 ft) led to the preservation of the old city beneath the new, a literal city beneath the city. New pavements were constructed on top of brick arches; glass-filled lights embedded in them illuminated the subterranean spaces; and the underground city took on a new life of its own as many merchants carried on their business in the lowest floors of the buildings that had survived the fire. In 1907, fearing an outbreak of bubonic plague, Seattle's municipal authorities condemned the underground spaces and they were mostly abandoned, save for storage or for illicit activities such as shelters for the homeless, gambling dens and illegal bars.

The more recent exposure of Seattle's city beneath the city has largely been the result of one man's enterprise. In 1965 a local resident, Bill Speidel, set up his 'Underground Tour': for a fee, customers could visit part of the subterranean city beneath Pioneer Square while being regaled by Speidel's lurid stories of the spaces' former denizens.[15] That tour continues to be popular to this day, and has been expanded and diversified to include thematic excursions such as the adults-only

'Underworld Tour', which explores the space's former reputation for prostitution, drugs and other nefarious activities.[16]

In one sense, Underground Seattle makes concrete (and exposes) the peculiar fantasy of imagining a city's 'double' – one that structures China Miéville's novel *The City and The City* (2011) and Gerald McMorrow's film *Franklyn* (2008). In these fictions, an imagined city shares space with its 'real' counterpart, and in both cases those that mediate the two cities create breaches that result in strange and dangerous events. Miéville's imagined cities are both modelled on late Cold War Berlin, with its myriad of borders, some literal, others metaphorical; while the Londons in *Franklyn* are both contemporary and futuristic, the latter a religion-dominated dystopia. The fantasy of mediating two urban worlds – one banal and known, the other exotic and secret – is fuelled by the desire to expand the range of understanding of the city. Thus, exposing the urban underground to view – as with Seattle's Underground tours – might reflect not just the increasing touristification of the city's once secret spaces, but rather the desire to multiply readings of the city. As the French semiologist Roland Barthes made clear, this work of multiplying readings of the

View through a skylight from Seattle's underground spaces to the city above.

city is not merely about leading us into new urban spaces, but rather a fundamental tenet of urban existence itself.[17] Without it, our cities would become sterile environments rather than the poems they are meant to be for each of us.

EDGES

different kind of exposure takes place at the edges of cities and of undergrounds themselves, whether one is a few metres away from the Baltic Sea, several metres down in the centre of New York or on the tip of the African continent. Edges are peripheral, but not only in the traditional sense of geography; they can be located physically in the outskirts of a city but also figuratively as forgotten places that spring back to mind with the right trigger: a name, perhaps, or a sound, or even through the contemplation of an eighteenth-century painting that suddenly brings a new thought to the fore.

Exploring urban undergrounds through the notion of edges also presents us with the very qualities of the unintended: the stretch of metro infrastructure connecting to Petržalka, one of the largest housing estates in Bratislava, unfinished but now turned into a firing range; a long-forgotten lake drawing explorers and city mayors alike into a renaissance of urban history in Brescia, northern Italy, a city with an important Roman past. Edges are also suggestive of the sealed and of the slightly off-the-map, that which is off-centre or, in other words, eccentric.

Moreover, the edges of cities, whether in metropole or colony, testify to the ongoing process of mutual affectation where centre and periphery fold into each other, changing aspects in one, creating new characteristics in the other, deploying the force of mixture and cross-pollination in both.[1] Edges are also evocative of other imaginaries that resurface once we're reminded of their presence: a sealed corridor beneath New York's Grand Central station; the passages beneath a mid-seventeenth-century Dutch fort in Cape Town; or the control panels, handles and meters that once controlled the water and heating of Senate House Library in London.

In his *Invisible Cities*, Italo Calvino explores the essence of Eudoxia, a city where 'a carpet is preserved in which you can observe the city's true form.' Eudoxia is a city rising upwards and downwards, 'with winding alleys, steps, dead ends, hovels'.[2] The carpet, as a representation of the city, and the city itself, with all its practices, mirror each other; both change in time. Through the edges that undergrounds are we get a fuller sense of how city, representation and viewpoint connect. For it is at the edges that all three are joined.

Urban Rhythms: St Petersburg Metro
Anna Plyushteva

Metro systems are typically constructed at great financial cost. They require the mobilization of all available engineering and political ingenuity. They are often discussed in terms of the proud histories of which they are part, and of the powerful tropes of nation, identity and progress they are supposed to embody. Yet, for most users, underground railways mainly stand for the definitive routine of everyday urban life: the ordinary, repetitive task of getting from A to B and back again.

Russian metro systems in particular tend to be discussed in terms of the grandeur of their spaces, their spectacularly decorated stations and the memorable underground vistas that reveal themselves to a visitor's eyes. Arguably, this makes it especially difficult to write about the St Petersburg Metro while at the same time drawing attention to the everydayness of mundane underground urban transport. As I sought to reimagine the St Petersburg Metro as a familiar thing, my focus shifted to those parts of the city that do not form part of the St Petersburg 'brand'; I started looking more closely at the places where transport is more about moving people and things, and less about the way that the city wants to be seen. That is how Primorskaya station came to be at the centre of this story.

Primorskaya ('by the sea') station is in a residential area, at the end of the M3 St Petersburg metro line, only a short walk from the shore of the Baltic Sea. At 71 metres (233 ft) below street level, Primorskaya is not one of the deepest metro stations in St Petersburg (Admiralteskaya, the deepest, descends an impressive 86 metres/282 ft below ground); neither is it the oldest station, having been built in 1979, more than two decades after the first section of the city's metro began operating, in 1955. The paragraphs dedicated to it in the numerous publications on the city's metro system tend to be some of the shortest, as trivia is scarce: 'One of only two Metro stations in Saint-Petersburg where opening hours vary between odd and even dates.'[3] Even though it is adjacent to the city's Metro Museum, tourists are hardly ever spotted on Primorskaya's single platform. As to the museum itself, it was closed for a long renovation, and during my time in St Petersburg I failed to find a single person who had been inside.

The station's interior is modest. Its columns are seemingly designed and lit with the sole intention of revealing as little as possible of the beauty of the marble cladding. The metal sculpture of an anchor at the far end of the platform, celebrating the station's nautical name and location, is the only notable decoration. Compared to the classical bas-reliefs of Ploshchad Vosstaniya (Uprising Square) station, or the futuristic new vestibule of Gorkovskaya station, Primorskaya seems entirely forgettable.

However, a trip to an unremarkable metro station is, in itself, remarkable. It is a shortcut to obtaining a glimpse of the everyday rhythms of a city. It is an opportunity to take a hasty stroll in the midst

Ticket office in Primorskaya station, part of the St Petersburg Metro.

of those who know their way around in intimate and embodied ways. The area around Primorskaya has undergone a transformation in the three and a half decades since the station was built, and the lives of local residents have changed to no lesser extent. Since the end of the Soviet Union, in 1991, neon signs and supermarkets have gradually taken over the area. When Primorskaya opened, the neighbourhood to the west, between the station and the sea, was an urban wasteland; its marshes had not yet been drained to make room for the high-rise apartment blocks that have recently mushroomed. The older apartment blocks to the east suffered serious subsidence following the construction of the metro station, and had to be reinforced in the late 1970s and early 1980s. Such small, familiar nuisances were of course pervasive across the city for decades with the expansion of the metro, as St Petersburg's complex geology and the government's subterranean ambitions clashed time and time again. Some of these conflicts had dramatic effects, as new technology for digging and reinforcing deeper tunnels was tested, occasionally with the result that entire streets collapsed into the city's marshy soil.

In the context of this history, Primorskaya is peripheral territory. The neighbourhood around it, swept by freezing winds from the harbour, knows only the trivial incidents of cracked walls and skewed staircases. And yet, these peripheral places and histories are rich and evocative. To the visitor to St Petersburg, the short ride to Primorskaya station offers a unique insight into the life of the metro and the city. If you remain unconvinced, the revamped St Petersburg Metro Museum might help to change your mind; it reopened in November 2015.

Unruly Spaces: Cairo Metro
Alexandros Tsakos

The last time I found myself in Cairo's Tahrir Square, in 2012, I had ignored warnings against travelling there. Riots were erupting constantly and developing in unpredictable ways. Yet, on this particular day, I needed to visit both the Egyptian Museum and the office of the Organization for the Salvage of the Monuments of Nubia, and Tahrir Square was close by, luring me with its obvious dangers and excitements. So I gave into the temptation. I was confident that if trouble started I could easily bolt into the nearest metro station.

However, when I saw stones being thrown, fights breaking out and people running, and heard explosions in the distance, I realized that the metro entrance I knew of was blocked, so I ran as a voice called to me:

Platform of Al Shohadaa station in Cairo's metro.

'Run to the next one.' As police officers moved in to secure the entrance to the station, I fled downstairs and found my body squeezed reassuringly between hundreds of others in the safety of the underground.

In a metropolis of approximately ten million inhabitants, commuting takes a lot of energy and time. With chronic congestion above ground – five million journeys are made every day on Cairo's public transport system – commuting underground is the only relatively efficient way of travelling across the city. It also gives confidence to strangers: a month before my arrival in Cairo I felt assured enough to arrange an appointment at the Coptic Museum, even though I knew I would be living at the other end of the city.

Yet, like many other spaces in the city, the Cairo Metro is now infused with fear of civil unrest, political violence and revolution. The metro may be one of the only forms of urban transport where civility is the norm, where people with opposing political ideas and social backgrounds and differing genders can travel without fear of conflict. Yet, in Cairo, the metro is notorious for its sexual discrimination; Egyptian men regularly harass female passengers (particularly foreign ones) in the underground trains. Were these underground spaces truly a refuge from the turmoil above ground?

Sensing danger, I decided to get off the train at the next station, Al Shohadaa (The Martyrs), named Mubarak until the revolution of

2011 that spelled the end of that president and his corrupt regime. I moved along with the waves of other passengers, but slowly, so that, before reaching the exit, I was left almost alone on the platform. I stopped and stared at the wall of tiles that carried the name of the station. Al Shohadaa opened in 1989, and was part of the first section of Cairo's metro; Cairo was at that time one of only two cities in Africa to provide mass transportation (the other being Tunis, where a light railway started operation in 1985).

In Cairo, less than 5 kilometres (3 mi.) of the metro's total length of 45 kilometres (28 mi.) is actually underground. At Al Shohadaa station, I realized that I could change from Line 1 to Line 2, the second metro line to be built, completed in 1991, and the first and only part of the system to descend beneath the river Nile. I checked the metro map at the station, reading off the names of other stations: Al Shohadaa Massara, Road El-Farag, Sainte Teresa.

'Sainte Teresa?' I thought. 'Isn't that the name of the Catholic church at Shubra that my mother was named after?' My grandparents, born and raised in Egypt under British rule, praised the serenity of the place. And so off I went. But the Shubra of 2012 was very different from the one of the colonial past. I found the church, and in it refuge and peace, an escape from the danger of the tumultuous city centre.

I retraced my steps to the metro station, where I realized that the metro could not take me back to my home at Heliopolis. The new Line 3, beginning northeast of Attaba station on Line 2, will not reach Heliopolis (and the airport) before the beginning of the next decade, according to the most recent plans.

Edge of Existence: Abandoned Bratislava Metro
Petr Gibas

In Bratislava, you cannot ride on the metro. This, however, does not mean that there is no underground transport system in the city. Indeed, the metro cuts through Petržalka, Bratislava's largest housing estate, none of whose more than 100,000 inhabitants could ever ride on it. Despite that, Petržalka was shaped by the metro; its rows of *paneláky* – concrete-built, pre-fabricated blocks of flats – are distributed with reference to the course of the metro beneath. Yet you cannot ride on this metro or pass under the Danube from the city centre to Petržalka. The announcements at the city's five metro stations are heard by no one. In short, the Bratislava metro is special: it is present in Petržalka only in its absence.

The plans to build a metro – or 'rapid transit system', as it was originally called – in Bratislava date back to 1974, when the strategic report 'Conception of the Development of Bratislava Public Transport System' was approved by the city's governing bodies.[4] Discussions about different projects as well as competitions were held throughout the 1980s; in 1988 the decision was finally made and construction started. In a documentary from 1989 – the year state socialism collapsed in Czechoslovakia – one of the architects of the metro explained that

> the [Bratislava] rapid transit system is in fact designed as a true metro. It runs under the ground and intersects all other transport systems without physically crossing with them while servicing the housing estates. Simultaneously, with the building of the metro the main compositional axis of Petržalka is to be finalised. Here a lively residential boulevard will be created with all the facilities, which are moreover linked to the metro and public as well as individual transport.[5]

A couple of months later, state socialism in Czechoslovakia collapsed and the promise of a technologically and socially advanced socialist future turned to dust. Within weeks the new government had halted the construction of the metro. The excavators, vans and cement mixers disappeared together with the workers, architects and planners. What they left in Petržalka was a metro on which you cannot ride. But what you can do is follow it as it weaves in its absence through the housing estates.

On a bright and sunny late-summer morning, the Danube was on the rise. Bratislava was braced for flooding and we crossed above the whirling, hastening waters to look for the metro. At first a vast, empty stretch of land nearly led us astray, as we thought it to be the beginnings of the metro's journey (and ours) through Petržalka. We pondered and then continued until we came across what we knew from the newspaper was part of the metro – a pile of concrete hollow prefabs half overgrown with bushes and trees in the middle of a vast low-cut lawn. In front of us a space – green and brown, as lawns are when burned by late summer – opened up, piercing the housing estate, cutting it in half and inviting us for a journey, not exactly a ride.

This is the visible part of the Bratislava metro – depressions in the ground surrounded by bushes, trees, walkways and rows of *paneláky*, with dark-brown metal pipes protruding here and there from the ground and sandy paths created in the grass by people walking their dogs or going to nearby shops, churches or homes. The green shades of the plants, the sandy brown of the pathways, the blue of the sky

Entrance to an
abandoned tunnel
of the Bratislava Metro.

and the white of the sharp sunlight: these are the colours of the metro,
surrounded by colourfully repainted *paneláky* (although some are still
grey, kept as they were originally built in the 1980s).

We arrived after midday, weary, having reached the end of the
metro's course. Behind the last row of flats and the road circling the
city was a narrow path trodden in wild grass. Finally we reached a
half-finished train shed, leading from the grass to the darkness of wet
and mouldy underground tunnels. Today the tunnels are used as a firing
range for airsoft geeks or as a vast canvas for graffiti artists – the only
underground vestiges that remain of the Bratislava metro.

Mystic Caverns: Grand Central Terminal, New York
Julia Solis

'What's behind this door?' I asked. I was standing on the mezzanine level of the M42 substation, the deepest cavern beneath Grand Central Terminal in the heart of New York City. An employee had offered to show me around his notoriously well-protected workplace, and he had come to a dead stop in front of a little door with green paint peeling off. 'I don't know,' he said, 'it's just some long dark passage. Every time I open the door I get a blast of air, but I've never actually gone inside.'

Rarely has any space in New York City mystified its population to the degree that Grand Central station has. No wonder – all you have to do is turn it into a pivotal part of daily life in the city, throw in enough majestic splendour to attract hordes of visitors (building designed in the Beaux Arts style from 1913, featuring an oyster bar with a Guastavino tile ceiling), spread conflicting information about its architectural layout (two levels deep? Five? Or fifteen, as has also been claimed), become the subject of popular books that mythicize and confuse the layout further (most infamously through the secret interconnecting passages mentioned in Jennifer Toth's book *The Mole People* of 1993), take three large sections out of commission until they give rise to wholly separate mythologies (such as the 'non-existent' Track 61, the final resting place of Franklin D. Roosevelt's private train and last stop on a special elevator to the Waldorf Astoria hotel above), and close most of it off to the curious under threat of arrest and prison.[6] Add all these factors together and you get not only baffled tourists but also employees who over years of working in one section have concocted their own mental maps of the station. Whether these coincide with reality is almost irrelevant. Perhaps more interesting is the vast imaginary construct of tunnels, ladders, crypts and squats, buried stations and forgotten emergency shelters, sewer entrances and ghost trains that populate this alternative world.

The M42 substation was for a long time the main power supply for the railway network that originated here. Until the recent construction for the East Side Access project – to connect the two major commuter railway systems in Manhattan under one roof – this sub-basement beneath the main concourse was where the deepest excavations for Grand Central took place. Accessible only via an elevator or a couple of emergency stairways, it is nestled inside a stone-walled pit that in some areas still shows blast marks on the bedrock. Because this was where the system's electricity was controlled, it was always kept out of public awareness and off maps of the terminal. In the Second World War, soldiers with shotguns were stationed at the entrances to prevent sabotage of the system. Of course, security hasn't exactly let up in New York's underground in recent years, and public access to this part of the station is still prohibited.

'Homeless guys living inside the tunnels', my friendly tour guide said, 'used to come in through that door to steal the copper right out of this station. I don't know why this door isn't locked.' For the last two hours I had crept through the substation looking at every pile of junk, every closet, hatch and drain opening in this confined space, not only to see what was actually the deepest point of Grand Central, but also to see if there wasn't a forgotten passage somewhere. Amazingly, M42 itself consists of three levels: a giant hall containing turbines and switchboards with a cramped utility level beneath its floors, and then a balcony section wrapping around the hall. For someone who wanted to unlock more of the terminal's mysteries, M42 was a feast for the senses and the imagination.

Under Grand Central Station, New York City.

'Can we take a look?' I asked. It was true – the moment he opened the door, a blast of cold air enveloped us. In contrast to the well-illuminated station, this was a pitch-black corridor, devoid of signs and graffiti, heading straight back across a water-filled pit and then turning a corner. Since one of us was wearing high heels and neither wanted to encounter floating rats, we searched the mezzanine for a plank to lay across the pit. It probably wasn't necessary: this may have been the cleanest space in the entire station, a disused subterranean artery with not even a hint of trash.

The journey wasn't long; after a few turns the passage ended against a wall and slanted skyward; high above us was a grid from which the warm station light and train sounds filtered down into the tunnel. This was also the source of the air, and, at one time, an adventurous slide for copper thieves. But far from satisfying my curiosity, the space actually raised more questions. How many of these passages were there? What was in them? Did any of them lead to vaults of ancient treasure, like old blueprints, rusty tools, discarded Christmas decorations from 1953? Perhaps a menagerie of taxidermized rats wearing little conductor's outfits and riding decrepit model trains? Were there connections to sewer tunnels after all, or maybe some brick-lined crawlspaces connecting to an old-time actress's dressing room beneath the stage of a Broadway theatre?

Taking the elevator back up into the throng of rush-hour commuters, one thing was certain – some underground spaces awaken a sense of curiosity that no amount of exploration can satisfy. The boundaries of M42 may be clearly defined in physical space, but its dark and winding tentacles extend far into unconsciousness. Never mind the track plans, blueprints and excavation diagrams – Grand Central Terminal will continue to inhabit a special place in the subterranean imagination of New York, one whose mystery only deepens with each newly discovered corridor.

Buried Waterways: Brescia Underground
Caroline Bâcle

'So, have you found the platform yet?' is a question I've been asking Andrea Busi from time to time since 2012. Back then, my producer and I were making a documentary film about waterways buried under cities. Admittedly, at first the subject petrified me. As a film-maker, how am I to tell the story of something we can't see? Granted, a buried river is a fascinating main character with a tumultuous story, but it makes a tough interview subject.

Yet as research progressed, it became clear that the film in progress wasn't about buried rivers, but rather about the evolution of our relationship with them – about the change in our perception of water in the urban environment. It was a collection of stories about people searching for lost nature, a group of love stories; and one of them would lead us to northern Italy to meet a group called Brescia Underground.

Every urban explorer knows about Brescia Underground. The heart, brains and ambition behind it is Andrea Busi. His picturesque hometown of Brescia – population just under 200,000 – is tucked away in the mountainous region of Lombardy. When he was a child, he started reading the Italian comic about the adventures of Cattivik, an anti-hero who took the form of a drop of sewage. From that point on,

Overleaf
Beneath Brescia.

FUTURES

One of the notions central to the German historian Reinhart Koselleck's exploration of the relationship between the past and the future is what he called a 'horizon of expectation' (*Erwartungshorizont*) – that is, the imagined domain that structures action in the present in the interest of a vision of the future over which a monopoly – religious, political, cultural or otherwise – keeps a tight hold.[1] An important aspect of the planning, building and use of the undergrounds discussed in this book is that they forecast the future, structuring a horizon of expectation that gives purpose to action not by the consistency of how real the forecast is but rather by the commonality of directing change. That direction often involves a future that is iconoclastic and which, just as often, is the realization of political will. Take the examples of the metros of cities such as Sofia, Washington, DC, Pyongyang and Dubai: the architecture of stations, the signs and decor, how deep the system is and where lines connect, the timing of the inaugural ride – all are part of the means that governments have used to articulate a vision of their own future, whether that future is seen through a red Communist star, or based on US president Lyndon Johnson's Great Society, the EU's European Regional Development Fund or the will of a Middle Eastern sheikh.

At the same time, if the materiality of undergrounds shapes the future of our cities, societies and governments, so do the use and meaning that are attached to those undergrounds. A particularly striking example of this is Mariam Al Safar, one of the few female underground train drivers in Dubai and, indeed, the entire Middle East. Sheikh Mohammed bin Rashid Al Maktoum might say that 'anyone who does not attempt to change the future will stay a captive of the past', but the really challenging question is whom to include in that future, and whose pasts project a vision that is both fair and inclusive. Fairness and inclusiveness also relate to broader issues such as gender: how does gender equality enter the scientific station at CERN, and what does it mean to understand 'everything', as scientists (over 80 per cent of them male) claim their experiments with the Large Hadron Collider will help them do? Unsurprisingly, perhaps, exclusivity is replicated in the future, when our hopes and fears of an apocalyptic event turn the 'end' into a real structure at the top of the world, sealed by concrete walls and steel doors, a 'sanctuary' of the Arctic Circle fit for Doomsday, come frost, flood or nuclear mayhem. Just as excluding and exclusive is the underground timepiece of the Long Now Foundation, enticing a handful of visitors to witness the movement of the century hand and the millennium cuckoo of a 10,000-year clock.

What future horizons are there, then? In whose power do they rest, and what insights do undergrounds give us into our own selfhood, our fears and the timelessness of futures we did not invent?

Futures Past: Pyongyang Metro
Darmon Richter

The doors slam shut, not with the pneumatic hiss of gears and the dull slap of rubber seals closing, but rather with a heavy thud of wood hitting splintered wood. On the platform a girl in a crisp, blue uniform blows a whistle and the train pulls noisily away, diving nose first into darkness. I catch one last glimpse of austere marble halls, glass chandeliers and gaudy socialist murals. On the train, arranged along wooden benches that run the length of the rattling wagon, two dozen pairs of eyes are pretending not to stare at me.

This is the Pyongyang Metro: a vision of the future, as imagined in the 1950s. At an average depth of 110 metres (360 ft), it's the deepest metro in the world, with palatial stations that take their cue from the Soviets: in their richly nuanced designs they echo themes of independence, military strength and the boons of socialist philosophy. The trains, meanwhile, are old DDR stock, bought en masse from Berlin in the late 1990s; although your guides will probably tell you they're Korean-made. Portraits of Kim Il-sung and Kim Jong-il hang high on the lacquered wooden prow of each carriage.

It was President Kim Il-sung who built the metro, opening the first stations between 1969 and 1972. In an official English-language guidebook released in 1994, the system is described as 'not only the traffic means but also the place for ideological education'. The murals, the painted tableaux, even the stations' names could have told you as much. As the guidebook explains, 'its inside decoration is depicted artistically so as to convey to posterity the glorious revolutionary history and the leadership exploits of the great leader President Kim Il Sung.'[2]

Of the system's two lines – Chollima and Hyoksin – it was Chollima that came first, named after the mythical winged horse that appears far and wide in the folklore of East Asia. In North Korea, Chollima is a symbol of speed and efficiency. In the aftermath of the Korean War, during the reconstruction of Pyongyang, Kim Il-sung urged workers to 'rush as the speed of Chollima', and so the 'Chollima Movement' was born – a nationwide effort that paralleled Chairman Mao's Great Leap Forward. The Chollima line was completed in 1973, featuring among its eight stations those with names such as 'Red Star', 'Comrade', 'Triumph' and 'Glory'.

My own journey along these tracks started at Puhung, or 'Revitalization': a vaulted hall of steel, stone and marble, set about with hidden ambient lights and punctuated with a series of futuristic chandeliers – clusters of orbs that glowed in hues of purple, gold and grey, like strange, metallic orchids – to channel an art deco ethos through the pomp and splendour of old-school imperialism. From the guidebook:

Interior of Yonggwang station, Pyongyang Metro.

> The works of art at Puhung Station represent the appearance
> of the country which is prospering day by day and the happiness
> of the working people who enjoy the equitable and worthwhile
> creative life to their hearts' content thanks to the popular policy
> of the Workers' Party of Korea and the Government of the
> Democratic People's Republic of Korea.

We moved on, next, to Yonggwang, which opened in 1987. This
station's name translates as 'Glory', and, if anything, it was more
glorious than the last. Here, the lights – metal-stemmed chandeliers in
starburst formation, resplendent in shades of pink, green and yellow –
symbolize fireworks. 'The illuminations', reads the guide, 'bring to view
the victory celebrations after the war.' Kim Il-sung looks fondly on from
a mural that depicts him striding through a scene of booming industry
and happy workers.

Onwards, again, we rush at the speed of Chollima to Kaeson station.
This station is named 'Triumph', for the triumphal arch (the tallest in
the world, our guides assure us) positioned directly above it. Here are
more scenes of celebration – smiling workers, citizens and soldiers –
while a bronze statue of the Eternal President watches the trains
come and go.

The tour concludes here; we've seen half the Chollima line, and
not even glimpsed the newer Hyoksin ('Innovation') line. There are
theories, however, that the Pyongyang Metro extends far beyond
these two public lines; even beyond the disused 'ghost' stations such
as Kwangmyong (situated beneath the mausoleum of Kim Il-sung
and closed since 1995).

In 2009 Hwang Jang-yop – a defector, and former secretary of
the Workers' Party of North Korea – told a South Korean radio
station about Kim Jong-il's secret metro. According to Hwang, 'About
300 m [985 ft] below ground in Pyongyang, there exists a second
underground world which is different from the subway level.'[3] Another
source describes a vast subterranean command centre, featuring
'state-of-the-art communications equipment and billeting facilities . . .
comparable in area to the Kim Il Sung Square, which can accommodate
a rally of over 100,000 people'.[4]

Given the extent of militarization here, coupled with Kim Jong-
il's well-reported paranoia (the leader spent much of his reign on a
constantly moving armour-plated train), such theories, extravagant
though they may sound, nevertheless feel tantalisingly plausible.[5]

Sleeping Dragons: Future Ruins of CERN
Camilla Mørk Røstvik

During the Cold War, European physicists, engineers, politicians and bureaucrats sought to create a utopian research situation in the countryside outside Geneva, Switzerland. By utopian, I mean the goal of encouraging peaceful non-applied scientific research of an international and non-commercial kind, in order to probe the Standard Model of physics, which explains how the basic building blocks of the universe interact. Understanding this completely is CERN's main goal.

The literal meaning of utopia is 'no place', and the European Organization for Nuclear Research, known as CERN, hidden underground and destined to become a ruin, is utopian in all facets of its work. Built on the twice-excavated Gallo-Roman site of Cessy, the laboratory has over the course of its existence required the building and rebuilding of intrinsically short-lived structures. Thus, if one were to picture a cross-section of underground CERN one would see the Large Hadron Collider and other machines under or at the same level as the Roman city that once thrived there. The rapidly evolving technology of bubble chambers and colliders means that they have short lives, thus creating a plethora of underground ruins together with their hypermodern successors.

The tunnels of CERN in Switzerland, destined to be ruins.

Perhaps part of the undoubted fascination with CERN relates to the fairy-tale qualities of this enormous, yet mostly invisible project. There is something odd about these large coiled dragons firing matter together underground, surrounded by the misty mountains of Geneva, and on their collective quest to discover why the universe has mass. Our fascination with CERN, like that for fairy tales, is connected to our love of the mysterious, the undiscovered and magical, as well as to our interest in social justice. CERN can be viewed as an independent enclave of scientists battling military and commercial science in its utopian quest to understand, as it puts it, 'everything'. But fairy tales have twists, and dragons sometimes wake up. Is CERN really a maverick undertaking of blue-sky research, controlling the dragons of nature, or is it creating a capitalist creature of the future? Physics, after all, is big business.[6] Most perceive CERN as a haven of research, as made popular by Brian Cox in the UK and a number of other professional science communicators worldwide, but some have misgivings.

CERN, after all, is engaged in a careful balancing act between the above-ground world of seemingly perpetual financial crisis and the underground world of high-energy physics. As CERN's European member countries struggle to pay their annual membership fees, conspiracy theories abound and questions of purpose collide with the organization's strong press office. Amid all this, the underground movements of the 27-kilometre (17-mi.) Large Hadron Collider ring have received praise, especially when those movements revealed the elusive Higgs boson particle.

CERN, furthermore, is both hypermodern and old-fashioned. As a social and cultural experiment, alongside its scientific quest, it has yet to succeed in truly changing its demographic make-up. At 17 per cent, the representation of women at CERN is shocking, although not unusual in this 'culture of extreme objectivity'.[7] Perhaps the lack of women in the organization mirrors CERN's attitude to the natural world in some way. The many underground machines have been sunk into the countryside below the Swiss–French border outside Geneva since 1954. Local political and environmentalist groups have been frustrated by this, and social justice movements have asked why European countries should spend so much money on understanding invisible matter, in the context of what some see as more pressing social concerns. CERN's function is to undertake an invisible underground quest to understand the invisible world. Should we be surprised that now, after years of expansion, the creatures it has spawned supervise their own power structures?

Even greater questions linger. As humans, are we even essential to the undertaking of CERN's goals, or is it the machines and instruments of science that drive proceedings? Destined to become out of date and be replaced or altered, the physical underground manifestation of CERN has a sell-by date that will arrive at some point. Once this happens, humans will have to leave, although the structures will remain in some way.[8] What is left are (and will be) ruins in a landscape that is hypermodern, yet also outdated and defunct. The space, however, might yet change into a site of science-based tourism. CERN claims to be at the forefront of human knowledge, but it lags far behind in terms of social responsibility. As long as the organization continues to display patriarchy in its dealings with the environment and women, can we trust it to discover 'everything' on behalf of us all? As an organization that thrives underground, it is increasingly important to bring CERN's goals and values to the surface.

Segregating Symbols: Dubai's Metro
Carlos López Galviz

> 'Anyone who does not attempt to change the future will stay
> a captive of the past.'
> Sheikh Mohammed bin Rashid Al Maktoum

Reporting for a nine-hour shift that starts at 3 am is a familiar story for millions of workers, including those whose workplace is in underground metro systems. It is perhaps a less familiar story for women drivers, and an even less likely story in the Middle East. However, for more than five years this has been the story of Mariam Al Safar, who left a career in banking to become the first and so far only woman driver on the Dubai Metro. In December 2013 she became supervisor of operations for Dubai's trams, a powerful symbol reinforcing the trend of 'young women overturning a traditionally patriarchal culture to find their feet in the workplace'.[9]

Symbolism has been important to Dubai's metro from the outset. The opening took place on 9 September 2009, at nine seconds past nine o'clock in the evening, although only ten out of the planned 29 stations of the Red Line opened that day and, following a fault in one of the train cars, several passengers were stranded for two hours before being re-routed.[10] The design of the underground stations is based on the four elements – earth, fire, water and air – and on a vision of heritage that plays on the theme of pearls. Pearls are one of the commodities that smugglers and merchants in this area have traded for centuries. The symbolism continues: in early 2014 the city's Roads and Transport Authority launched a photographic competition for babies born on

9 September 2009, as part of the events commemorating the metro's first five years of operation.

Besides ceremonies and celebrations, Dubai's metro is also intent on making class segregation very clear: carriages are divided into gold and silver classes, and the latter include areas marked out for the exclusive use of women and children. Dubai is not new to class contrasts. Modernization of the self-proclaimed 'pearl of the Middle East' draws on a labour force with low wages and few rights but that, nevertheless, continues to build the dream of the biggest, tallest, largest and most luxurious accommodation for the exclusive use of millionaires and billionaires (among them rock stars such as Rod Stewart). Dreams take the form of buildings, islands or cities within the city, such as Media City or the International Humanitarian City, whose chairperson is Princess Haya bint Al Hussein, herself the holder of a driver's licence for heavy trucks.[11]

Segregation helps to make sense of contrast in an orderly manner, one that perpetuates differences, however close the dividing lines may be. Twelve of the 47 stations are underground; eight out of the twelve are on the Green line, which serves the area bordering Dubai Creek,

'Gold class' section on a platform of the Dubai Metro.

and including older districts such as the Bastakia Quarter, where, more than a century ago, pearl merchants built their imposing houses. At the other end of the metro, southwest on the Red line, Ibn Battuta station is named after the indefatigable traveller and chronicler who, in the fourteenth century, visited all the Islamic countries of his time 'from Mali to Sumatra and from Kenya to the Russian steppes'.[12] Lines that divide gold from silver, underground from above, also connect past travels and future visions.

But what about the future? Dubai's 76-kilometre (47-mi.) metro is the world's largest fully automated system, and there are plans for its substantial expansion in preparation for the World Expo in 2020. Driverless cars and automated transport systems are no longer a vision of the future from the past. Soon, let's hope, female faces –

the Mariams and Princesses of today – will enjoy the rights that have been denied them for centuries. To paraphrase Sheikh Mohammed bin Rashid Al Maktoum: anyone who refuses to see the limitations and constraints of the past is captive to envisioning futures where change is selective and exclusive, glittering to a few but both impervious and opaque to the large minority.

The Great Society: Washington's Metro
James Wolfinger

Most subway travellers in the United States are used to the tunnels of New York City, Boston, Philadelphia and Chicago. For the most part, they have a similar look and feel: low ceilings, lots of steel supports, clattering trains. They seem to be the very embodiment of Gilded Age technology, and in fact in many ways they are. It is the familiarity with those systems that makes riding on Washington, DC's metro something notably different, but without an understanding of the origins of the system it is difficult to grasp why it is so unusual.

First-time riders usually focus on the look of the stations. The Chicago architect Harry Weese designed them – in contrast to those of New York City and Philadelphia – to be modern, well-lit and free of the hidden spaces where crime can take place. Some architectural critics have dubbed them an unfortunate example of the Brutalist school, but most people find the vaulted layouts open, airy and passenger-friendly. Each station is 183 metres (600 ft) long and finished in granite and bronze, with high ceilings and soft, indirect lighting. They all offer, as the historian Zachary Schrag has written, 'a coffered ceiling reminiscent of the Pantheon, Corbusian concrete curves, and practical details, such as lights on the platform edge that begin to flash as the train approaches . . . [The effect from] the mezzanine is like gazing from a balcony down to a ballroom below.'[13]

The attention to surroundings that riders notice most did not happen by chance. Instead, contemporary observers should see these tunnels and their public spaces as the physical embodiment of an American political moment. When planning for the Washington Metro took off in the late 1950s and early 1960s, most Americans had a strong belief in the efficacy of their government and the nation's ability to do great things. Most famously, this was the era when President John F. Kennedy vowed that the United States would land a man on the moon and President Lyndon Johnson embarked on the most ambitious domestic programme in the nation's history, dubbed the 'Great Society'.

Overleaf
Metro Center station,
Washington, DC.

Many people remember Johnson's programme for its promotion of civil rights legislation, its war on poverty and its funding of education and healthcare, but in his initial speech about the Great Society, what Johnson focused on first was urban America. The country, Johnson told those assembled at the University of Michigan in 1964, would double its urban population by the end of the century, and the nation would have to 'rebuild the entire urban United States'. The president surveyed the land and found cities with 'decay of the centers and the despoiling of the suburbs. [Everywhere] open land is vanishing and old landmarks are violated.' In these cities, people felt 'loneliness and boredom and indifference'. He continued:

> Our society will never be great until our cities are great. Today the frontier of imagination and innovation is inside those cities and not beyond their borders . . . It will be the task of your generation to make the American city a place where future generations will come not only to live, but to live the good life.

President Johnson emphasized the final point by quoting Aristotle: 'Men come together in cities in order to live, but they remain together in order to live the good life.'[14]

Planners and architects, then, built Washington's metro at a propitious moment. They enjoyed a federal commitment to the common wealth that has now largely disappeared from American politics, one that translated into substantial funding and a greater attention to architectural detail. If subways in San Francisco, Milan and Stockholm were widely believed to contribute to the beauty of the urban environment, then so should Washington's. The system's detailing matched the aesthetics of the American capital, extending underground the city's environment built of granite, marble and limestone. Cost was always a consideration, but as early as 1969 initial estimates budgeted $2.5 billion to construct the system, and that number had risen to $10 billion by 2001. Planners also thought big about the size of the system, eventually building it out to 166 route kilometres (103 mi.).

Some commentators have criticized the 'extravagance' of the Washington Metro, calling it a 'boondoggle' that does not move enough people to justify its high cost. That is a fair financial criticism, but one that is ultimately ahistorical. It misses the point that the metro was built during a particular time when faith in the government and the need to revitalize urban America worked hand in hand. Washington's metro was built to move people, no doubt, but symbolically it supported President Johnson's Great Society commitment to make urban America 'a place where the city of man serves not only the needs of the body and the demands of commerce but the desire for beauty and the hunger for community'.

Slow Modernity: Sofia Metro
Anna Plyushteva

It had been a long and sticky July afternoon in the Bulgarian State Archive when I stumbled upon the correct record. It was a folder of official letters and reports from 1975 – around the time when extensive and rather heated correspondence was taking place between different departments and agencies of then-Communist Bulgaria. The topic of discussion was the plans of the Sofia Municipal People's Council for bringing an underground railway to the rapidly expanding and increasingly congested capital. The first feasibility studies dated back to 1968, but it was not until the mid-1970s that a specific plan had been drawn up. It was evident from the archival documents that everyone had an opinion about it. The most intriguing official letter I read that day came from an agricultural collective on the northern edge of Sofia, its managers clearly unimpressed with the oncoming pressure of urbanization and modernity: 'We do not agree with the proposal for building a depot for Sofia Metropolitan on the indicated land. This is Class A land and it was recently sown with lucerne [alfalfa].'[15]

The Sofia Metro took a long time to come into being, but not because of opposition from farmers. The first short section did not open until 1998 – and it was so short, in fact, that it had to endure years of mockery from the press and the public: 'a really expensive fair ride', local newspapers declared, 'going from nowhere to nowhere'.[16] But by 2009 things had begun to change. With a big cash injection from the European Union Regional Development Fund, and under the rather sceptical gaze of Sofia residents and Brussels bureaucrats alike, the metro started going places. Its second line opened in 2012, and a new kind of opinion of the underground rail system could be heard: 'Once there is a transfer station, it feels real, it feels like a proper metro.'[17]

The transfer station between Line 1 and Line 2, called Serdika, is a striking space. Located a short stroll from the State Archive building, it provided me with a highly appropriate, if somewhat unusual, location to spend my breaks in, while researching the history of the Sofia Metro project. The unusually placed café (recently opened on one of the concourses and overlooking both platforms, which are housed in a single huge tunnel), the station offered unusually expansive underground views as well as a respite from the pomp of 1970s bureaucratic correspondence, not to mention the July heat. Apart from this underground piazza-like experience, Serdika station aims to immerse visitors and commuters in the city's history. The cool, neutral-coloured walls of the tunnel are decorated with cabinets exhibiting ancient Roman ruins. When taken in alongside the Russian-made underground trains, the perplexing abundance of digital clocks and the contemporary placelessness of the station's architecture, it is possible to perceive within Serdika station a sense of historic continuity. This makes it a significant space, particularly in a city whose memory has been dominated by shocks and jolts at least since the fourteenth century.

On to the present and the future, then. 'People aren't having enough children here in Bulgaria. The population is shrinking. My dream for this project is for people to meet in the metro, fall in love, and have babies', a French civil engineer said to me after Line 2 opened in 2012. He soon left Sofia for North Africa, to work on his next project. The construction of Line 3 of the metro, due to begin in 2014, was delayed because the tendering process attracted criticism from Bulgaria's competition watchdog. As one of the biggest infrastructure projects

Interior of Serdika
Metro Station, Sofia.

in the country, the metro appears to have retained an air of controversy through each of the contrasting political periods its development has spanned. In the last decade, however, the shift of public opinion has been overwhelming, and the transformation of its image from extravagance into necessity has ensured construction on the network's extensions hardly ever stops. The year 2015 was another milestone in terms of both city prestige and transport accessibility (both of which are sought-after and scarce commodities for Sofia's local government), as the metro's Line 1 reached the city's airport. If transfer points are indeed what makes transport infrastructure real, the Sofia Metro is now assuming the role first intended for it in the urban imaginary more than thirty years ago.

Time Underground: The Clock of the Long Now
Carlos López Galviz

There is a tunnel in Mount Washington, Eastern Nevada, adjoining the Great Basin National Park; nothing like an urban centre. On the contrary, it is remote and hardly visited – a place for silent pilgrimage and contemplation. Just as remote is a limestone mountain near Van Horn, Texas: nature at its best, including tunnels and an underground in the making. Both mountains will change, although not in the near future, thanks to their owner, the Long Now Foundation. Their idea? Housing 'a mechanism and a myth' – a 10,000-year clock.

In a way, this project is reminiscent of medieval cathedrals and of the impact they must have had on visitors seeing them rise above the landscape of cities across Europe. Begun nearly twenty years ago, the Foundation's 10,000-year clock is an ambitious project with the idea of promoting long-term thinking. A prototype of the clock is now on loan to the Science Museum, London. It was completed in 1999, in time for the Millennium. The clock has since chimed only twice, the tenets of slowness and precision being key to the Foundation's understanding of timekeeping.

Once inside either mountain (Texas being the first option, still under construction in early 2016), and once two separate doors have been closed to act as a lock against dust and animals, two tunnels will direct visitors a few hundred feet into darkness and then to a vertical ascent – 150 metres (500 ft) up a 'continuous spiral staircase', at the end of which is a light: inviting, anticipating, promising. The staircase will reach into the clock, so that people encounter first the counterweights, and then the winding station, where, depending on when the clock was

First prototype of the Clock of the Long Now, Science Museum, London.

last wound, visitors may push the horizontal windlass or capstan that winds the mechanism. Continuing upwards, you reach the wheels, where a mechanical and – importantly to the clock's designer, Danny Hills – very slow computer operates the mechanism behind the chimes. The wheels consist of gears incised with 'an elaborate system of slots and sliding pins': in other words an automaton, an architectural musical box with over three million melodies to choose from.

Finally, at the apex of their ascent, visitors will reach the 'primary chamber', where the actual face of the clock (2.5 m/8 ft in diameter) shows astronomical time and the movement of stars and planets, including 'the galactic time of the Earth's procession'. Getting the actual time of the day and date will again depend on the last visit, and so another winding action of the clock, should it be needed, will show the updated time.

The way in which the clock's mechanism is described, its architectural scale and the experience of ascending into and out of it (for there will be an exit) remind me of Martin Scorsese's homage to the early cinema pioneer Georges Méliès, *Hugo* (2011). In the film, Hugo lives in the clock tower of the Gare Montparnasse in Paris. His uncle, a drunkard, has taught him how to wind the clock, keeping trains and passengers to time. Hugo's father was a clockmaker. The stationmaster is the quintessential timekeeper, his prosthetic leg signifying the oddity of his own synchronicity with time and the uneven rhythm of his steps across the station. Pocket watch in hand, he counts minutes and seconds, paying attention to everyone, ensuring they all observe order and excluding those who do not: most tellingly among the latter orphans, who are sent to the police immediately after their capture – think Charles Dickens's Oliver or Joe in *Bleak House*, Cadine and Marjolin in Émile Zola's *Le Ventre de Paris*, and Hugo himself.

Time will be different at the Long Now mountains. The clock includes a century hand and a cuckoo that will spring out once every millennium – just ten times in all, if everything goes according to plan. Here time is not kept, but re-enacted at a different speed, with a different purpose and in a different space – hidden out of sight, so that visitors of the future might be turned into time pilgrims inside a mountain, and including an underground ascent.

The 'experience', which includes a day's hike starting at dawn, is being developed by Jeff Bezos, founder and chief executive of Amazon. As comforting is a statement by Kevin Kelly, Long Now board member: 'The biggest problem for the beating Clock will be the effects of its human visitors.'[18] This is, then, a timepiece that bans, or at its very best selects, the very beings for whom timekeeping has any meaning and function; and so is an experience that differs significantly from what pilgrims encountered in the cathedrals that housed the mechanical clocks of medieval Europe.

After the End: Svalbard Global Seed Vault
Alexander Moss

Despite a comparatively modest budget (in global infrastructure terms) of about £5 million, the creation of the Svalbard Global Seed Vault has captured the world's imagination in a way that very few infrastructure projects ever manage. This has no doubt come about through a (mis)recognition of its extremity, and in particular the careful manner in which this extremity has been mediated through global news networks. Superlatives have abounded in its description as a project 'designed to withstand all natural or human disaster', safeguarding 'every known variety of crop'.[19] It has become lodged in the popular imagination as the 'Doomsday Vault', a reliquary or 'Noah's Ark' of plant life that may one day provide the lifeline to rescue humanity from the consequences of irremediable famine, whether brought about by war, bioterrorism, climate change or natural disaster. This narrative is as compelling as it is sensational, arising from the context in which the idea for a global central vault at Svalbard was first mooted;

around the time that seed banks in Afghanistan and Iraq were being destroyed by warfare, and those in the Philippines by flood damage. The 'Doomsday Vault' offered a curious emotional uptick in the seemingly limitless panorama of horror and despair that informs the news media, with its perpetual narrative cycle of bloodshed, disease, catastrophe and misery – even as it refers obliquely to that cycle in creating the meaning of its 'good news' stories.

This theme – a powerful admixture of hope and fear – has galvanized around the concrete particularities of the Vault's construction and logistics, burnishing the project with an almost mythical allure of forbidding isolation, secrecy and securitization. Descriptions have almost always emphasized its geographical extremes: its location, 79° above the equator, deep in the Arctic Circle, accessible only via the airstrip for the northernmost permanently inhabited city in the world, in the Svalbard archipelago; and the selection of the site for the impregnability of its natural defences, tunnelled 125 metres (410 ft) into the side of a mountain, 130 metres (430 ft) above sea level in a region of permafrost untroubled by seismic activity. The Vault boasts 1-metre-thick (3-ft) reinforced-concrete tunnel walls, and is designed to withstand even nuclear attack (although this scenario has already been calculated as unlikely, given Norway's globally renowned political neutrality and resource-rich economic self-sufficiency). In addition to its formidable array of thick steel blast doors and video surveillance systems, early reports also suggested the presence of a permanently stationed armed guard to 'keep away people [and polar bears] who aren't supposed to be [there]'.[20] Small wonder that the project has captured the imagination of so many, when it would seem to herald the physical materialization of a speculative fantasy from the mind of an Ian Fleming supervillain.

The Vault, then, is a kind of sanctuary excavated into a mountain at the top of the world, eccentrically beyond the vicissitudes of life and fortune, and unique, an apogee of its type to which all others are, nonetheless, concentrically referred. It is this pattern of flows in the architectonic design of the Global Seed Vault, as infrastructure, that is its defining criterion. Contrary to the overwhelming majority of infrastructure projects, which are modelled on the distributed pattern of networked systems, the Vault adopts a centralized and centripetal structure, unidirectional in flow; isolating rather than connecting; and designed, ultimately, to safeguard its cargo in one place over an extended duration rather than between places, in an effort to shave time off logistical operations.[21]

The centripetal motion of the structure is apt to the project of shoring up interests in the creation of a global treasure-hoard of

The Svalbard Global Seed Vault.

bio-information secured against the dominant infoscape of fear and precariousness. The Svalbard Global Seed Vault is a consolidation, ultimately, of power. We might do well to question the motivation of the arbiters of this power, arbiters that include the Rockefeller Foundation, Monsanto and Syngenta, all of which have been instrumental in funding the development of the project.[22] In an overpopulated world of diminishing resources, political instability and potentially irreversible climate change, it provides a draught of comfort, and a (possibly baseless) reassurance that should the worst ever happen, the pieces of the puzzle will be saved so that the survivors of a final catastrophe might rebuild this world, and life itself. We might also do well to question this logic, since it springs, like so many proposed solutions to the impending disaster of climate change, from a reactive attitude to our predicament now that we find ourselves at the brink.

Overleaf
Arsenal station on the Paris Métro, closed to passengers on 2 September 1939.

REFERENCES

INTRODUCTION

1 See Bradley L. Garrett, *Subterranean London: Cracking the Capital* (London, 2014).

2 Rosalind Williams, *Notes on the Underground: An Essay on Technology, Society and the Imagination* (Cambridge, MA, 1990).

3 Stephen Graham and Lucy Hewitt, 'Getting Off the Ground: On the Politics of Urban Verticality', *Progress in Human Geography*, XXXVII/1 (2013), pp. 71–2.

4 Stephen Graham, 'Super-tall and Ultra-deep: The Cultural Politics of the Elevator', *Theory, Culture and Society*, XXXI/7–8 (2014), pp. 239–65.

5 Eyal Weizman, *Hollow Land: Israel's Architecture of Occupation* (London, 2007; revd edn 2012).

6 See, for example, Peter Adey, 'Vertical Security in the Megacity: Legibility, Mobility and Aerial Politics', *Theory, Culture and Society*, XXVII/6 (2010), pp. 51–67; and Stuart Elden, 'Secure the Volume: Vertical Geopolitics and the Depth of Power', *Political Geography*, XXXIV/6 (May 2013), pp. 35–51.

7 Gavin Bridge, 'Territory, Now in 3D!', *Political Geography*, XXXIV/6 (May 2013), p. 55.

8 See, for example, C. López Galviz, 'Mobilities at a Standstill: Regulating Circulation in London, *c.* 1863–1870', *Journal of Historical Geography*, XLII/1 (October 2013), pp. 62–76. On communications and networks, see Richard Dennis, *Cities in Modernity: Representations and Productions of Metropolitan Space, 1840–1930* (Cambridge, 2008); Simon Guy, Simon Marvin and Timothy Moss, eds., *Urban Infrastructure in Transition: Networks, Buildings, Plans* (London, 2001); Joel A. Tarr and Gabriel Dupuy, eds, *Technology and the Rise of the Networked City in Europe and America* (Philadelphia, 1988).

9   Peter Sloterdijk, *Sphären III: Schäume* (Frankfurt, 1999).

10 Williams, *Notes on the Underground*, pp. 212–13.

11 Kristian H. Nielsen, Henry Nielsen and Janet Martin-Nielsen, 'City under the Ice: The Closed World of Camp Century in Cold War Culture', *Science as Culture*, XXIII/4 (2014), pp. 443–64; also quoted in 'Under the Ice: Polar Undergrounds', below.

12 Austin Zeiderman, 'Securing Bogotá', *Open Democracy*, 14 February 2013, www.opendemocracy.net. See also an interview with Alberto Granada, former sewer-dweller, in 'Sewers of Bogotá', 23 April 2007, www.vice.com.

13 See, for example, Sarah Cant, '"The Tug of Danger with the Magnetism of Mystery": Descents into "the Comprehensive Poetic-Sensuous Appeal of Caves"', *Tourist Studies*, III/1 (2003), pp. 67–81; and Maria Alejandra Pérez, 'Exploring the Vertical: Science and Sociality in the Field among Cavers in Venezuela', *Social and Cultural Geography*, XVI/2 (2015), pp. 226–7.

14 Not least, our global search for underground spaces has practical limitations of, for example, language. The References include websites that we came across and that readers might find worth checking. Among these, we highlight the superb collection of photographs and descriptions of underground spaces in Córdoba, Argentina, available at www.speleotunel.com.ar. See also the publications of the Association Française des Tunnels et de L'Espace Souterrain, www.aftes.asso.fr.

15 The French translation from Latin reads: 'Cette clarté nocturne vient du Firmament, qui n'est autre chose que le revers de la surface de la Terre, dont l'hémisphère donne une lumière pareille à celle, que la Lune rend chez nous; de sorte qu'à ne considérer que cela, on peut bien dire, que sur le globe en question les nuits diffèrent peu des jours, si ce n'est que pendant la nuit le Soleil est absent, & que cette absence rend les soirées un peu plus fraîches.' Ludvig Holberg, *Voyage de Nicolas Klimius dans le monde souterrain, contenant une nouvelle téorie de la terre, et l'histoire d'une cinquième monarchie inconnu jusqu'à-present* (Copenhagen, 1753), p. 16.

ORIGINS

1   David R. Olson and Ellen Bialystok, *Spatial Cognition: The Structure and Development of Mental Representations* (New York, 2014), pp. 69–71.

2   Edward Soja, 'Cities and States in Geohistory', *Theory and Society*, XXXIX/3–4 (2010), pp. 361–76.

3   Ruth Whitehouse, *The First Cities* (London, 1977), pp. 71–2.

4   Anthony Clayton, *Subterranean City: Beneath the Streets of London* (London, 2000); and David L. Pike, *Subterranean Cities: The World Beneath Paris and London, 1800–1945* (Ithaca, NY, 2005).

5 See R. Chudley and R. Greeno, *Advanced Construction Technology* (New Jersey, 2006), p. 179; and see Richard Trench and Ellis Hillman, *London Under London: A Subterranean Guide* (London, 1993), pp. 105–15.

6 See A.E.J. Morris, *History of Urban Form before the Industrial Revolution* (London, 2013), pp. 17, 60–61.

7 See John Hopkins, 'The "Sacred Sewer": Tradition and Religion in the Cloaca Maxima', in *Rome, Pollution and Propriety: Dirt, Disease and Hygiene in the Eternal City from Antiquity to Modernity*, ed. Mark Bradley (Cambridge, 2012), pp. 81–102.

8 On the history and legacy of the Cloaca Maxima, see Hopkins, 'The "Sacred Sewer"', and Emily Gowers, 'The Anatomy of Rome from Capitol to Cloaca', *Journal of Roman Studies*, LXXXV (1995), pp. 23–32.

9 See, for example, L. Volloresi, 'Roma Sotteranea', *National Geographic Italia*, XVIII/1 (2006), pp. 2–25.

10 Pliny the Elder, *Natural History, Books 36–37*, trans. D. I. Fichholz (Cambridge, MA, 1989), pp. 104–8.

11 Victor Cunrui Xiong, *Sui-Tang Chang'an: A Study in the Urban History of Medieval China* (Ann Arbor, MI, 2000).

12 See 'Going Underground', in Neal Bedford and Simon Sellars, *The Netherlands* (London, 2007), p. 281.

13 Information on these tours can be found at www.maastrichtunderground.nl.

14 Steve Pile, *Real Cities: Modernity, Space and the Phantasmagorias of City Life* (London, 2005), p. 8.

15 Petrus Gyllius, *The Antiquities of Constantinople: With a Description of its Situation, the Conveniencies of its Port, its Publick Buildings, the Statuary, Sculpture, Architecture, and Other Curiosities of that City. With Cuts Explaining the Chief of Them. In Four Books*, trans., enlarged and with a large explanatory index by John Ball (London, 1729), pp. 147–8.

16 Georgius Dousae, *De Itinere Suo Constantinopolitano Epistola* (Leiden, 1599); quoted in Jean Ebersolt, *Constantinople Byzantine et les Voyageurs du Levant* (Paris, 1919), pp. 108–10.

17 Ömer Ayden and Reşat Ulusay, 'Geotechnical and Geoenvironmental Characteristics of Man-made Underground Structures in Cappadocia, Turkey', *Engineering Geology*, LXIX/3 (2003), pp. 245–72.

18 A. Erdem and Y. Erdem, 'Underground Space Use in Ancient Anatolia: The Cappadocia Example', in *Underground Space Use: Analysis of the Past and Lessons for the Future*, ed. Y. Erdem and T. Solak (London, 2005), p. 38.

19 Stephen Starr, 'How the Ancient Underground City of Cappadocia Became a Fruit Warehouse', *The Guardian*, 30 May 2014, www.guardian.com.

20 Milton Santos, *La Naturaleza del Espacio* (Barcelona, 2005).

LABOUR

1 Lewis Mumford, *Technics and Civilization* [1934] (Chicago, 2010), pp. 77, 69–70.
2 Paul Dobraszczyk, *Into the Belly of the Beast: Exploring London's Victorian Sewers* (Reading, 2009), pp. 103–5.
3 See Iain Sinclair, *Hackney, That Rose-red Empire: A Confidential Report* (London, 2010), pp. 404–16.
4 Eyal Weizman, *Hollow Land: Israel's Architecture of Occupation* (London, 2007; revd edn 2012).
5 Williamson's life and the history of his tunnels are dramatized in David Clensy's book *The Mole of Edge Hill* (Liverpool, 2006).
6 On the history of the tunnels and their role today as a tourist attraction, see the website of the Williamson Tunnels Heritage Centre, www.williamsontunnels.co.uk.
7 All research materials for this entry, including the quotations, come from the file 'Broad Street Subway' in the *Evening Bulletin* Morgue, Urban Archives, Temple University, Philadelphia.
8 Alexander von Humboldt, *Memoria Razonada de las Salinas de Zipaquirá. Dispuesta para uso de los Visitantes de las Salinas por Luis Orjuela* (Bogotá, 1888), p. 23.
9 Manuel Ancízar, *Peregrinación de Alpha: Por las Provincias del Norte de la Nueva Granada en 1850 i 51* (Bogotá, 1853).
10 Aprecuz Canal, 'Virgen de Guasa (Zipaquirá)', 25 October 2012, www.youtube.com.
11 M. Singh, A. J. Burchell and K. Nayan, 'Delhi Metro: Tunnels and Stations on the 11km Underground Metro Corridor', in *Tunnels and Underground Structures*, ed. Jian Zhao, J. Nicholas Shirlaw and Rajan Krishnan (Rotterdam, 2000), pp. 169–70.
12 Matti Siemiatycki, 'Message in a Metro: Building Urban Rail Infrastructure and Image in Delhi, India', *International Journal of Urban and Regional Research*, XXX/2 (2006), pp. 277–92.
13 The films were *Bewafaa* (2005), *Black and White* (2008), *Dilli 6*, *Dev.D*, *Love Aaj Kal* and *Paa* (all 2009). *Times of India*, 28 December 2009, available at www.timesofindia.indiatimes.com.
14 See 'Benchmarking', at www.cometandnova.org (accessed 18 February 2015).

DWELLING

1 Gaston Bachelard, *The Poetics of Space* [1958], trans. Maria Jolas (London, 1994), pp. 17–18.
2 Indeed, early social surveys of marginalized groups often led straight

into the underground. See, for example, Henry Mayhew, *London Labour and the London Poor* [1861] (Oxford, 2000).

3   Rosalind Williams, *Notes on the Underground: An Essay on Technology, Society and the Imagination* (Cambridge, MA, 1990), p. 212.

4   Peter Seidel, Klaus Klemp and Manfred Sack, *Underworld: Sites of Concealment* (Santa Monica, CA, 1997), p. 132.

5   Patrick Keaney, 'Colombia's "Dirty War" against Trade Unions', MIT Western Hemisphere Project, 13 February 2002, www.web.mit.edu.

6   Juan Forero, 'Bogotá Says Army Killed Union Chiefs', *New York Times*, 8 September 2004.

7   Stan Yarbro, 'The Sewer Kids of Bogota: The Underclass Underground', *Los Angeles Times*, 6 November 1990.

8   Karen McIver, 'Thousands of Homeless Massacred, Forced to Live in Sewers', Care2 Petitions, 5 December 2002, www.care2.com.

9   Russel Ward, *The Australian Legend* (Melbourne, 1958).

10 Philip Butterss, 'From Ned Kelly to Queens in the Desert', in *Social Justice: Politics, Technology and Culture for a Better World*, ed. Susan Magarey (Kent Town, Adelaide, 1998), pp. 65–79.

11 Robert B. Cervero, *The Transit Metropolis: A Global Inquiry* (Chicago, 1998).

12 Gary Presland, *The Place for a Village: How Nature Has Shaped the City of Melbourne* (Melbourne, 2009).

13 See 'Infiltration', www.infiltration.org (accessed 2 January 2016).

14 This article relies on several decades of reporting in the *Chicago Tribune*.

15 Jacob Riis, *How the Other Half Lives* (New York, 1890).

16 Terkel quoted in Cindy Richards and Diane Struzzi, 'Lower Wacker to Shut its Gates on Homeless', *Chicago Tribune*, 22 January 1999, http://articles.chicagotribune.com.

17 'Odessa Catacombs', www.katakomby.odessa.ua (accessed 8 January 2015).

18 'Odessa Catacombs', www.showcaves.com (accessed 8 January 2015).

19 Jarrod Tanny, *City of Rogues and Schnorrers: Russia's Jews and the Myth of Old Odessa* (Bloomington, IN, 2011).

20 David Brandenberger, *National Bolshevism: Stalinist Mass Culture and the Formation of Modern Russian National Identity, 1931–1956* (Cambridge, MA, 2002).

REFUSE

1 David L. Pike, *Subterranean Cities: The World Below Paris and London, 1800–1945* (Ithaca, NY, 2005), p. 13.

2 Henri Lefebvre, *The Production of Space* [1974] (Oxford, 1991), p. 242.

3 Stephen Halliday, *The Great Stink of London: Sir Joseph Bazalgette and the Cleansing of the Victorian Metropolis* (Stroud, 1999), p. 107.

4 See Donald Reid, *Paris Sewers and Sewermen: Representations and Realities* (Cambridge, MA, 1991), pp. 37–52.

5 R. Raj Singh, *Heidegger, World, and Death* (London, 2012), p. 42.

6 On the streams and their presence in the system today, see urban explorer Steve Duncan's 'The Forgotten Streams of New York', www.narrative.ly (accessed 19 July 2014); for a map of the system, see 'Sewer Drainage Area Types Map', www.nyc.gov (accessed 19 July 2014).

7 'New York City's Wastewater', www.nyc.gov (accessed 19 July 2014); 'History of New York City's Water Supply System', www.nyc.gov (accessed 19 July 2014); and 'Subway FAQ: Facts and Figures', www.nycsubway.org (accessed 19 July 2014).

8 David Grann, 'City of Water', *New Yorker*, 1 September 2003, p. 88.

9 *C.H.U.D.* (1984, dir. Douglas Cheek). *Teenage Mutant Ninja Turtles* was created by Kevin Eastman and Peter Laird; the comic ran from 1984 to 2010, the first animated television series was broadcast from 1986 to 1997, and the first three features (live action) were released in 1990, 1991 and 1993. For the Morlocks, see www.uncannyxmen.net (accessed 10 July 2014).

10 See Thomas Kelly, *Payback* (New York, 1997), p. 64.

11 Jimmy Breslin, *Table Money* (New York, 1986); Colum McCann, *This Side of Brightness* (New York, 1998).

12 *Taxi Driver* (1976, dir. Martin Scorsese, screenplay by Paul Schrader); Alan Moore and Dave Gibbons, *Watchmen* (1986–7).

13 Edward Bazelgette, dir., 'Sewer King', episode 4 of *The Seven Industrial Wonders of the World*, BBC2, 2 October 2003.

14 'London's Victorian Sewer System', Thames Water, 11 December 2012, www.thameswater.co.uk.

15 'Thames Tideway Tunnel', Thames Water, 12 December 2012, www.thameswater.co.uk.

16 'Waste Water Treatment Plants: Thames Tideway Tunnel', *National Infrastructure Planning*, 7 July 2014, www.infrastructure.planningportal.gov.uk; Paul Dobraszczyk, *London's Sewers* (Oxford, 2014), pp. 22–3.

17 Pike, *Subterranean Cities*, p. 216.

18 The quotation is from John Hollingshead, *Underground London* (London, 1862), p. 2. For Mayhew on mudlarks, toshers and other

sewer-men and cleaners, see Henry Mayhew, *London Labour and the London Poor*, 4 vols (London, 1861–2; New York, 1968), vol. II, pp. 155–8, 383–464.

19 Hollingshead, *Underground London*, p. 58.

20 John Vidal, 'Fatberg Ahead! How London was Saved from a 15-tonne Ball of Grease', *The Guardian*, 6 August 2013, www.theguardian.com.

21 David L. Pike, 'London on Film and Underground', *London Journal*, XXXVIII/3 (2013), pp. 236–41.

22 An incomplete list of historical fiction and fantasy works includes Clare Clark's *The Great Stink* (2005); Terry Pratchett's alternative *Oliver Twist, Dodger* (2012); Anne Rice's *Dark Assassin* (2006); Eleanor Updale's high/low crime series *Montmorency* (2003–14); K. W. Jeter's steampunk riff on *The Time Machine, Morlock Nights* (1979); and the Doctor Who storyline 'The Talons of Weng-Chiang' (26 February– 2 April 1977). Present-day sewers figure prominently in, among others, dark fantasies by Neil Gaiman (*Neverwhere*, 1996) and China Miéville (*King Rat*, 1998); the horror films *The Sight* (2000) and *Creep* (2004); the children's comedies *Garfield: A Tail of Two Kitties* (2005) and *Flushed Away* (2006); and Ben Aaronovitch's urban fantasy police procedural (*Whispers Underground*, 2012) and Michael Robotham's psychological thriller *Lost* (2005).

23 Zahi Hawass, *Valley of the Golden Mummies* (Cairo, 2000), pp. 94–7.

24 Andrew Kiraly, 'The Yucca Mountain Hangover', KNPR Nevada Public Radio, 29 July 2014.

25 As an interesting subterranean aside, of the 928 nuclear tests that took place on the Nevada Test Site, 828 were conducted underground.

26 Chris Whipple, 'Can Nuclear Waste be Stored Safely at Yucca Mountain?', *Scientific American*, June 1996, pp. 72–9.

27 Vincent F. Ialenti, 'Adjudicating Deep Time: Revisiting the United States' High-level Nuclear Waste Repository Project at Yucca Mountain', *Science and Technology Studies*, XXVII/2 (February 2014), pp. 27–48. On Native American land claims and disputes over the site, see D. Endres, 'The Rhetoric of Nuclear Colonialism: Rhetorical Exclusion of American Indian Arguments in the Yucca Mountain Nuclear Waste Citing Decision', *Communication and Critical/Cultural Studies* VI/1 (2014), pp. 39–60.

28 Douglas Cruickshank, 'How Do You Design a "Keep Out!" Sign to Last 10,000 Years?', *Salon*, 10 May 2014.

MEMORY

1 Sigmund Freud, *Civilization and its Discontents* [1930] (London, 2002), p. 9.

2 Michel Serres, *Conversations on Science, Culture and Time: Michel Serres Interviewed by Bruno Latour* (Detroit, 1995), p. 59.

3 Tim Edensor, 'The Ghosts of Industrial Ruins: Ordering and Disordering Memory in Excessive Space', *Environment and Planning D: Society and Space*, XXIII/6 (2005), pp. 829–49.

4 James P. O'Donnell, *The Bunker* (Boston, MA, 1978), p. 3.

5 Samuel Merrill, *Excavating Buried Memories: Mnemonic Production in the Railways under London and Berlin*, PhD thesis, University College London, 2014.

6 Michael Braun, 'Ein Tragischer Baugrubeneinsturz beim Bau der Berliner Nordsüd-S-Bahn', *Bautechnik*, LXXXV/6 (2008), pp. 407–16.

7 Karen Meyer, *Die Flutung des Berliner S-Bahn-Tunnels in den Letzten Kriegstagen: Rekonstruktion und Legenden* (Berlin, 1992).

8 Monica Black, *Death in Berlin: From Weimar to Divided Germany* (New York, 2010).

9 See Rosalind Williams, *Notes on the Underground* (Cambridge, MA, 2008); David L. Pike, *Subterranean Cities: The World Below Paris and London, 1800–1945* (Ithaca, NY, 2005).

10 Christian Boros interviewed in *Freunde von Freunden*, video by Christian Fussenegger and Maren Sextro (2011).

11 According to the timeline presented by Sammlung Boros at www.sammlung-boros.de (accessed 12 November 2014).

12 On the work of the Survey, see www.nottinghamcavessurvey.org.uk.

13 See 'About the Nottingham Caves Survey', ibid. (accessed 2 January 2016).

14 See 'A Walk through the Underworld', ibid. (accessed 2 January 2016).

15 These objects were collected and published in the art publication *A Box of Things* (2014).

16 Duncan Sayer, *Ethics and Burial Archaeology* (London, 2000), p. 131.

17 Julian Jonker and Karen E. Till, 'Mapping and Excavating Spectral Traces in Post-apartheid Cape Town', *Memory Studies*, II/3 (2009), pp. 307, 328.

18 Klaus Grosinki, *Prenzlauer Berg: Eine Chronik* (Berlin, 1987); and Jens U. Schmidt, *Wassertürme in Berlin. Hauptstadt der Wassertürme* (Cottbus, Germany, 2010).

19 Wolfgang Benz and Barbara Distel, eds, *Der Ort des Terrors: Geschichte der Nationalsozialistischen Konzentrationslager* (Munich, 2005).

GHOSTS

1 Mike Crang and Penny Travlou, 'The City and Topologies of Memory', *Environment and Planning D: Society and Space*, XIX/2 (2001), pp. 161–77.

2 Steve Pile, *Real Cities: Modernity, Space and the Phantasmagorias of City Life* (London, 2005), p. 150.

3 Henri Lefebvre, *The Production of Space* [1974] (Oxford, 1991), p. 231.

4 Italo Calvino, *Invisible Cities* [1972] (London, 1997), pp. 98–9.

5 Ibid., p. 110.

6 See www.auldreekietours.com for a list of its tours.

7 See Jan-Andrew Henderson, *The Town Below the Ground: Edinburgh's Legendary Underground City* (Edinburgh, 1999), pp. 21–8.

8 Ibid., pp. 35–49.

9 See 'Edinburgh Vaults', www.haunted-scotland.co.uk (accessed 12 January 2016).

10 Henderson, *The Town Below the Ground*, p. 123.

11 On dark tourism, see Richard Sharpley and Philip Stone, *The Darker Side of Travel: The Theory and Practice of Dark Tourism* (Bristol, 2009).

12 Pile, *Real Cities*, p. 131.

13 On the London catacombs, see David L. Pike, *Subterranean Cities: The World Beneath Paris and London, 1800–1945* (Ithaca, NY, 2005), pp. 130–44.

14 One of the most bizarre private lines was the London Necropolis Railway, which carried cadavers between London and the Brookwood Cemetery in Surrey, southwest of the city.

15 Petr Gibas, 'Uncanny Underground: Absences, Ghosts and the Rhythmed Everyday of the Prague Metro', *Cultural Geographies*, XX/4 (September 2012), pp. 485–500.

16 J. E. Connor, *London's Disused Underground Stations* (London, 2008), pp. 28–33.

17 Alain Corbin, *Le Miasme et la Jonquille* (Paris, 1986), p. 226.

18 BBC News, 'London's Brompton Road Tube Station Sold for £53m', 28 February 2014, www.bbc.co.uk.

19 I would like to thank Stefka Patchova, Dragomir Gospodinov, Todor Dragolov and my parents, who helped greatly with the research for this text.

20 All the information about the shelter was provided by the Safety and Crisis Management Department, Prague City Hall, the organization responsible for the city's civil protection.

FEAR

1   Steven Graham, *Cities under Siege: The New Military Urbanism* (New York and London, 2011).
2   Paul Virilio, *Bunker Archaeology* [1975] (Princeton, NJ, 2009), p. 38.
3   Dominic Waghorn, 'US Families Prepare for "Modern Day Apocalypse"', *Sky News*, 23 December 2014.
4   Marie Cronqvist, 'Survival in the Welfare Cocoon: The Culture of Civil Defense in Cold War Sweden', in *Cold War Cultures: Perspectives on Eastern and Western European* Socities, ed. Annette Vowinckel, Marcus M. Payk and Thomas Lindenberger (New York and Oxford, 2012), pp. 191–212.
5   See 'Atomic Bomb Defences – Underground City in Stockholm – Mountain Bases', *Manchester Guardian*, 27 March 1953, p. 1.
6   *Vi Går Under Jorden* (1959), www.youtube.com (accessed 8 August 2014); see 'Swedish Nuclear Defense' (1959), www.euscreen.eu (accessed 8 August 2014).
7   Marie Cronqvist, 'Utrymning i Folkhemmet: Kalla Kriget, Välfärdsidyllen och den Svenska Civilförsvarskulturen 1961', *Historisk Tidskrift*, CXXVIII/3 (2008), pp. 451–76.
8   Robert McMillan, 'Deep Inside the James Bond Villain Lair that Actually Exists', 21 November 2012, www.wired.com.
9   See Mark Poster, *What's the Matter with the Internet?* (Minneapolis, 2001).
10 Douglas Alger, *The Art of the Data Center: A Look Inside the World's Most Innovative and Compelling Computing Environments* (Boston, MA, 2012).
11 'The World Beneath the City', *Global Times*, 24 September 2012, www.globaltimes.cn.
12 Michelle Lhooq, 'How a Bomb Shelter Became Shanghai's Grittiest Nightclub', *Thump*, 23 September 2013, www.thump.vice.com.
13 John McPhee, *La Place de la Concorde Suisse* (New York, 1983), p. 21.
14 Jean-Jacques Rapin, *L'Esprit des Fortifications. Vauban – Dufour – Les Forts de Saint-Maurice* (Lausanne, 2003), p. 89.
15 Imogen Foulkes, 'Swiss Still Braced for Nuclear War', BBC News, 10 February 2007, www.news.bbc.co.uk. On individual shelters, see Richard Ross, *Waiting for the End of the World* (Princeton, NJ, 2004).
16 Elaine Scarry, *Thinking in an Emergency* (New York, 2010).
17 On the use of the London Underground as a shelter during the Second World War, see David L. Pike, *Subterranean Cities: The World Beneath Paris and London, 1800–1945* (Ithaca, NY, 2005), pp. 173–89; and Richard Trench and Ellis Hillman, *London Under London: A Subterranean Guide* (London, 1993), pp. 11–21.
18 See the website of the Cabinet War Rooms, www.iwm.org.uk.
19 On the history of Paddock, see Nick Catford and Ken Valentine,

'SiteName: Paddock (Alternative Cabinet War Room)', *Subterranea Britannica*, www.subbrit.org.uk (accessed 4 August 2015).

20 Beyond agreement that the numbers are very large, there is no consensus on exact figures. I cite these numbers from Fabrizio Gallanti, Elina Stefa and Gyler Mydyti, 'Concrete Mushrooms: Transformations of the Bunkers in Albania', *Abitare* 502 (2010), p. 118.

21 Bill Fink, 'NOT SUCH A JOKE/Accidentally Enjoying Albania/ Experience the Passion, the Courage and the Brutality of a Newly Democratic Nation', *San Francisco Gate*, 1 October 2006, www.sfgate.com.

22 Ismail Kadaré, *The Pyramid* (New York, 1996), p. 160.

23 Elina Stefa and Gyler Mydyti, *Concrete Mushrooms: Reusing Albania's 750,000 Abandoned Bunkers* (Barcelona, 2013). See also the project's Facebook page at www.facebook.com/concretemushrooms.

24 A general history of the development of mass transportation in Tokyo can be found in Alisa Freedman, *Tokyo in Transit: Japanese Culture on the Rails and Road* (Stanford, CA, 2011). On the subway in particular, see Sato Nobuyuki, *Chikatetsu no Rekishi* (Tokyo, 2004).

25 I discuss the difference between the underground and the street – notions of surface and depth – in Mark Pendleton, 'Subway to Street: Spaces of Traumatic Memory, Counter-memory and Recovery in Post-Aum Tokyo', *Japanese Studies*, XXXI/3 (2011), pp. 359–71.

26 Haruki Murakami, *Underground: The Tokyo Gas Attack and the Japanese Psyche*, trans. Alfred Birnbaum and Philip Gabriel (London, 2000), p. 206.

SECURITY

1 Stuart Elden, 'Secure the Volume: Vertical Geopolitics and the Depth of Power', *Political Geography*, XXXIV/6 (2013), p. 35.

2 Ryan Bishop, 'Project "Transparent Earth" and the Autoscopy of Aerial Targeting: The Visual Geopolitics of the Underground', *Theory, Culture and Society*, XXVIII/7–8 (2011), p. 279.

3 David L. Pike, *Subterranean Cities: The World Below Paris and London, 1800–1945* (Ithaca, NY, 2005), p. 16.

4 John Beck, 'Concrete Ambivalence: Inside the Bunker Complex', *Cultural Politics*, VII/1 (2001), p. 94.

5 Simon Guy, 'Shadow Architectures: War, Memories, and Berlin's Futures', in *Cities, War, and Terrorism: Towards an Urban Geopolitics*, ed. Stephen Graham (Oxford, 2004), pp. 75–92. John Lennon and Malcolm Foley, *Dark Tourism: The Attraction of Death and Disaster* (London, 2000).

6 Most notable here have been the three series of the History Channel's *Cities of the Underworld* (2007–9).

7 Cited in Andrew Webb, 'Roswell Missile Silo Reborn as Data Storage Center', *Albuquerque Business First*, 30 March 2003.

8 See Ian Daly, 'Nuclear Bunker Houses World's Toughest Server Farm', *Wired*, 5 October 2010; and Simson Garfinkel, 'Welcome to Sealand. Now Bugger Off', *Wired*, July 2010.

9 Don DeLillo, *Underworld* (London, 1997), p. 248, cited in Beck, 'Concrete Ambivalence', p. 95.

10 Bryan Finoki, 'Tunnelling Borders', *Open Democracy*, www.opendemocracy.net, 26 November 2013.

11 Bryan Finoki, 'Subterranean Urbanism', www.subtopia.blogspot.co.uk, 2 April 2006.

12 The term 'security theatre' comes from Finoki, 'Tunnelling Borders'.

13 Neilsen's crimes were portrayed in Ian Merrick's film *The Black Panther* (1977).

14 See www.oxfordcastleunlocked.co.uk.

15 See the transcript of Bush's Speech on Immigration, *New York Times*, 15 May 2006, www.nytimes.com.

16 See www.americanborderpatrol.com.

17 See 'Walls of Shame – US/Mexico', *Al Jazeera English*, 5 November 2007.

18 Slavoj Žižek, 'Rolling in Underground Tunnels', *Mondoweiss: The War of Ideas in the Middle East*, 24 August 2014, www.mondoweiss.net.

19 Stephen Graham, *Cities Under Siege: The New Military Urbanism* (London, 2011), p. 171.

20 Eyal Weizman, *Hollow Land: Israel's Architecture of Occupation* (London, 2007).

21 Ibid., p. 257.

22 Doug Suisman, Steven Simon, Glenn Robinson, C. Ross Anthony and Michael Schoenbaum, *The Arc: A Formal Structure for a Palestinian State* (Santa Monica, CA, 2005), p. 33.

23 Weizman, *Hollow Land*.

24 China Miéville, *The City and the City* (Basingstoke, 2009).

RESISTANCE

1 Gavin Bridge, 'Territory, Now in 3D!', *Political Geography*, XXXIV/6 (May 2013), p. 55.

2 Alastair Bonnett, *Off the Map: Lost Spaces, Invisible Cities, Forgotten Islands, Feral Places, and What they Tell us about the World* (London, 2014), p. 171.

3 Iain Sinclair, 'Into the Underworld', *London Review of Books*, XXXVII/2 (2015), pp. 7–12.

4 Channapha Khamvongsa and Elaine Russell, 'Legacies of War',

Critical Asian Studies, XLI/2 (2009), pp. 281–306.

5   Colin Long, 'Heritage as a Resource for Pro-poor Tourism: The Case of Vieng Xay, Laos', in *World Heritage and Sustainable Development: Proceedings of Heritage 2008 International Conference*, ed. Regerio Amoeda, Sergio Lira, Cristina Pinheiro and João Pinheiro (Vila Nova de Foz Coa, Portugal, 2008), pp. 227–36.

6   Oliver Tappe, 'Memory, Tourism, and Development: Changing Sociocultural Configurations and Upland-Lowland Relations in Houaphan Province, Lao PDR', *Journal of Social Issues in Southeast Asia*, XXVI/2 (2011), pp. 174–95.

7   Oliver Tappe, 'From Revolutionary Heroism to Cultural Heritage: Museums, Memory and Representation in Laos', *Nations and Nationalism*, XVII/3 (2011), pp. 604–26; Rosalind Williams, *Notes on the Underground: An Essay on Technology, Society and the Imagination* (Cambridge, MA, 1990).

8   In 2009 the author participated in a field school in Viengxay organized by Deakin University. See also www.visit-viengxay.com (accessed 13 August 2014).

9   Unexploded ordnance is a particular problem at the Plain of Jars heritage site in Xieng Khouang and is a general issue for the country as a whole. See Gabriel Moshenska, 'Charred Churches or Iron Harvests?: Counter-monumentality and the Commemoration of the London Blitz', *Journal of Social Archaeology*, X/1 (2010), pp. 5–27.

10 Tappe, 'Memory, Tourism, and Development'.

11 Wantanee Suntikul, Thomas Bauer and Haiyan Song, 'Towards Tourism: A Laotian Perspective', *International Journal of Tourism Research*, XII/5 (2010), pp. 449–61.

12 Cai Guo-Qiang, *Bunker Museum of Contemporary Art, Kinmen Island: A Permanent Sanctuary for Art in a Demilitarized Zone* (Taiwan, 2006).

13 For a history of the Prague metro, see Evžen Kyllar, *Praha a Metro* (Prague, 2004).

14 'The Diggers', 2007, www.spirit-of-moscow.com.

15 On the Tartars, see John F. Richards, *The Unending Frontier: An Environmental History of the Early Modern World* (Los Angeles, 2006). On the Battle of Klushino, see Tomasz Bohun, *Moskwa w Rękach Polaków. Pamiętniki Dowódców i Oficerów Garnizonu w Moskwie* (Moscow, 2005).

16 'The Diggers'.

17 Tamara Eidelman, 'Vladimir Gilyarovsky', *Russian Life*, XLVIII/5 (2005).

18 All quotations in this essay are derived from Caroline Bacle's film *Lost Rivers* (2015). Available at www.vimeo.com.

RENDERINGS

1 Henri Lefebvre, *The Production of Space* [1974] (Oxford, 1991), p. 93.
2 Rosalind Williams, *Notes on the Underground: An Essay on Technology, Society and the Imagination* (Cambridge, MA, 1990), pp. 83–97.
3 A key text on *Roden Crater* is Craig Adcock, *James Turrell: The Art of Light and Space* (Los Angeles, 1990).
4 Quoted ibid., p. 158.
5 Many of these are reproduced in *The Art of Light and Space*, together with Adcock's own reconstructed imaginary, which has guided this text. See also more recent images available in Michael Govan, Christine Y. Kim et al., *James Turrell: A Retrospective* (New York, 2013).
6 For a complete list of these shelters, see Keith Warrender, *Below Manchester: Going Deeper under the City* (Timperley, Manchester, 2009), pp. 60–131.
7 See 'Underground Manchester', www.newmanchesterwalks.com (accessed 12 January 2016).
8 Keith Warrender, *Underground Manchester* (Timperley, Manchester, 2007), p. 26.
9 On the Chislehurst Caves, see Eric R. Inman, *Chislehurst Caves: A Short History* (London, 1996).
10 *El Mundo*, 2 October 1928, p. 7.
11 J. Víctor Tommey, 'En el subterráneo', *PBT*, 13 December 1913, n.p.
12 Wendy Lesser, *The Life Below Ground: A Study of the Subterranean in Literature* (Boston, MA, 1987), p. 25.
13 David L. Pike, *Subterranean Cities: The World Beneath Paris and London, 1800–1945* (Ithaca, NY, 2005), p. 288.
14 See '3.Manntour', www.drittemanntour.at.
15 Further information on LACMA and *Levitated Mass* can be found at 'Levitated Mass', www.lacma.org (accessed 20 August 2014).
16 Mark C. Taylor and Michael Heizer, *Double Negative: Sculpture in the Land* (New York, 1997).
17 Details of the film can be found at www.levitatedmassthefilm.com (accessed 20 August 2014).
18 Charles Baudelaire, *Les Fleurs du mal* (Paris, 1857).
19 Matthew Gandy, 'The Paris Sewers and the Rationalization of Urban Space', *Transactions of the Institute of British Geographers*, XXIV/1 (April 1999), pp. 23–44.
20 Félix Nadar, *Le Paris Souterrain de Félix Nadar: Des os et des eaux* [1861] (Paris, 1982).
21 Victor Hugo, *Les Misérables* [1862] (Paris, 1962), p. 55.
22 Adam Clarke Estes, 'Paris Unclogs its Sewers with Giant Balls of Iron', *Gizmodo*, 22 September 2014, www.factually.gizmodo.com.

EXPOSURE

1 John Hollingshead, *Underground London* (London, 1862), p. 2.
2 Bradley L. Garrett, *Explore Everything: Place-hacking the City* (London, 2013), pp. 114–16, 126.
3 The phrase is from Kristian H. Nielsen, Henry Nielsen and Janet Martin-Nielsen, 'City Under the Ice: The Closed World of Camp Century in Cold War Culture', *Science as Culture*, XXIII/4 (2014), pp. 443–64.
4 David L. Pike, '*Paris Souterrain*: Before and After the Revolution', *Dix-Neuf*, XV/2 (2011), pp. 183–5, 181.
5 David L. Pike, *Subterranean Cities: The World Beneath Paris and London, 1800–1945* (Ithaca, NY, 2005), p. 117.
6 For more on these novels and other related fiction, see ibid., pp. 104–5, 119–23.
7 Ibid., p. 175.
8 Sean Michaels, 'Unlocking the Mystery of Paris's Most Secret Underground Society', *Gizmodo*, 21 April 2011, www.gizmodo.com. See also Jon Henley, 'In a Secret Paris Cavern, the Real Underground Cinema', *The Guardian*, 8 September 2004, www.theguardian.com; John Lackman, 'The New French Hacker-Artist Underground', *Wired*, 20 January 2012, www.wired.com; and Alex Billington, 'This is Awesome: Photos of the Secret Cinema Club Underneath Paris', *FirstShowing.Net*, 14 July 2013, www.firstshowing.net.
9 Duncan Campbell, *War Plan UK: The Truth about Civil Defence in Britain* (London, 1982).
10 Nick McCamley, *Secret Underground Cities* (Barnsley, 2000).
11 Elizabeth Leane, *Antarctica in Fiction: Imaginative Narratives of the Far South* (Cambridge, 2013); and Robert McGhee, *The Last Imaginary Place: A Human History of the Arctic World* (Chicago, 2013).
12 Nielsen et al., 'City under the Ice'.
13 Martin Siegert, 'Antarctic Subglacial Lakes', *Earth-Science Reviews*, L (2000), pp. 29–50.
14 Henry Pollack, *A World Without Ice* (New York, 2010).
15 Speidel also published his own history of the city's subterranean space: *Seattle Underground* (Seattle, 1968).
16 See 'Bill Speidel's Underground Tour', www.undergroundtour.com.
17 Roland Barthes, 'Semiology and the Urban' (1967), in *Rethinking Architecture: A Reader in Cultural Theory*, ed. Neal Leach (London and New York, 1997), p. 171.

EDGES

1 Jane M. Jacobs, *Edge of Empire: Post-colonialism and the City*
   (London, 1996).
2 Italo Calvino, *Invisible Cities* [1972] (London, 1997), pp. 86–7.
3 'St-Petersburg Metro', www.metro.spb.ru (accessed 30 August 2014).
4 See the history of the Bratislava metro at the official webpages of
   Bratislava's municipal government: www.bratislava.sk (accessed 30
   August 2014; in Slovak).
5 'Rýchlodráha v Bratislave' [Rapid Transit System in Bratislava],
   Kinožurnál [CineNews] documentary 44 (1989).
6 Jennifer Toth, *The Mole People: Life in the Tunnels Beneath New York City*
   (Chicago, 1993).
7 On the Cape Town tunnels, see Ross Parry-Davies, 'Tunnels of Table
   Mountain: The Mother City's Water Tunnels', in *Tunnelling in Southern
   Africa*, ed. Anthony Boniface and Norman Schmidt (Cape Town, 2000),
   pp. 37–40.
8 Reif Larsen, *The Selected Works of T. S. Spivet* (London, 2010), p. 374.

FUTURES

1 Reinhart Koselleck, *Futures Past: On the Semantics of Historical
   Time* [1979], trans. and with an introduction by Keith Tribe
   (New York, 2004).
2 'Pyongyang Metro Guidebook', 1994, www.pyongyang-metro.com.
3 'Kim Jong-il "Has Secret Underground Escape Route"', *The Chosunilbo*,
   9 December 2009, www.english.chosun.com.
4 'Underground Backup Command Center Under Taesong',
   www.nkeconwatch.com, 21 July 2006.
5 'Kim Jong Il's Russian Trip Sends Message to US', www.voanews.com,
   8 August 2001.
6 Although CERN is not a commercial organization, it draws on funding
   from all its European member states and non-European observer states.
   Having invented the Internet, the W, Z and Higgs bosons, CERN has
   acquired both financial and cultural capital in the form of Nobel prizes
   (and prize money), celebrity and royal visits, popular cultural reference,
   artist interest and massive media coverage. It employs thousands of
   scientists around the world, and receives funding from hundreds of
   universities and states.
7 Sharon Trewaak, *Beamtimes and Lifetimes: The World of High-energy
   Physics* (Boston, MA, 1992).
8 I have not been able to find out if there is a plan for this at CERN,
   other than building and changing machines.

9 Kerry McQueeney, 'Breaking Down the Barriers: Woman, 28, Becomes First Female Train Driver in the Whole of the Middle East', *Mail Online*, 30 January 2012, www.dailymail.co.uk.

10 'Dubai Ruler's Trial Run', *Railway Gazette*, 1 November 2008, www.railwaygazette.com.

11 Mike Davis, 'Fear and Money in Dubai', *New Left Review*, 41 (September–October 2006), www.newleftreview.org.

12 Ibn Battûta, *Voyages I. De l'Afrique du Nord à La Mecque*, trans. C. Defremery and B. R. Sanguinetti [1858] (Paris, 1982), p. 4.

13 Zachary Schrag, *The Great Society Subway: A History of the Washington Metro* (Baltimore, MD, 2006), p. 65. The present article draws mostly on personal experience and on Schrag's fine history of Washington's metro.

14 Lyndon Johnson, 'The Great Society', 22 May 1964, www.pbs.org.

15 Bulgarian State Archive, St Kolev, Agrarian-Industrial Complex 'Sredets' letter to Metropolitan Directorate of the City People's Council, 14 November 1975.

16 'Emergency Pre-election Spending Begins', *Capital*, 7 March 1998, www.capital.bg.

17 Author's interviews with Sofia commuters, conducted 2012–14.

18 See www.longnow.org (accessed 5 November 2014).

19 '"Doomsday" Vault Opens its Doors', BBC News, 26 February 2008, www.news.bbc.co.uk; Tom Clarke, 'Arctic Seeds of Future Renewal', Channel 4 News, 31 August 2007, www.channel4.com.

20 'Doomsday Vault Tunnelled into Arctic Mountain to Protect World's Seeds', *Associated Press*, 25 February 2008, available at www.rainforestportal.org.

21 See Paul Baran, 'On Distributed Communications: I. Introduction to Distributed Communications Networks', Memorandum RM-3420-PR, The Rand Corporation, August 1964, p. 2, available at www.rand.org.

22 F. William Engdahl, '"Doomsday Seed Vault" in the Arctic', *Global Research*, 4 December 2007, www.globalresearch.ca.

NOTES ON CONTRIBUTORS

Caroline Bacle has a career in documentary and children's programming that spans fifteen years. She has collaborated with British, American, French and Canadian broadcasters including the BBC, Channel 4, PBS, Canal+, France 5, Bravo, CBC and CTV. Her award-winning documentary *Lost Rivers* (2012) has screened in festivals around the world.

Nick de Pace teaches architecture at the Rhode Island School of Design.

Paul Dobraszczyk is visiting lecturer at The Bartlett School of Architecture in London. His research covers ornament and iron, visual representations of London's Victorian sewers, and the relationship between real and imagined urban ruins. He has published widely on these subjects, including *Iron, Ornament and Architecture in Victorian Britain* (Farnham, 2014) and *Into the Belly of the Beast: Exploring London's Victorian Sewers* (Reading, 2009). He is currently working on a monograph, *The Dead City: Urban Ruins and the Spectacle of Decay* (forthcoming, 2017).

Klaus Dodds is Professor of Geopolitics at Royal Holloway, University of London and co-author of *The Scramble for the Poles: The Contemporary Geopolitics of the Arctic and Antarctic* (Cambridge, 2015).

Sasha Engelmann is a geographer of art, exploring creative experiments with the poetics and politics of air. In 2015 she completed site-based fieldwork at Studio Tomás Saraceno in Berlin, and is collaborating on Saraceno's long-term project *Becoming Aerosolar*. Engelmann lectures on multidisciplinary art practice at the Institut für Architekturbezogene Kunst (IAK) at the Technische Universität Braunschweig and is pursuing a DPhil in the School of Geography and the Environment at the University of Oxford.

Carlos López Galviz is a Lecturer in the Theories and Methods of Social Futures at Lancaster University. Since October 2014 he has led the project Reconfiguring Ruins (www.reconfiguringruins.blogs.sas.ac.uk), funded by the Arts and Humanities Research Council. He has published widely on nineteenth-century London and Paris, including *Going Underground: New Perspectives* (co-editor; London, 2013).

Matthew Gandy is Professor of Geography at University College London. His publications include *Concrete and Clay: Reworking Nature in New York City* (Cambridge, MA, 2002), *Urban Constellations* (as editor; Berlin, 2011), *The Acoustic City* (co-editor; Berlin, 2014) and *The Fabric of Space: Water, Modernity, and the Urban Imagination* (Cambridge, MA, 2014). He is currently writing a book about the interface between the cultural and scientific aspects of urban biodiversity.

Bradley L. Garrett is a geographer at the University of Southampton with a passion for photography of off-limits places. Working as an archaeologist for five years, he became interested in the politics of designating and controlling access to sites of urban heritage and began infiltrating 'closed' locations and sharing them with the public. His book *Explore Everything: Place-hacking the City* (London, 2013) is an account of his adventures trespassing into ruins, tunnels and skyscrapers in eight different countries. His second book, *Subterranean London: Cracking the Capital* (Munich, 2014), is a photographic dissection of what lies underneath the streets of London, layer by layer. The year 2016 marks the release of the final book in his urban exploration triptych; *London Rising: Illicit Photos From the City's Heights* (Munich, 2016), which documents the social, infrastructural and corporate verticalities of the city.

Petr Gibas is currently finishing his PhD in social anthropology at Charles University in Prague, Czech Republic. He works at the Institute of Sociology of the Czech Academy of Sciences, where he specializes in the sociology of home and homelessness. He is the co-author of *Non-humans in Social Science: Animals, Spaces, Things* (Červený Kostelec, 2011), *Non-humans in Social Sciences: Ontologies, Theories and Case Studies* (Červený Kostelec, 2014) and *Allotment Gardens: Shadow of the Past or a Glimpse of the Future?* (Prague, 2014).

Stephen Graham is Professor of Cities and Society at the School of Architecture, Planning and Landscape, Newcastle University. His interdisciplinary background links human geography, urbanism and the sociology of technology to explore the political aspects of infrastructure, mobility, digital media, surveillance, security and militarism, with an emphasis on how these work to shape contemporary cities and urban life. His books include *Splintering Urbanism: Networked Infrastructures,*

Technological Mobilities and the Urban Condition (co-author; London, 2001), *Disrupted Cities: When Infrastructures Fail* (Abingdon, 2009), *Cities Under Siege: The New Military Urbanism* (London, 2011) and *Infrastructural Lives: Urban Infrastructure in Context* (co-editor; London, 2015). He is currently working on a book entitled *Vertical: Sewers, Skyscrapers, Satellites (and Everything in Between)*, on the political aspects of verticality.

Kim Gurney used to travel the London Underground as a financial journalist until she switched tracks to study fine art; recent projects include the curation of an underground performance work and making artwork on the notion of disappearance. She is the author of *The Art of Public Space: Curating and Re-imagining the Ephemeral City* (London, 2015) and is a research associate at the University of Cape Town and the University of Johannesburg.

Henriette Hafsaas-Tsakos is a Norwegian archaeologist with experience carrying out fieldwork in Norway, Sudan and Palestine. Her doctoral thesis was on the subject of war on the southern frontier of the emerging state of ancient Egypt. Her research specializes in the Bronze Age cultures of the Nile Valley, with a focus on the ancient peoples of Sudan.

Harriet Hawkins's research focuses on the geographies of artworks and art worlds. She has produced artist's books, participatory art projects and exhibitions with both individual artists and a range of international arts organizations, including Tate, Arts Catalyst, Iniva, Furtherfield and Swiss Artists-in-Labs. She is the author of *For Creative Geographies: Geography, Visual Arts and the Making of Worlds* (London, 2013) and *Creativity* (London, 2015), co-editor of *Geographical Aesthetics* (Farnham, 2014) and Senior Lecturer in Geography at Royal Holloway, University of London.

Mariëlle van der Meer is the managing director for Europe and the Middle East at Minerva Schools at KGI in San Francisco. Originally from the Netherlands, she now lives in London after years of extensive travel around the world; she has a passion for International Higher Education and has worked in the sector for over ten years. She has an MA in Cultural Anthropology from the Universiteit van Amsterdam, obtained in 2000 after a period of fieldwork in Australia.

Samuel Merrill is an interdisciplinary researcher working on the cultural memories, heritages and geographies of a widely conceived underground. He is currently investigating the digital memories of contemporary European anti-fascist groups at the Department of Sociology of Umeå University, Sweden. He won the 2014 Peter Lang Young Scholars Competition in Memory Studies and his book *Excavating Buried Memories: Mnemonic Production in the Railways Under London and Berlin* will be published in 2016.

Camilla Mørk Røstvik is a PhD candidate in the Centre for the History of Science, Technology and Medicine and the Art History and Visual Studies department at the University of Manchester. She runs the university's Feminist Reading Group and parallel to her academic work she is a researcher in residence at the People's History Museum, Manchester.

Alexander Moss is an artist and writer based in London. As a medievalist at the University of Oxford his research focused on the ontology and psychology of numinous experience. Most recently he has been interested in the phenomenology of cities, infrastructure and networked information from perspectives in German idealism and Lacanian psychoanalysis.

Matthew O'Brien is an author, journalist and college instructor who has lived in Las Vegas since 1997. His first book, *Beneath the Neon: Life and Death in the Tunnels of Las Vegas* (Las Vegas, 2007), chronicled his adventures in the city's underground flood channels. His second book, *My Week at the Blue Angel* (Las Vegas, 2010), is a creative non-fiction collection set in off-the-beaten-path Vegas. He is the founder of Shine a Light, a community project that provides housing, drug counselling and other services to people living in the drain tunnels of the city.

Mark Pendleton teaches East Asian history and cultural studies at the University of Sheffield. His work has appeared in a range of publications, including the journals *Japanese Studies*, *Asian Studies Review* and *M/C Journal* and, most recently, in the edited volumes *Death Tourism: Disaster Sites as Recreational Landscape* (London, 2014) and *Historical Justice and Memory* (Madison, WI, 2015).

David Pike teaches literature and film at American University, Washington, DC, and has published widely on nineteenth- and twentieth-century urban literature, culture and film. His books include *Metropolis on the Styx: The Underworlds of Modern Urban Culture, 1800–2001* (Ithaca, NY, 2007); *Subterranean Cities: The World beneath Paris and London, 1800–1945* (Ithaca, NY, 2005) and *Passage through Hell: Modernist Descents, Medieval Underworlds* (Ithaca, NY, 1997).

Anna Plyushteva is an urban geographer and doctoral candidate at University College London. Her research interests are mobility, infrastructure, change and everyday urban life and her thesis focuses on the expansion of the metro in Sofia, Bulgaria, and its role in reconfiguring habits and technologies of commuting. She has published on post-socialist urbanism, public transport socialities and public space.

Darmon Richter is a writer and photographer with a passion for immersive, first-hand travel stories; his own work has ranged from the exploration of drug culture in North Korea to Vodou pilgrimages in Haiti.

He writes The Bohemian Blog and is currently working towards a PhD on the subject of 'Dark Tourism in Post-Soviet Space'.

Julia Solis is the author of *Stages of Decay* (Munich, London and New York, 2013) and *New York Underground: The Anatomy of a City* (London, 2005). A selection of her underground photos is at www.sunkenpalace.com.

Alexandros Tsakos is a Greek archaeologist and historian of religions who has taught and conducted fieldwork in Greece, Sudan and Norway, and has also worked in the fields of culture and tourism. He is currently a postdoctoral fellow at the University of Bergen with a project entitled 'Religious Literacy of Christian Nubia'.

James Wolfinger holds a joint appointment in History and Education at DePaul University, Chicago, and is the author of the book *Philadelphia Divided: Race and Politics in the City of Brotherly* (Chapel Hill, NC, 2011) as well as numerous articles and reviews. He is currently working on an urban and labour history of the Philadelphia public transportation system.

Dhan Zunino Singh is a sociologist and historian. He is a research assistant at the Universidad Nacional de Quilmes, Argentina, and focuses on the cultural history of urban mobility. He gained his PhD from the University of London in 2012 with a thesis on the history of planning, construction and use of the Buenos Aires Underground.

PHOTO ACKNOWLEDGEMENTS

The author and publishers wish to express their thanks to the below sources of illustrative material and/or permission to reproduce it.

Reproduced by permission of Archivo General de la Nación, Buenos Aires: p. 181; Strategic Environmental Assessment for Cavern Development UID: 487016, Hong Kong. © Arup: p. 100; Caroline Bâcle: p. 168; Wayne Barrar: p. 135; Rodrigo Booth: p. 148; captured by Bresciaunderground: pp. 224–5; Bundesarchiv, Berlin: p. 90; Paul Dobraszczyk: pp. 31, 42, 106, 109, 132, 146, 170–71, 179, 184–5; © Marc Dozier/Corbis: p. 58; Steven Engelmann: pp. 92–3; Carlos López Galviz: pp. 29, 125, 215, 246; Matthew Gandy: p. 102; Bradley Garrett: pp. 8, 16, 22–3, 74–5, 82–3, 111, 164–5, 190, 194–5, 198, 206–7, 250–51; Petr Gibas: pp. 118, 162, 220; © Google Earth: p. 176; Kim Gurney: pp. 96, 189, 229; Henriette Hafsaas-Tsakos: p. 128; Sebastián Iannizzotto: p. 38; reproduced with kind permission of the Kaysone Phomvihane Memorial Caves Office (www.visit-viengxay. com): p. 157; © Barry Lewis/In Pictures/Corbis: p. 62; courtesy of the Library of Congress, Carol M. Highsmith photographer: pp. 240–41; Lee McGrath: p. 36; Mariëlle van der Meer: pp. 49, 238; Samuel Merrill: p. 122; Camilla Mørk Røstvik: p. 235; Alexander Moss: pp. 201, 203; Peter Muzyka: pp. 522–3; NordGen/Dag Terje Filip Endresen: p. 249; reproduced by permission of the Nottingham Caves Survey: p. 96; Matthew O'Brien: p. 60; Mark Pendleton: p. 138; David L. Pike: pp. 131, 159; Anna Plyushteva: pp. 116, 244; Darmon Richter: pp. 66, 70; courtesy of PhillyHistory.org, a project of the Philadelphia Department of Records: p. 45; © Popular Science. Reproduced by permission: p. 209; Julia Solis: pp. 26, 80, 114, 211, 222; Alexandros Tsakos: p. 218; James Wolfinger: p. 68.